20/4/22

DECADES

The
Bee Gees

in the 1960s

Andrew Môn Hughes, Grant Walters & Mark Crohan

D1477463

SONICBOND

sonicbondpublishing.com

Sonicbond Publishing Limited
www.sonicbondpublishing.co.uk
Email: info@sonicbondpublishing.co.uk

First Published in the United Kingdom 2021
First Published in the United States 2021

British Library Cataloguing in Publication Data:
A Catalogue record for this book is available from the British Library

ISBN 978-1-78952-148-1

Typeset in ITC Garamond & ITC Avant Garde
Printed and bound in England

Graphic design and typesetting: Full Moon Media

DECADES

The
Bee Gees
in the 1960s

Andrew Môn Hughes, Grant Walters
& Mark Crohan

sonicbondpublishing.com

Authors' Note

This volume is the first in a series of four books in the 'Decades' series dedicated to The Bee Gees' lengthy career.

Acknowledgements

The authors would collectively like to thank the following:

Stephen Lambe and Sonicbond Publishing for giving us the opportunity to take on this project. Your faith in us is very much appreciated and we believe that it will ultimately be rewarded.

Spencer Gibb, who has been a critical connection between the authors and his family's work, and a committed, ardent supporter of this entire project from start to finish.

Vince Melouney and Jonathan Lea for the continual time and care they've invested in this volume.

Lee Meadows, Reinhard Wenesch, and Frank Stiller for their kind assistance with record sleeve scans; Luke Taiapa for providing valuable archive clippings; Jaesen Jones for his incredible *Go-Set* archives expertise; and Joe Brennan, whose *Gibb Songs* website remains one of the most important chronicles of Bee Gees history.

Marion Adriansen, Dick Ashby, Steve Barry, Tony Bates, Melinda Bilyeu, Dennis Bryon, Hector Cook, David Fedor, Hazel Gibb, Justine Gibb, Gerard Groux, Milton Hammon, Beth Kujala, Kitt Larue, David Leaf, Brett Leslie, Mary Merrill, Erling Paulsen, Tim Roxborogh, Andrew Sandoval, Bob Stanley, Faye Ward, Blue Weaver, Peta Gibb Weber and Minako Yoshida, for their many heartfelt contributions and conversations along the way.

The 'Oh No' Group - Dan Box, Mark Byfield, Judy Farrar, Michelle Gibson, Ann Grootjans, Linda Keane-Bacon, Paul Mann, Darrin Mitchell, Richard O'Donoghue and Ronnie Olsson for their friendship, banter, and shared love of the Gibbs' music. This book series was written with all of you in our hearts.

Albhy Galuten and Karl Richardson for so many candid, helpful conversations in which their technical, behind-the-scenes insight has breathed so much life into many aspects of this series.

And last, but never least: Barry, Robin, and Maurice Gibb for their unfathomable talents that gifted the world with one of the greatest musical legacies of all time. Every word written here is dedicated to you with our utmost respect and admiration.

Thanks to...

Andrew would like to thank ... my wife Judy, for her love, patience, understanding and making my life so complete, and Bella and Patch, our wonderful furry companions for the joy that they bring; my mother and father Enid and Mervyn for encouraging my love of music – the record player for Christmas in 1970 was the start of it all, but I guess the headphones a few years later showed that my tastes were changing; my sons Jonathan and Christopher, whose laughter is infectious – but usually at my expense. I love you all.

Special thanks to Jon Owen for working his techie magic like no other; Colin Trueman of VOD Music and record fairs; fellow music book authors Toni Schiavone and Malcolm C. Searles, and community radio presenters Dai Sinclair (Môn FM) and Steve Snelling (Radio Aber).

Extra special thanks for extra special friends - Frank & Manuela Stiller.

Grant would like to thank ... my wife Julie for her love and encouragement; my parents Gordon and Wendy, whose Bee Gees albums and turntable inspired a lifetime of listening; my brother Andrew for his enthusiasm and listening ear; Spencer Gibb for his friendship and many long late nights talking shop; Justin Chadwick, Quentin Harrison, Andy Healy, and all of my fellow scribes at *Albumism*; Walker and Anne Evans, Susan Post, and the staff at *Columbus Underground* who gave me my very first writing gig; Stacy Oliver-Sikorski for equal measures of support and sarcasm; and my colleagues at ACUHO-I who patiently listened to me lament over deadlines and eye strain. Thanks also to Bob Stanley, Grant-Lee Phillips, Juliana Hatfield, Edie Brickell, Brad Houser, Brandon Aly, David Wild, Libby Kober, Jacki Andre, Whitney Gear, Jenny Johnson, Sarah McNeal, Paul Stelzer, Jimmy Mak, Russ Bradley, Michael Gerbrandt, and so many others who have taken such a keen interest in this project.

Mark would like to thank ... my father, the late Joseph Gabriel for giving me my love of music; my three children Bree, Edan, and Daina and their respective spouses Dale, Michelle, and James for their enduring patience over the past few years. I would also like to acknowledge my six grandchildren Eliza, Ava, Archie, Darcy, Oliva, and Poppy, for the joy they have given me; and Lisa Maddocks, my friend and muse who has constantly inspired and encouraged me.

DECADES | The Bee Gees in the 1960s

Contents

Foreword 9

Prologue 15

1960 30

1961 35

1962 40

1963 45

1964 58

    Brilliant From Birth 70

1965 74

    The Bee Gee's Sing And Play 14 Barry Gibb Songs (1965) 85

1966 89

    Spicks And Specks (1966) 103

    Inception/Nostalgia (1970) 112

1967 122

    Bee Gees' 1st (1967) 135

    Turn Around, Look At Us (1967) 157

1968 160

    Horizontal (1968) 161

    Rare, Precious And Beautiful (1968) 182

    Idea (1968) 185

    Rare, Precious and Beautiful – Volume 2 (1968) 205

1969 209

    Rare, Precious And Beautiful – Volume 3 (1969) 210

    Odessa (1969) 212

    Best Of Bee Gees (1969) 236

Epilogue 242

Bibliography 252

Foreword

When I was first asked to write this foreword, I must admit I was a little intimidated. Not because of the subject matter itself, but because I assumed that it would be just as hard for me to discuss The Bee Gees on an impersonal level as to attempt the opposite. I then had an epiphany of sorts: it turns out I do it all the time. I reference them often when I'm producing or engineering a record for someone, working on my own material, or even when I'm teaching a class on the music business, songwriting, or production.

The Brothers Gibb are naturally ingrained in me, but not specifically as family. I've realised that I've always been able to separate the music and the talent from my personal relationships. I judge their achievements for what they are. This is important because I feel that's what every musician, performer, producer, and especially songwriter, should do. I'm often asked – usually because I am related – how The Bee Gees have influenced me. My response is always, 'How are they not influencing *you*? And if they're not, then you need to start listening'. Of course, I'd be lying if I said there weren't personal exceptions. Losing my uncle Andy and the music his brothers wrote relating to that, will touch me forever. There are certain songs that connect to my parents' divorce, and naturally, many others that occurred at pivotal moments in my life. My dad playing me 'Nights On Broadway' is one of my earliest memories, and I have a humorous virginity story related to 'You Win Again' that I won't share here. I could go on and on.

Don't get me wrong – as someone who chose a career as a musician, songwriter, and producer, I did have the luxury of a front row seat to not just some of the best recordings of all time, but the opportunity to discuss those elements with many of the people involved. Of course, that includes the Gibb brothers themselves, each with their individual perspectives – and legends and great minds such as Arif Mardin, Albhy Galuten, Brian Tench, Femi Jiya, and so many others over the years. Another question I often get is 'How do you live up to your family?'. The teenage 'artist' in me definitely felt like I was in their shadow, but the adult answer is 'You don't' or 'You can't'. The truth is, nobody can live up to them. The Bee Gees are a truly unique phenomenon.

There are no other artists in history that have achieved what they accomplished. Not only because of their history of decades working together, but also because they were the first to achieve so many milestones. At the height of their career, when many or all of their hugely successful predecessors or peers had either broken up or faded away – for example, The Beatles or Elvis Presley – they went on to become the biggest artists of a generation. They broke world records, including the greatest number of songs in the top ten at one time; the number of weeks on a top ten singles chart; and, of course, the biggest-selling album of all time until it was surpassed by Michael Jackson's *Thriller* a few years later: itself a record that might not have existed without the impact the Gibb brothers had on pop culture.

The obvious downside of being the first to achieve something, is that there was no rule book. It meant they were also the first artists to experience a public backlash for their success. Sadly, in my opinion, they were unfairly labelled as the face of 'disco': a genre I personally believe they weren't even a part of. That 'rule book' they were never given ended up becoming the one they inadvertently wrote. It served as a road map for so many other artists in the years to follow, including myself – the knowledge that things can turn on a dime. Understandably, being the first to experience something like this, the brothers were hurt – professionally, artistically and personally.

Nonetheless, where others might have disbanded or quit entirely, The Bee Gees persevered and endured – and as they had before, they reinvented themselves. They wrote and produced countless hits for other artists and then regrouped as performers, only to have more and more success in the decades to follow. If my father and my uncle Maurice were still alive today, there would without a doubt be new Bee Gees records still being released. Regardless of that, to this day – and depending on the chart or list you're looking at – you can often see them listed as the most successful songwriters of all time. I believe that is the achievement and legacy they would care about the most. Their songs are still being covered or re-released, documentaries are being made, and movies are in the works.

This book – the first of a forthcoming series – is important for so many reasons, and I'll name a few. I feel others will hit you as you read. One is that it needed to be written and should probably have been written a long time ago. To reference my earlier point, there are no other artists in modern history to have written and recorded together over multiple decades, so breaking that down doesn't just deserve to be documented – it is vital.

Another – and this is me being a little 'nerdy' as an engineer/producer – is that this book breaks down every record, track by track, with backstory and details from a time when studio technology was changing almost daily. Producers, artists, and engineers were striving tirelessly every day to come up with new sounds and new standards. Who better to follow than the career of these brothers and the teams in which they worked? They were present at the infancy of modern recording and were a part of the innovations that took us into the digital age; perfectionists who achieved that goal of discovering and changing sounds.

I once witnessed a session where my uncle Barry was producing a vocal part my father was singing. It sounded flawless to me, but Barry wasn't happy. He made Robin do it again, and honestly, I couldn't tell the difference, but Barry was ultimately satisfied. They then swapped roles, and Robin began supervising Barry's performance. Identical story. Those brothers understood things about each other, heard things in each other, and drove each other in a way that's probably impossible for most people to understand – all of this from three brothers who couldn't read or write music but instead relied on gut feeling, intuition, and passion.

My last point is that this book gives an insight into the brothers' process and so much more. It's something that will appeal to multiple audiences. If you're interested in recording and the history behind it, you'll learn something. If you're interested in music history in general, you'll learn something. If you were already a Bee Gees fan and thought you knew a lot, then I guarantee there are many things you'll discover – maybe even something about a closet favorite song of yours that wasn't a huge hit. Finally, if you weren't a fan to begin with, or didn't know too much about the history, then I believe there's even more of a reason to read. I promise it will make you want to listen.

When I was initially asked to write this, the premise was for a single book from the authors that would cover the entirety of The Bee Gees' career. Since then, it's evolved into multiple volumes that will cover different eras, which in my mind, is absolutely the right decision considering everything I have previously mentioned. The career of these brothers is so unique, long and extraordinary, that a single book or documentary couldn't do it complete justice. Once I found out there would be a book series, I went back to rewrite this and tailor it for this specific volume. Other than the addition of this paragraph, I decided not to. While some of what I wrote is not related to The Bee Gees' 1960s era, I believe it serves as an introduction to the series and who they were as artists and professionals, regardless of the decade. Because I was not alive for this period of their career and have no fly-on-the-wall experience of it, I can appreciate this era through stories that have been passed down to me, but mostly as just a music lover and audio geek witnessing music history unfold just by listening.

This was the beginning of a decades-long career covering revolutions in recording technology; a time when managers and labels nurtured and developed talent because they had nothing to lose; dramatic shifts in how radio and promotion, in general, were handled; the early days of artists being able to write for themselves as well as other people; the ups and downs of being a family while dealing with fame and success for the first time – an incredible insight into not only what was the dawn of the modern music industry, but also a pivotal understanding of the dynamics and evolution of these three brothers and what The Bee Gees ultimately became.

The three authors that have come together to create this project have left no stone unturned. In addition to getting to the bottom of all the information they could about these tracks, sessions and albums spanning multiple decades, they've also created a narrative that will make you feel closer to The Bee Gees and undoubtedly have a new perspective on the music, the story, and the legacy. I may have been intimidated to write this at first, but I sign off being proud to have been asked.

Spencer Gibb
(Yep, my dad was Robin fuckin' Gibb)
Austin, Texas, USA
May 2021

I first met Barry, Robin, and Maurice Gibb in 1964 on the set of the popular Australian TV show *Sing, Sing, Sing*, which was hosted by legendary Australian rocker Johnny O'Keefe. I was there with my band Billy Thorpe & The Aztecs, and together with the Gibbs and JO'K, we performed The Beatles' arrangement of 'Money (That's What I Want)'. It was amazing to hear Beatlesque harmonies coming out of the mouths of such young people. They were very friendly and funny, doing and saying silly things, but also driven and determined to be successful in the music business. Little did I know then that I'd eventually get to know them much better.

In late 1966, despite having had big hits on the Australian music charts with Billy Thorpe & The Aztecs (in addition to several releases of my own), I left Australia for the UK, where all the music that was turning me on was coming from. I wanted to be where The Yardbirds, The Pretty Things, The Rolling Stones, The Beatles, The Animals, John Mayall's Bluesbreakers, Them, and others were happening.

Shortly after I arrived in London, I was happy to find that my friends, Australian rock group The Easybeats, were in town. I was able to track them down and they told me that the Gibb brothers had just arrived in London, and they had a phone number for them. I called and spoke with Maurice, who told me that they'd just been signed to a contract with a guy called Robert Stigwood at Brian Epstein's NEMS Enterprises, and they were going to be recording in a few days' time. He then asked me if I would come and play guitar during the session. I, of course, said 'Yes'. What I didn't tell him, was that I had no guitar, as I had sold mine to help pay the fare to London. Fortunately, Harry Vanda of The Easybeats graciously helped me out and lent me his cherished Gibson guitar.

The address Maurice had given me was in the centre of London, at what turned out to be a world-class recording studio called IBC, where it was great to see the Gibbs again; there was so much to talk about. They told me about 'Spicks And Specks', which was released just as they were leaving Oz and that it was getting a lot of airplay. It was really good to reconnect with the guys. I also met drummer Colin Petersen for the first time at this session. Colin had played in a popular band in Australia called Steve & The Board, but we'd never crossed paths. He'd also been a child film star, starring in the title role in the movie *Smiley*. He was a great drummer, the perfect man for the job. That night at IBC, the five of us recorded 'New York Mining Disaster 1941', which would become an international hit when released only a month later. That night completely changed my life. The next day, I went out and bought a new guitar and returned Harry's Gibson.

At first, I was paid as a session musician, as there were contractual issues that needed to be dealt with, so I missed the group's first photo and video sessions. But a very short time later, I became an official member of The Bee Gees. We always had a great time in the studio. There was lots of laughter, good vibes and excitement. We would try out many ideas, try different instrumentation – one had to tear the Mellotron away from Maurice – and we each had the freedom to play what we wanted, with all of us having input in the song arrangements and recording production. The songs that the brothers were writing were unique – songs such as 'Lemons Never Forget', 'Indian Gin And Whisky Dry', 'The Earnest Of Being George', and of course all the singles: 'Words', 'To Love Somebody' and 'I Started A Joke', to name just a few. We must not forget Bill Shepherd. Bill was the man that wrote all the orchestrations, which I thought were tremendous. 'Less is more' was his approach. It's so fantastic that the chemistry between this group of people created songs that are remembered and still appreciated over fifty years later.

Less than two years on, unfortunately, the non-stop whirlwind of constant travel, concert tours, recording sessions, TV and radio appearances, photoshoots, press interviews and business meetings caught up with us. By that time, the immediate and enormous success had taken a mental and physical toll on everyone – it really was 'such a shame'. I felt, for my own health and well-being, that I had to leave the group. Robin quit a few months after, with the remaining three disintegrating later in 1969. The Gibb brothers reunited as a trio in 1970, by which time I had formed Fanny Adams and signed to MCA Records.

Sadly, Robin and Maurice are no longer with us, but their memories live on. I'm proud to say that Barry and Colin remain friends of mine to this day. All the many things we accomplished during those two incredible years of my life are included in this fantastic book. I sincerely hope you enjoy reading about those years as much as I enjoyed living them.

Vince Melouney
Somerset, England
May 2021

Prologue

The Bee Gees' musical reach now extends across more than 60 years and a multitude of generations. Their influence and identity are contextual depending on when listeners happened to discover them. For some, they were the very definition of 1970s culture, rising to stratospheric fame on the shoulders of their contributions to the *Saturday Night Fever* soundtrack. Others unearthed their lengthy catalogue in the 1980s and 1990s when the group had already been declared industry icons as consummate contemporary pop singers, songwriters, and producers.

Before they mastered their crafts as performers, songwriters, and recording artists, The Bee Gees spent a decade climbing their way out of their commonplace working-class upbringing in Britain to forge a path for themselves as career songwriters and musicians. This volume will tell the story of the Brothers Gibb in the 1960s – a decade they began as fledgling performers and ended rather painfully disassembled as colleagues and family members. In between, they rose from obscurity to find bona fide success as internationally recognised artists. It's a fascinating chapter in The Bee Gees' story, and the music that evolved from it is equally compelling.

However, exploring the group's 1960s legacy requires a few backward steps to unearth their family roots: beginning with Hugh Leslie Gibb, the family patriarch, born 15 January 1916. He was considered an 'oddball' in his family. 'I liked music, and the attitude was that it would never do you any good', he recalled of his aspirations. 'The main theme then was to go to work, have a steady job, and bring your wages home every weekend. To deviate from that wasn't right in their eyes. To be a musician was like the old days, you know, when they were considered vagabonds, and that's all I ever wanted to do'. Much to the chagrin of his conservative parents, Hugh sought work as a drummer. While in his early twenties, he eventually gained enough experience and credibility to build and lead his own band. By 1940, The Hughie Gibb Orchestra was well-known on the circuit of Mecca ballrooms, playing mainly in the north of England and Scotland.

Hugh's work also led him to his future bride, Barbara May Pass (born 17 November 1920), at the Stretford Trades & Labour Club in 1941. It was a match made in big-band heaven. Barbara was an occasional vocalist who happened upon Hugh's gig on a night off. Mr. Gibb was entranced to the point that he left the stage to dance with her during their performance. After a courtship of three years, they married at St. Matthew's Church in Stretford on 27 May 1944.

Their first child, and only daughter, Lesley Barbara, was born on 12 January 1945. Hugh's work took the young family to Scotland, where they lived for a short while before returning to Manchester at the end of World War II. From there, the family moved to the Isle of Man – a small enclave in the Irish Sea – after Hugh was offered steady stints at the Douglas Bay, Alexandra, and Glen Helen Hotels on the island.

Hugh and Barbara's first son, Barry, was born at 8:45 a.m. on 1 September 1946 at the Jane Crookall Maternity Home in Douglas, the island's capital. Christened Barry Alan Crompton Gibb, the first of his middle names, was in honour of Hugh's youngest brother, who died on 14 February 1929 of pneumonia, aged just ten months. The second was in honour of the Gibbs' purported famous ancestor, Sir Samuel Crompton, who had invented the spinning mule in Lancashire in 1779.

Robin Hugh Gibb came into the world at 3:15 a.m., and his fraternal twin, Maurice Ernest Gibb, debuted twenty minutes later, on 22 December 1949, at the Jane Crookall Maternity Home.

Although the brothers would later recall their formative years on the Isle of Man with great clarity and fondness, that period was tumultuous for the family. The availability of work for Hugh's band on the small island proved to be inconsistent. As a holiday destination during the summer months, it was a hive of activity, with mainlanders seeking a break from post-World War II recovery. However, during the winter months, tourists were exceptionally scarce. Even though Hugh was prepared to turn his hand to anything – working on board the local tourist ferry, The Thistle, which went from one end of Douglas Bay to the other; nursing at the local mental hospital; selling insurance; and delivering bread – the family's fortunes would fluctuate wildly at times. After nine years as Manx residents, the Gibbs – now numbering six – returned to Manchester in 1955 in search of better opportunities.

Shortly after, the children were all enrolled at Oswald Road School: Lesley and Barry (recorded as 'Barrie' in the admissions register) in the Junior School on 5 September, and Robin and Maurice in the Infant School on the same date. Barry recalled having 'a very bad experience at school', evoking a memory of a teacher who he felt was 'particularly unkind to children' as the reason for dodging school and being chased by the truant officer, who would, on occasion, come knocking on the Gibb family's door. Conversely, Robin recalled his days at Oswald Road School quite differently: 'I enjoyed my time at Oswald Road. It was the first school where I made really good friends'.

Living in a semidetached house at 51 Keppel Road in the middle-class south-Manchester suburb of Chorlton-cum-Hardy, the Gibb family was still struggling to make ends meet. Hugh was working two jobs, while Barbara also worked part-time. However, life for the Gibb children was one of fun, exploration, and occasionally, mischief. Barry:

> We were street kids. Our parents had no control over us. I had a great fear of the law, which you did have in those times, but I was also very rebellious. Life on the street became more fun, and we wouldn't come home until eleven or twelve at night, because in the summers, it didn't get dark until eleven o'clock at night, so kids around my age didn't go home. We'd be on the streets every night.

Robin was disarmingly candid with his recollections: 'I was a little swine actually. I didn't know it at the time, but I look back now and I know I was. For the things I did, they put kids in reform school. I was the same as Barry; we used to go and set fire to golf courses and things like that. We never did anything that could have harmed people, but we did a lot of damage to open land. We were very young and came from the kind of area where we weren't the only kids like that. My best friend, who lived down the road from us in Northen Grove in Manchester in '57, went with us. We used to go into houses that had been vacated and do a lot of wrecking. My friend was found the following day walking down the road and was picked up and sent to reform school because he'd had a previous record. Barry and I went to court, and we were put on probation'.

Maurice, however, always made it clear that his elder brothers' problems with the police did not involve him: 'I was the goody-goody really. I never got into any bother. Once, I stole a bottle of orange juice at the store, but I got caught. It was the first and last time I ever nicked anything'.

Abandoned car wrecks and advertising billboards were all fair game to the boys. But Hugh and Barbara's blissful ignorance of their sons' activities came to a sudden end when the local police came knocking, citing Robin as the culprit who had burned down a shed at the back of a butcher's shop. With threats of being sent to reform school, the brothers' well-documented activities as junior arsonists, were no more.

Thankfully, Barry, Robin, and Maurice's attention turned to other less-destructive hobbies, at least for now, and their parents' adoration of music began to surface in their young sons.

As far as anyone knows, the origin of The Bee Gees' prodigious singing can be traced back to one of 51 Keppel Road's bedrooms. Barbara arrived home one day (although sometimes Hugh would appropriate the story) to competing noises from their television set being watched by her father-in-law, Hugh Gibb Sr., and what she thought were singing voices playing on a radio elsewhere in the house. 'We used to bring Hugh's father over to our place to watch the cricket', she remembered. Asking if Hugh Sr. wanted her to turn the radio off, he nonchalantly replied that the voices weren't coming from a radio but from his grandsons and further revealed that it wasn't the first time he'd heard them singing. A mystified Barbara went into the bedroom and, sure enough, she discovered nine-year-old Barry with six-year-old Robin and Maurice, sitting on the bed harmonising effortlessly. Robin mused later that 'Our father Hugh was a band leader, and he played the piano and the drums brilliantly. Neither of our parents were aware that we could sing in harmony'.

Barry remembered vividly the day the three brothers discovered their gift: 'The three harmonies, as such, was a beautiful sound. We wanted to do that; we started finding out what harmonies were. It was all instinctive. It wasn't a matter of looking at music or learning in school, though you did sing in assembly'. Singing together was more than just good fun, even at this young age. As Robin theorised, 'It was a bonding experience learning harmonies and practising in the echoed surrounds of the gents' lavatories in department stores, and even up sewerage pipes – anywhere the acoustics were good'.

To assist in the music-making, or perhaps to imitate Elvis Presley, Barry tried his hand at crafting a guitar from the bottom of an old cheese barrel: nailing a piece of wood to make a neck and using household fuse wire as strings.

Observing all this, compelled Hugh and Barbara to give Barry his first guitar for his ninth Christmas, in 1955. Guitar lessons from a neighbour – a British soldier recently returned to Manchester after being stationed in Hawaii – quickly followed. He showed his eager student chords that he'd learned there. He used an unconventional tuning often referred to as Hawaiian slack-key guitar or lap steel guitar tuning. To this day, Barry has always favoured the open-D tuning (i.e. D-A-D-F#-A-D). When Maurice later learnt the guitar, his traditional tuning against Barry's method would produce a unique and rich tonal contrast when they'd play on stage and in the studio.

The brothers continued to sing and experiment while the twins used homemade instruments or toy guitars next to Barry's real one. Soon, their new musical diversion included their neighbourhood friends Kenny Horrocks (who lived across at 50 Keppel Road) and Paul Frost, who joined them on drums and tea-chest bass. Using older sister Lesley's and their parents' records as their guide, the group – which they decided to call The Rattlesnakes – continued to practice their repertoire in the cellar of Frost's house, with the drum kit he'd received in 1956 as a Christmas present, as the centrepiece.

Common to many British cinemas at the time, was spotlighting local children, who would go on stage between the day's films and mime current pop hits. Chorlton-cum-Hardy's Gaumont Theatre, located near Manchester Road and Nicholas Road, was about 200 yards from the Gibbs' house on Keppel Road. On the morning of Saturday 28 December 1957, The Rattlesnakes decided they would try their hand at performing 'live' in front of an audience and made the quick trek downtown.

The boys planned to mime to a record: a Christmas present Hugh and Barbara had given to the brothers' elder sister Lesley. Over the years there have been different recollections from the brothers of what the actual record was – Barry insisted it was Paul Anka's 'I Love You Baby' for a period, but in a 1968 interview, he remembered it as The Everly Brothers' 'Wake Up Little Susie'. Memories of who actually dropped and broke the fragile 78-rpm shellac record on the street corner opposite the cinema, nearly thwarting their debut, have also fluctuated over the years. However, the prevailing consensus now seems to be that it was Maurice. Unperturbed, the five boys took the setback in their stride and performed the song themselves, unaccompanied.

Recalling their performance as 'awful', the band did, at least, receive a shilling each from the theatre manager and were told to come back the following week. Barry would recall that for the next performance, they were more organised: the three brothers singing, with their two friends making choreographed moves while clapping their hands. They also expanded their repertoire, adding 'Lollipop' (The Mudlarks), 'That'll Be the Day' (The Crickets) and '(Who Wrote) The Book of Love' (The Monotones). These two performances were followed over the next few months of 1958 by similar shows at the Odeon Cinema on Withington Road in Whalley Range, and the Palatine Picture House on Palatine Road in Withington.

However, The Rattlesnakes would be a fleeting phenomenon, disbanding a short time later with the departure of Horrocks and Frost. The three Gibbs adopted a new name – Wee Johnny Hayes & The Blue Cats, with Barry assuming the Wee Johnny Hayes stage persona.

Barry began to write his own songs with his guitar around this time. 'Turtle Dove' was the first of what would eventually become hundreds of Barry Gibb-penned original compositions. Today, he can only recall the title.

With Barry's acoustic guitar in hand, the three Gibb boys became quite a common sight around Manchester, in cinemas and even on street corners, harmonising on songs like 'Lollipop'. Hugh now began to recognise his sons' potential and assisted where he could. One of these opportunities was the Russell Club in the nearby ward of Hulme, where Hugh was the drummer in the resident band. One night – aided by the club owner Ivor Derbyshire – Hugh smuggled his three young sons into the club, where they sang a few songs to thunderous applause from the patrons. 'I paid them the princely sum of two and six', said Ivor, 'and had to smuggle them up the back stairs because the premises were licensed'. Barry would later recall: 'We did our first sort of evening live thing for the audience; and goodness, they liked us!'.

Barry says that he now realises the audience's response had more to do with their age and very little to do with their talent. 'We were doing something nobody had ever seen before – we were three kids singing in three-part harmonies. Kids and animals', he laughed, 'You can't go wrong! From then on, our father became devoutly supportive of what we were doing. He played on the drums for us that night and has done after that, even when we went to Australia'.

Though very supportive, Hugh Gibb would also be the aspiring trio's most vocal critic. 'One thing about Dad is that we would come off stage, and he will always find the criticisms', Barry recalled. 'He would never say, 'Great show!' – he would say, 'You messed it up again, didn't you?'. Our objective became to please Dad. And if we pleased him, we knew we were on the right track. These things would become implanted in our minds. It's not that he never gave us a pat on the back, 'cause I'm sure he did in his own way ... but he always complimented the audience. When we came off stage and it had been a good show, he would always say, 'The audience was great tonight'. That was his way of complimenting us'. Maurice concurred: 'Our father never once told us that we were good. Every time we came off stage, he told us we were terrible, and I think this is what stopped us from being big-headed'.

Apart from his guidance as a performer, Hugh's music collection was of major consequence to his sons' evolving sound as a singing group. 'My father was always bringing great records home', Barry said. 'He was actually an opera fan as well as a big band fan, and it would either be Bing Crosby, who was his idol, or The Mills Brothers. It was from The Mills Brothers that we heard all about harmonies, and he would play these records non-stop'.

'What Dad did, unknowingly, was to play a lot of music that was inspirational to writing', Maurice added. 'I would say The Mills Brothers, regarding my dad's input from them to us, was probably when you are on stage, was to smile. If you feel like crap and look like crap, people will feel like crap too. Dad would always be down the back holding a smiley face because that's what the Mills Brothers did. I really did think that Dad wanted us to be little white Mills Brothers'.

However, the brothers' growing passion for performing wasn't keeping them out of the occasional skirmish with the law. More local police visits to the family home followed, possibly suggesting that Hugh and Barbara should consider moving to a new environment – or perhaps even a different country – before the boys got into serious trouble. The boys' issues with the local constabulary were not the only reason for the decision to leave the United Kingdom. Barry:

Mum and Dad were looking for a better way of life. You know, rather than sitting in the back streets of Manchester, which was not all that pleasant at the best of times. That's not really a put-down on Manchester, because we love Manchester, but, at that period of time, Dad wasn't earning an awful lot of money. Dad hadn't been able to get very good work, and Australia's New Life scheme came around where you could emigrate for about £10 in those days.

It was against this background that the Gibb family began making plans for emigration. Barbara's sister Peg had moved to Australia a few years before, and Hugh and Barbara Gibb were already giving migration to the southern continent serious consideration. It seemed like the perfect opportunity for a fresh start in a new land. The idea of leaving behind the cold, damp British winters appealed to the whole family.

The family booked their passage to the island continent under the Assisted Passage Migration Scheme, which enabled British citizens to emigrate to Australia from 1945 to the early 1970s for just £10 per adult, with family members under eighteen travelling free. The Gibb family – now numbering seven with the addition of youngest brother Andrew Roy Gibb (born 5 March 1958 at the Stretford Memorial Hospital in Manchester) – were among more than a million Britons that migrated to Australia. Having been told that it could take some time for the necessary paperwork to be processed, the Gibb family was pleasantly surprised to be on their way within weeks. 'Sometimes you had to wait two years; we got it in six weeks', Hugh would recall.

And so, on Tuesday 5 August 1958, the Gibb family – Hugh, Barbara, Lesley, Barry, Robin, Maurice and baby Andy – boarded the Sitmar line ship the *M.V. Fairsea* at the Port of Southampton, and departed Britain for the five-week voyage to Australia.

'An adventure' was how the brothers would later describe the journey to Australia. Like hundreds of other families arriving at Southampton docks that August morning, excitement would have been evident, perhaps mixed with sadness whilst waving goodbye to family and friends.

Aboard the ship, Barry, Robin, and Maurice wasted no time performing for the other passengers. Whether they joined in with the concerts organised by the crew for the children, or just found other places on the ship that suited their requirements, the three brothers could regularly be heard and seen harmonising to Barry's guitar-playing.

Hugh remembered: 'We used to put them to bed because kids were supposed to be off the decks by 9:00 p.m. Then, later on, we would find a crowd had gathered, and in the middle were our little boys in pyjamas singing away. It happened every night – we couldn't do a thing about it'.

One of the highlights of the journey was passing through the 101-mile-long Suez Canal. Years later, Barry would still recall its impact on him and his brothers: 'I think it was the journey as well. I mean we saw the pyramids and all these exotic countries at such an early age. So, we've always had a feeling that that's had something to do with our songwriting, you know. We drew on all of that experience when we got older'.

Once *Fairsea* had passed through the canal, there was a brief stopover in Aden – a seaport city in Yemen – the voyage's only port of call before Australia. After the Gulf of Aden lay the journey's final leg, across the wide expanse of the Indian Ocean. Finally, on Monday 1 September, *Fairsea* came into Australian waters. It was a double celebration for the Gibb family, being Barry's twelfth birthday as well. According to the family's recollections, Maurice couldn't join in the celebrations, as he'd been ill for the latter part of the journey.

Fairsea docked the next day at Fremantle: the major port city in Western Australia located twelve miles southwest of Perth. It was here that those immigrants from the ship who'd decided to settle in Western Australia disembarked. Having been promised a 'land of sunshine', the Gibb family's first day in Australia was somewhat disappointing. With heavy rain setting in and visibility poor, it was more typical of what the British migrants on board thought they'd left behind.

After departing Fremantle, *Fairsea* continued on Sunday 7 September to Melbourne's Station Pier, where many of the remaining passengers disembarked, including those intending to settle in Adelaide, who were then required to travel back to South Australia by train from Melbourne.

Travelling up the east coast of Australia, *Fairsea* finally arrived in Sydney Harbour on Thursday 11 September, docking at Woolloomooloo Finger Wharf's berth No. 7, at approximately 8 a.m. With other families travelling to Queensland, the Gibb family were bussed to Sydney's central rail station, where they boarded a train that would take them overnight to Brisbane. From Brisbane, they travelled on to the Redcliffe Peninsula, fourteen miles away.

With many beautiful white sandy beaches, hot sub-tropical weather and picturesque parks, the Gibb family – unlike many English migrants – actually settled in a part of Australia that was actively promoted in the brochures issued by Australia House in London. Redcliffe was a relative paradise, albeit one with a generally working-class population, shared with many other English migrants on the same peninsula. Their immigration papers show the Gibb family settled in at 14 Portwood Street. However, they didn't stay there long, soon moving to King Street, Margate, and again to Fifth Avenue, Scarborough: Redcliffe's northernmost suburb. Another move a short time later would land them at 395 Oxley Avenue in central Redcliffe.

By this time, Hugh had found work – which was also suited to his creative side – as a 'bush photographer'. This line of work involved him travelling in caravans to the remote Queensland outback, providing goods and services, including family portraits and school photographs, that would otherwise be unavailable to the rural population. Unfortunately, this meant Hugh would be away from his family for long periods. Robin would later recall of this time, 'Dad had to leave for about six months, leaving us to look after mum and Lesley'.

After moving to Oxley Avenue just in time for the new school year, Barry, Robin, and Maurice were enrolled in nearby Scarborough State School on

11 February 1959: the start of the Australian school year. One of Barry's friends at the time was a boy of the same age called Ken Griggs, who lived on Ella Street near Suttons Beach, not far from the Gibb family home. Like all children eager to make some pocket money, Barry and Ken, with the twins in tow, started selling soft drinks at the nearby Redcliffe Speedway, where car racing had become an increasingly popular sport, with crowds attending in large numbers.

Ken recalls, 'We'd each grab a case with a strap around our shoulders and walk around selling them. Then we came up with a better idea! We would grab a few cases at the interval, and under the grandstand, set up a little stall, whereby Barry and the twins would sing and I would do the selling. People would stop to watch the singing and we'd get quite a crowd and sell the drinks. It went quite well, much better than walking around selling'.

Having seen the potential of a wider audience attending the small grass oval track, Barry asked a driver named Bob McMahon if they could sing a couple of songs between the races that night using the track's amplification system. Bob, in turn, approached the race promoter Bill Goode, saying he knew three young boys who 'could sing a bit' and wanted permission to sing during the interval. Goode was always looking for ways to entertain the crowd between races, and undoubtedly was encouraged by the boys not expecting payment. He quickly agreed and arranged for them to perform on the back of a flatbed truck supplied by local fruit wholesaler Duke Bowman. As a further incentive – as if they needed one – the brothers were told they could have any money people threw on the track. Barry: 'We weren't interested in the money anyway – we just wanted to do it. We did three songs, our own songs, which were 'Let Me Love You', 'Twenty Miles ToBlueland' and one other. We picked up about £3/10 off the track out of the sawdust'.

The three brothers became regulars at the racetrack over the next few weeks. Barbara was totally unaware of what they were doing on those balmy Friday and Saturday evenings: 'I thought they were just going to watch the races, until one night they came home with the pockets of their jeans stuffed with pennies – their pockets so full they couldn't walk, and they were complaining 'Nobody's discovered us yet!''.

During one of their earliest racetrack performances, Bill Goode would recall hearing 'these melodious voices over the track P.A. system. I happened to be rushing around the pits, organising motorcycles for the first event after the interval, and I heard the kids singing, and the absolutely beautiful harmony of the voices just made me stop dead in my tracks, and I said, 'Holy smokes, this is good!''.

Goode was already a well-known and successful businessman in the area, with a real estate and construction business. He was also a successful racing car driver, which he did on a part-time basis, and he also promoted the speedway events at Redcliffe, and later at the Exhibition Grounds in Brisbane.

The next week, he invited his friend Bill Gates – a disc jockey at Brisbane radio station 4BH – to participate in a celebrity race for charity, and to provide an expert opinion on the prospects of the singing trio. Goode had initially befriended Gates while advertising his business through the station, but they also had a mutual interest in speedway car racing. Gates' own recollection of that evening was crystal clear: 'Bill invited me down to attend this charity thing at Redcliffe Speedway, and he and I were walking around down there having a yarn, and on came these kids. They were singing on the back of a truck, and that's when we heard how good they were. The thing that really stood out, was their natural harmonies, and how wonderful they sounded over this old tinny P.A. system. Bill and I both remarked on that, and we decided to see if we could help them in some way'.

At the end of the evening, the two Bills obtained the Gibbs' home address, and according to Barry, sent them home with the message 'Tell your mum to ring this number – it's to do with recording'.

After Barbara Gibb contacted Goode the next day, he and Gates visited the family home on Oxley Avenue. Following Barbara through the veranda into the lounge, the two Bills once again met the brothers. Although Barry had his own guitar at this stage, Goode's recollection is of 'Barry playing with a bass fiddle made from an old tea chest with a piece of 3' x 2' nailed on it, and Maurice with a fruit case constructed the same way. To these *instruments*, a fishing line was attached to provide the necessary twangs. Robin had a couple of old oil tins, which he had adapted to make drums'.

After introductions, Barry produced dozens of pieces of paper that contained songs he'd written. Goode recalls both he and Gates were then 'treated to an evening of beautiful music somehow produced from those homemade instruments, and melody from the throats of the three young boys that had to be heard to be believed'.

With some prodding from her excited sons, Barbara had agreed to Goode and Gates' visit, with one proviso. With Hugh still out working in the bush, and Barbara not wanting to be the only adult representing her sons, her cousin came over from his nearby home to be present when the visitors arrived. As Barbara recalls, 'They came and listened to the boys, and they were absolutely knocked out'.

Meanwhile, hundreds of miles away in a remote part of Queensland, Hugh received telegrams asking him to come home quickly. By the time he returned, arrangements had already been made for him to accompany his three sons to an audition at the 4BH radio station studios in Brisbane one Sunday afternoon. Keith Fowle was the sound engineer for the session booked by Bill Gates. He would describe the recording facilities as 'a very basic recording situation in one of the on-air studios'. The recordings were transferred onto acetate: an aluminium-based disc with a lacquer coating, used mainly for short-term use and demonstrations.

Fowle remembers that initially, Barry recorded four songs. In all likelihood, three of the four songs, which the two Bills had heard them performing at the Redcliffe Speedway and at the home audition, included 'The Echo Of Your Love', 'Twenty Miles To Blueland' and 'Let Me Love You'. Fowle: 'There was just Barry's guitar and the three voices, with Barry singing lead and the twins harmonising. Very impressive for their age – very good harmonies'.

However, Gates wanted two more songs in addition to the four Barry had already written. 'I sent the two kids out to buy a hamburger and gave Barry an hour to write them', he reminisced. 'He did it in half the time'. One of them was '(Underneath The) Starlight of Love', which would come to have greater significance some four years later.

Goode recalls: 'At that time, 'doughnut'(acetate) records had just arrived, and the volunteer studio operator Keith Fowles cut several records for us. Their very first recording was 'Twenty Miles To Blueland'. We sent the donuts on to several record companies, who all answered, 'The harmony is good, but they are too young, call us in a couple of years.' However, as all parties agreed, no one wanted to wait that long'.

Regardless, Gates was very impressed with the studio recordings and started playing them on his *Platter Chatter* radio show: 'I tape-recorded six songs of theirs and played the hell out of them on 4BH. The response was so good that I sent the songs to top Sydney DJ Bob Rogers on 2UE and he played them to death too. The raw talent was apparent. The harmonies were fantastic, and Barry was able to write a new song in five minutes'. In 1991, Gates presented the original acetate of the 4BH recordings to Barry when The Bee Gees were honoured on the British *This Is Your Life* television programme. Now framed, the acetate hangs proudly in Barry's Miami home.

The response to the six songs receiving airplay on Gates' 4BH radio show in Brisbane, and Bob Rogers' 2UE radio show in Sydney, was very positive. Following that, the singing threesome received their first newspaper coverage in Brisbane.

Barry would later describe 'Let Me Love You' as not the first song he wrote, but as 'the first song I finished'. Whilst the recording has never been released formally, Barry has spoken of how its broadcast became somewhat problematic: 'Bill (Gates) began bashing our recording of the number across the air in Brisbane and it became very popular. People kept requesting it and asking where they could buy it, which was funny because there was only the one copy that Bill had made himself. He played it every day on his programme. Soon, the local TV studios started phoning and saying, 'We loved that song. Will you come and do it on the show?''.

After lying dormant for nearly fourteen years, an excerpt from the 'Let Me Love You' acetate was played as part of a 1974 Australian radio special on The Bee Gees. In 1991, during a British radio interview with all three brothers, they performed a short version of the song live with just an acoustic guitar.

It was now becoming apparent that a name for the group was essential and needed very quickly. Bill Gates recalls: 'Bill Goode and I met with the Gibb family and settled on the name 'Bee Gees'. At that time, I was calling myself 'BG on BH' (Brisbane radio station 4BH) and it was noted that at the meeting were Bill Goode, Bill Gates, Barry Gibb, Barbara Gibb and the Brothers Gibb (Robin and Maurice), and it was suggested that Bee Gees would sound okay'.

After hearing the Gibb brothers sing in the studio, both Bills agreed that they should put the boys on contract. Assuming Gates would assist Goode in promoting the trio, a third part of the management team who signed the contract was John Proctor: another employee in the 4BH marketing section. However, for reasons unknown, he would play no further part in The Bee Gees' story.

Whilst the group name does appear as 'Bee Gees' in the contract, in the earliest days of the group's new identity, it would be most frequently presented in the grammatically incorrect form: B.G's. However, they would be billed using a confounding number of variations on their name – including 'B-Gees' – on several occasions. The present spelling, Bee Gees, seemed to become permanent sometime in 1963.

Accordingly, Hugh and Barbara Gibb signed a five-year contract on 16 March 1959 with Goode, Gates, and Proctor on behalf of their children;

although Barry, Robin, and Maurice's signatures were also on the contract. The four-page contract was for the 'purpose of promotion and management in the field of radio, television, recording, theatrical pursuits and entertainment generally'. The contract stated that the management team would receive a third of the trio's earnings, with 'two thirds to the children to be paid to the parents in trust for the children'.

Gates remembers, 'We bought them a guitar, and got them as much work as we could around Brisbane, but as they were so young, opportunities were very limited'.

Now they were officially on their way, and according to Barry, it was all going to plan: 'We'd sit on each other's beds and plan our careers all night. We decided when we got to the top, we'd have our own office. We'd give it a fancy name and make important decisions', Barry recalled, chuckling. 'We wanted to get to a point where we never have to work again, and we'd sit back and enjoy what we'd done'.

With the tapes of The Bee Gees now being played on radio, more opportunities for live performances started to come in. Barry: 'Gates' show on Brisbane's 4BH was for a half-hour. We would tune in, and he might play one of our tapes – did us an enormous amount of good'.

Soon the brothers could be heard harmonising on another radio programme, called *Grand Talent Quest*, broadcast by another Brisbane radio station, 4KQ – their voices attributed to 'The Gibb Brothers'. 4KQ held an annual competition connected to the show at the former Ace of Clubs: a terrazzo-floored former ballroom on the second floor of the 1941-built Comino's Arcade in Redcliffe Parade. Years later, Barry could still recall the experience: 'I really have fantastic memories of the (4KQ) talent quest that we did at the Ace of Clubs – we lost the talent quest, I'll always remember that. I guess there's a lesson there somehow, which is, even if you lose a talent contest, it doesn't mean that you won't succeed later on at what you love'.

The Goode and Gates management team were also able to get The Bee Gees onto the bills of small outdoor concerts in Brisbane, including The EKKA – a hugely successful exhibition tent show held on cricket fields known as The Show Grounds – and The Fosters' Tent Show in Brisbane. Requests for performances at such places as the Ambassador Hotel and Moreton Bay Hotel followed. Filmer's Palace Hotel at Woody Point – run by the indomitable Mavis Filmer – was also a popular venue for the trio. For the next 30 years, Mavis would proudly show hotel visitors the same small stage that The Bee Gees performed on in 1959. Speaking in 2003 –

just a year before she died at age 84 – Mavis recalled the payment for their first performances were bottles of Coca-Cola.

Late in 1959, the Gibb family moved again, but only for a short stay. Their new abode was the Orient House Flats, on The Esplanade in Margate – just a ten-minute walk from Humpybong State School, where a young man named Colin Petersen was enrolled. The three brothers and Colin would not recall knowing each other at the time, but the paths of the four would cross again in the not-so-distant future.

1960

In mid-January 1960, The Bee Gees made one of their final appearances at the Redcliffe Speedway, which was duly reported in the 21 January issue of the *Redcliffe Herald*. The trio was paid a flat fee for entertaining the crowd, this time whilst the racetrack was being raked and holes filled. This was a good step up from chasing coins thrown to them by the patrons.

On the last Sunday in January, Barry, Robin, and Maurice completed their second recording session at the 4BH Auditorium at 45 Adelaide Street in Brisbane. Now with more confidence in their charges' potential, managers Goode and Gates arranged these recordings with the express aim of impressing American record companies.

This time the sound engineer was Don McKean, who recalls the whole Gibb clan were there to support the trio: 'The family were certainly there. Their father was driving me mad, coming into the panel booth wanting to change things all the time. I remember the mother being there with the toddler (Andy)'. McKean would also recall that it was a considerable effort to set it all up. 'The 4BH Auditorium was on the first floor above Chandlers shop. (It) was essentially for the live-to-air kid's show *Rumpus Room,* compered by Norm Llewelyn'. McKean, who believes Bill Gates organised this session in the small room, recalls, 'The booth was very small and only had inputs for a couple of microphones and a programme line to the upstairs control room. The tape-recording room, which I was responsible for, was up on the second floor, and I had to run extra mic cables to it up the stairs, especially to create an echo chamber through the tape machines there – stuff everywhere! I remember when the twins weren't harmonising, they were running around, like any ten-year-olds, knocking things over. It was a long hectic day!'.

McKean recalls that the recordings all went onto a magnetic tape of which Gates took control. McKean cut a couple of the tracks onto an acetate disc for his own reference – sadly lost many years ago. Both Gates and McKean thought the recordings were good and had high expectations: 'They were good. Really good, especially for their age, and I was amazed later when I heard that the record company in the USA didn't want to pick them up – wouldn't you kick yourself a few years later? It all seemed to die out sometime later, and Bill didn't discuss why with me. I left 4BH in June 1961 and that was that'.

In March 1960, the brothers made one of their earliest TV appearances on Russ Tyson's *Anything Goes* show on the ABC in Brisbane. Hugh would remember: 'We auditioned for one of the variety shows, *Anything Goes* on the non-commercial network, ABC (the Australian equivalent of the BBC in the UK and PBS in America). Right away, they signed us'. Hugh humorously recounted that 'to get a vocal balance, they had a boom mic, and the twins stood on boxes on either side of Barry to bring them up to the same height'.

Brisbane's commercial networks were also interested in the brothers, so they auditioned for a weekly variety show on Channel Nine called *Brisbane Tonight*. The open audition had attracted a studio full of excited children and ambitious parents. Hugh remembered that it was past ten o'clock before his sons had their chance to audition, describing how he 'cued the boys and said, 'Look, when you go in, don't mind all these people here. Work to this table where these two men are''. Wilbur Kentwell (Channel Nine's musical director) was at the table. 'It was a typical audition, the boys went up with the guitar, and they sang one of their own compositions while the two men were talking among themselves. After they sang, all the people in the studio just cheered. Wilbur took his glasses off and asked, 'Can you do another one?'. They sang all night for him'.

In early 1960, Barry, Robin, and Maurice would receive their only formal music lessons at the Queensland College of Music at Wickham Terrace in Brisbane, where they learned guitar. The title 'college' was perhaps slightly grand for what essentially was a shop that just sold musical instruments and accompanying lessons. Their teacher Robert Clark recalls the guitar lessons were free, courtesy of the 'college' manager Bill Lock, a friend of Hugh's. Barry was, according to Clark, 'already locked to playing the open chord way'. Every week, Barry would try to learn the traditional way, but he would struggle. Clark told Barry that way was too limiting, and every week Barry would come in with his guitar, he would have to retune it in the traditional way. On the other hand, the twins were very quick on the uptake, and were taught the basic chord rotation and were progressing quite well. Clark believes they attended about six lessons over a couple of months before moving on.

On 21 March, the Gibb brothers met one of their early music idols from England when 24-year-old Tommy Steele performed at Brisbane's Tivoli Theatre. Widely regarded as Britain's first teen idol and rock 'n' roll star, Steele was touring Australia on the Tivoli live theatre circuit. Though never as popular in Australia as he was in Britain, Steele – with hit singles including 'Rock With The Caveman', 'Singing The Blues', and

'Butterfingers' – and his unique vaudevillian style had influenced the Gibb brothers and their father Hugh considerably back in their Manchester days. A photo of Tommy with Robin and Maurice appeared in the Queensland daily newspaper *The Courier Mail* the next day.

After successfully auditioning on the regular Friday night talent quest segment of the *Cottee's Happy Hour* TV show, the brothers became part of the regular cast, singing popular hits of the day. Broadcast live at 5 p.m. each weeknight on Brisbane's BTQ7 channel, the show was sponsored by *Cottee's*: a soft drink and jam manufacturer. Hostess Nancy Knudsen recalls: 'The boys were not really showmen, as many of the kids were, but they just had a very nice harmony. Even though they were very young, they had real rhythm and a very nice harmonious tone. Their mother was almost never in evidence, and for a long time, I had no idea they even had a younger brother. Their father was always with them. He did all the talking for them, and while they were pretty wild by the standards then, they were very much under his thumb'.

But trouble was looming for the boys, as Nancy Knudsen recalled in the book *On-Air – 25 Years of TV in Queensland*: 'They always turned up at the studio in dirty chequered shirts and jeans, and boy, could they swear! They were only about ten or twelve years old, but four-letter words would be flying around everywhere! And this was at the time when four-letter words were just not acceptable, even in private conversation. I warned them about it several times because my audience had a lot of mums and teachers and schoolkids in it, and they were getting very upset. But the boys kept swearing – so I fired 'em! Now when The Bee Gees describe the early days ... they always mention radio but never TV – maybe that's the reason. I told them, 'If you continue behaving like that, you'll never get anywhere''.

But all was not lost. They were quickly picked up by *Swingin' School*: a TV show hosted by Lee Henderson, which replaced the Friday edition of *Cottee's Happy Hour*. *Swingin' School* was aimed at a slightly older audience and was essentially a new talent show where the local ballet schools always performed along with local children. The Bee Gees were the regular act and would perform three or four songs within their own segment for each show.

With Hugh still working at this time, Barbara became their chauffeur, if not their roadie. Although professional performers, the boys were also still very young and fun-loving, often causing minor commotion at the TV stations while waiting for their time to perform. Barbara remembers:

'They were naughty, and because Hugh had another job at the time, I often used to take them to the television studio alone. Before they went on to do the show, we used to sit in a little foyer, but they wouldn't sit:they used to disappear! At one point, they climbed up the television mast! When all the executives arrived, they'd say, 'This place is lousy with Bee Gees''.

As their TV appearances increased, so did their various nightclub stints. They expanded their repertoire to include standards like 'Bye Bye Blackbird' and Paul Anka's 'Diana', with Hugh occasionally backing them on drums. They were also starting to attract more gigs outside of Brisbane, including the Oxley Hotel and the Beachcomber Hotel on Queensland's Gold Coast. Barry also recalled performing at the Sandgate Hotel to the north of Brisbane: 'It was a galvanised roof, and the water was pouring in onto the stage, not just raining, pouring in. And we had to stand there, water pouring in, soaking, and singing, and people in front of us sitting and fighting – not standing, but punching each other sitting down. It was like *Crocodile Dundee*'.

In April, they appeared at the Bonny View Hotel in Bald Hills: a North Brisbane suburb between Brisbane and Caboolture, inland from Redcliffe. The advertising in *The Brisbane Telegraph* on 23 April reflected their growing fame: 'Introducing The Bee Gees – colossal new instrumental vocal act'. Two months later, on 29 June, the trio received their first mention in a national magazine, the *Teenagers Weekly*: a supplement to the big-selling *Australian Women's Weekly*. The article mentioned that the brothers were fast getting a name on all three television channels in Brisbane, with Barry referred to as a 'pocket edition of Tommy Steele'.

Following a recommendation from Lee Henderson, the brothers made their first televised appearance outside Queensland on 12 August, on the Sydney-based variety show *Strictly for Moderns*. The show was filmed at Sydney's TCN9 studios at Willoughby: a suburb on Sydney's lower North Shore. In the chat prior to their introduction, the host – former English actor Desmond Tester – who also produced the show, refers to the trio winning a recent Queensland talent show called *Limelight,* inferring their prizes included 'tickets with Ansett Airlines to fly down here today'.

The film clip shows the three brothers performing Barry's new composition 'Time Is Passing By': a country-pop ditty. The clip would be retained in Australia's *National Film and Sound Archive*, and has been shown countless times on many TV specials and documentaries on The Bee Gees. It remains a priceless time capsule of a precocious talent, in terms of both songwriting and performance. The film clip reveals a polite, almost shy Barry towering over his younger twin brothers, who were dressed in matching zipped jackets. As well as providing harmony, Robin and Maurice provide somewhat out-of-time finger-snapping movements to accompany Barry's guitar strumming.

In late December 1960, during the summer holidays (the start of the southern hemisphere summer), the three brothers made their debut on Queensland's small vaudeville circuit, appearing at Brisbane's Rialto Theatre in the pantomime *Jack and the Beanstalk*, produced by Ric Marshall. Like British pantomimes, it was customary that there was entertainment on stage in between scenes. Maurice would proudly recall that 'The Rialto Theatre billboard would read 'Featuring the BG's'. We'd go out and sing while they changed the set. We'd do 'Run Samson Run' or some other Neil Sedaka song, and one other song, and one of our own. We'd try to break our songs across to them. The kiddies loved it. They'd cheer, 'Hey, great!' and then they're back to *Jack and the Beanstalk* again'.

The show would usually play twice daily, at 10:15 a.m. and 2:15 p.m., but a special evening show was performed in front of the Governor of Queensland, Sir Henry Abel Smith.

1961

In early 1961, the Gibb family moved house again but remained on the Redcliffe Peninsula. Their new accommodation was in Ernest Street, Margate: a central-eastern suburb of Redcliffe.

The Bee Gees' first engagement of the year was on 21 January at Brisbane's Manhattan Hotel.

Brisbane singer Tony Worsley recalls the talent quests: 'I'd go to the Gabba [Woolloongabba, a suburb of Brisbane]Police Boys Club. They taught boxing there for free, and on Saturday afternoons, there'd be a guest act and a talent quest. I wasn't the only wannabe-recognised talent on the quest circuit. Billy Thorpe – known then as Little Rock Allen – strummed out his Gibson to Little Richard tunes. The Gibbs, Barry and his twin brothers Maurice and Robin, mightn't wear shoes but were breaking in their harmonies. Even child actor Colin Petersen used some of his *Smiley* movie fees to pay Harry Liebler for drum lessons. All these would twang, warble and thump through talent quests. As is usual in the Brisbane scene, it became more than a bit incestuous. Barry Gibb was my young sister's first boyfriend. We'd all go out to Cribb Island. There were the Cook sisters (later The Cookies), the Gibbs, Billy, even Ross D. Wylie came a few times. We'd set up a stage in this barn and play and sing to our families. Yeah, there was a bit of 'bet I make it before you do', but it was fun, just mucking around'.

Another of their early performances that year was at the Lands Hotel in Brisbane on 8 March. The Bee-Gees (sic) were part of the *Barry Erickson Show* along with fellow artists The Mighty Atom, Rod Ball and Frank Skiller.

Later in 1961, the Gibbs' management arrangement with Goode and Gates came to an end, as Bill Goode recalls: 'Disaster happened. My home building company was ravaged by a credit squeeze, and even though it was financially viable, creditors desperate to get their money, put us to the wall. The Gibb brothers' father Hugh was waiting for me at my office each morning. With the problems I had, I rang Bill Gates to see if he could help, but he had his hands full, having been promoted to 4BH's top DJ, and he was also running several record shops. I then asked Hugh if he would try to get them some gigs, and he was very successful'. Bill Gates agreed: 'I'm not a businessman, I'm a disc jockey', he told their father, 'and, I've done all I can for them on my side'.

With his sons maintaining a reasonably high profile on Brisbane TV, and a growing live performance schedule, Hugh began to appreciate that things were becoming serious. 'That's when I began to realise that it wasn't just a flash-in-the-pan craze'. Obviously, his sons required not just a loose management arrangement but someone working full time on their behalf who could also drive them to venues. Considering that many opportunities lay in performing in nightclubs and bars, they would require someone to look after their welfare, and Hugh was the obvious choice to fill the role. He would recall his own dilemma of the time: 'Is it my job or is it going to be them? I felt their future is going to be stronger than mine, so, to be quite frank, they kept us. I gave up my work just to drive them around, they were only kids – they had to have somebody. I never wanted to be their manager, but by force of circumstances, it had to be'. Maurice confirmed: 'My father had to give up his job to take us everywhere because we were underage. He had to take us into the various places, and it was all down to pointy-toed shoes and polish and bow ties and nicely dressed. We did that for about three years'.

Barry also would always remain very appreciative of his father's support and guidance: 'We had very strong parents. When we were young, there were a lot of places we weren't allowed to be in. When we went someplace where drinking was taking place, our father was always with us. We weren't allowed to come from backstage and blunder into the audience. We were all well-protected from the kind of adults who might have tried to talk us into drinking or anything like that'.

With Hugh now turning his full attention towards managing his sons, he also attempted to give them a profile in places outside of Queensland. If his young sons were to be exposed to the many unsavoury aspects of the entertainment world, then at least he would be there to guide them and counsel them. He also had some experience in show business and would be there to advise them on stagecraft, how to walk on stage and, on occasion, when to walk off stage. Maurice would later recall, 'Almost every time we came off stage, the audience was going 'More! More! More!' in the background – we'd go 'Oh!', and Dad would say 'You killed them tonight'. We'd go out there and do one more song, and they'd love it. Dad would say 'Always leave them wanting more', and he'd usher us out the back door. And the next week, we'd get another booking for that club because we left them wanting more as our father had said'. Hugh also taught them the basics, emphasising the need to smile, look like they enjoyed performing, and engaging the audience. When required, he'd even still sit in on the drums.

With the Gibbs now performing regularly at nightclubs and Returned Soldiers League (RSL) clubs, their stage act continued to evolve. Robin recalls: 'We had to appeal to adults, so my father, who was a very big Mills Brothers fan, had us do a lot of Mills Brothers songs on the nightclub circuit'. The trio's act at that time included Irving Berlin's 'Alexander's Ragtime Band' and two Lonnie Donegan songs: 'My Old Man's A Dustman' and 'Does Your Chewing Gum Lose Its Flavour (On The Bedpost Overnight?)'. When they could – which was not often by their own reckoning – the brothers would slip in something more contemporary from artists like The Everly Brothers, Ray Charles and Neil Sedaka, who were already influencing them.

Working the nightclub and hotel circuit, with Hugh's show business experience guiding them, their act became something that Barry would later term 'a comedy act with harmony'. It reflected a more vaudevillian style that might've contributed to Australian audiences' struggle to accept them as pop stars later. There was much musical comedy coming from the trio, as Maurice would relate: 'My father knew exactly what those audiences wanted. We were cute little kids; any bit of comedy would have them laughing their heads off, saying, 'They're so cute'. We used to do slapstick. For instance, we'd be singing 'Puff The Magic Dragon', and every time Robin sang 'Puff', I'd get sprayed in the face. Mums and dads loved that. We had a lot of comedy routines. I was always the one who got suckered; always the straight man, Robin was the funny one, the cheeky little cute look. Barry was the older brother, looking after us. It was always visual comedy. Sort of like Abbott and Costello'.

However, they were well sought-after for teenage dances also. One of those 1961 engagements was on 21 July at St Mary's Hall in the town of Warwick, 81 miles southwest of Brisbane. This time they were billed as 'The TV stars of the Y.C.W. (Young Christian Workers) Jazz Concert – The Fabulous Bee Gees'.

In August 1961, The Bee Gees would make one of their first appearances at the Surfers Paradise Garden Hotel. Some 60 miles south of Brisbane, Surfers Paradise – colloquially known as Surfers – is a suburb on Australia's Gold Coast, now famous for its many high-rise apartment buildings and long surf beach. Even in 1961, it was already a hive of entertainment opportunities, featuring many hotels, nightclubs and sports or RSL clubs.

Another appearance in August was at the Woolloongabba Railway Hotel, where they were billed as 'Brisbane's Own T.V. Sensation'. However, the main act that night was Edith Dahl, advertised as the 'Scintillating American Star of the 1961 *Ziegfeld Follies*'.

Barry would leave school about this time and undertake his first and only work outside of the entertainment world: 'Show business has always been in my blood, but I did get an ordinary job once. It was in Brisbane, and I had to cart materials to a tailor in a case. The tailor would give me the money, and I would have to take it back to the office. I got sacked because I went home one day and forgot to hand the money in. I really did forget, but they thought I'd nicked it. So, they sacked me'. By his own admission, Barry's heart was never in the job anyway: 'I wanted to write songs – songs are what make me tick'.

With Barry having reached the legal age to leave school, it may have taken some of the pressure off the family in keeping the ever-vigilant Queensland Children's Welfare Office away. The business of child performers had always presented a challenge. When Messrs. Goode and Gates oversaw their bookings, they even preferred using the term 'promoter', and avoided using words like 'manager' that may have had professional connotations which might attract undesired attention.

Barry now had more time to devote to his songwriting, and in September 1961, aged just fifteen, he signed a five-year 'composer's agreement', or a publishing contract, with Belinda Music, Ltd. At that time, the company was very active signing up local talent, such as other popular singer-songwriters, including Johnny Devlin and Lonnie Lee. Tony Brady – who had brought Barry down to Sydney to sign the contract – would recall: '(Belinda) had heard about him even then, as Barry was an amazingly quick songwriter'. Perhaps not by coincidence, Belinda's management included one Norman Whiteley: a pianist who had known Hugh since the 1950s when the two played the Manchester band circuit.

Inexplicably, for their appearance at the Toowoomba RSL's Grand Rock and Roll Floor Show on 5 November, The Bee Gees billing included the line 'Their last appearance before leaving for the USA'.

As 1961 closed, it had been another year of progress for the Gibbs. Still, it was a confusing one for popular music in Australia, with many competing genres and song styles making the charts – Elvis's 'Wooden Heart' and Del Shannon's 'Runaway' were in heavy rotation, along with Andy Stewart's 'A Scottish Soldier' and Ernest Gold's 'Theme Of Exodus'.

It was also the year in which the Gibb brothers heard Roy Orbison's 'Crying' for the first time. Barry would later say he was 'moved to tears' by the power of Orbison's hit, and all three brothers would become lifelong fans of the music legend. Orbison would later cover The Bee Gees' 1968 hit 'Words', and in 1983, he appeared as a guest vocalist on Larry Gatlin and the Gatlin Brothers' 'Indian Summer' – a track Barry would co-write and co-produce. Among other artists making hits in 1961 who were later to record Bee Gees' songs, were Australian performers Johnny O'Keefe and Bryan Davies, and international stars Gene Pitney, Cliff Richard and Elvis Presley.

With so much work for the brothers now coming from Queensland's Gold Coast, another move was imminent. After three years living there since migrating from England, it would be the Gibb family's last Christmas on the Redcliffe Peninsula. The time spent in Redcliffe had left a strong impression on the eldest Gibb son, as he recalled in 2015: 'That was my childhood, and I would wish that childhood on any other child – and if you lived in Redcliffe, you'll know exactly what I mean'.

In 1999, in response to a request from The Redcliffe Museum, Barry wrote a letter warmly reminiscent of his time on the Peninsula, recalling a carefree, barefooted childhood that none of the three brothers ever forgot. Barry's prose finished with, 'I have changed; the child inside me has not. I'm still here on Redcliffe Beach. I'm still fishing for the tiger shark on a pier long swept away by time and tide. I can still see the pie cart, the Saturday night dance, and the speedway, and first love. I remember visibly my childhood days here, and I will dwell on my Redcliffe for as long as I live'.

Redcliffe wouldn't forget The Bee Gees either, as commemorations and tributes in 2013 and 2015 would show.

1962

In early 1962, the Gibb family migrated south to Queensland's Gold Coast, which stretches 25 miles down the state's southern coastline to Tweed Heads in New South Wales. They settled at 23 Cambridge Avenue in Surfers Paradise.

Soon after settling in, the group secured a six-week residency, which was later extended to eight months, at The Beachcomber: a nightclub run by Gold Coast legend Bernie Elsey. The group's performances would alternate between the dining room and the underground Jolly Roger nightclub, which Elsey had excavated by hand under The Beachcomber's foundations, allegedly without council approval. Local legend also has it that the following March, management at another Surfers Paradise club received a letter from a 'Mr. Epstein' in Liverpool, England, asking if Elsey would be interested in arranging bookings for a good but little-known quartet who called themselves The Beatles. The price proposed was £60 per Beatle per week, in addition to their return fares from England and accommodation expenses. The letter enclosed an ordinary snapshot of four mop-haired youngsters. The club's management declined based on cost, citing Elsey, who the previous year had hired three Bee Gees for a total of £40 a week. In June 1964, The Beatles would make their only tour of Australia – for a great deal more money than was offered to Elsey.

Singer Regina King recalls: 'The Beachcomber had live entertainment late at night, so someone would get a gig after we finished our 7 p.m. to 11 p.m. shift. When I sang there, although they were still very young, The Bee Gees were often the headline act. They would be asleep in their father's old bomb parked outside The Beachcomber in Cavill Avenue. Their father would wake them up when it was their turn to go on and they would pounce on to the stage to sing their beautiful harmonies, blasting out old standards like 'Bye Bye Blackbird' and 'Bill Bailey Won't You Please Come Home'. They brought the house down every night'.

Barbara Gibb recalls another venue: 'We used to play the Southport Hotel, which was in the same area as The Beachcomber. The boys would really play me up. Just before they went on stage, they'd disappear into the gent's toilet where I couldn't follow them, to tune up, and I used to be petrified because their singing used to go right through the whole place. Everybody could hear them tuning up and singing. And I couldn't go in and tell them when it was time to go on stage. They knew very well I couldn't go into this place, so that's why they went. But they never missed a cue; they were very professional always'.

Across the road from the Beachcomber was the Chevron Hotel, which Barry remembered in a 2012 New Zealand radio interview with Tim Roxborough: 'When we were children, we worked (there) with a lot of Māoris like the Māori Troubadours in Surfers' Paradise and with Prince Tui, and we all hung out together and we learned an awful lot'.

RSL clubs now became very regular venues to play. Barry: 'We used to play Returned Soldiers clubs, and there'd be a juggler, a guy with dancing dogs, a comedian and us. We'd do a lot of comedy – in fact, we were billed as 'The Bee Gees Comedy Trio'. We'd sing 'Does Your Chewing Gum Lose Its Flavour (On the Bedpost Overnight?)' and do little comedy routines. If you were going down badly, the secretary would come on stage and pay you in the middle of your act. Then we worked in places like dockside clubs, where sailors would actually have beer-drinking competitions during the show. These places we were playing were full of one-armed bandits, which were positioned all around the stage. Then these two blokes started having a fight in the audience, but they were so drunk, they had to fight sitting down! Australians are great! They'll get into a fight for any reason whatsoever. That's the way it was back then in the fifties and sixties. Brutal! It really was an amazing place to be a kid'.

Barry continued, 'The big time to us, back then, was working in clubs, hotels, the RSLs. Let's face it, that was our life from the pre-teen years onwards. Australia also toughened us up as The Bee Gees. An Australian audience is the hardest to please in the world, and I always found that if you could please an Australian audience, you could please any audience in the world, so it was a good training for us as a group. We were into Col Joye, Johnny O'Keefe, Billy Thorpe and Normie Rowe; though I wouldn't say they influenced us a great deal musically. Maybe they did in the sense of competition. We really wanted to get out and prove ourselves against those acts. We were three kids, and everybody loves kids, you know – and a great dog act! I honestly feel synonymous with Australia. It's really everything I learned about songwriting'.

Another person working at The Beachcomber was entertainer Ian Turpie, who insisted Barry's unusual guitar style restricted his songwriting, as it only allowed him to play major chords. He showed him minor chords to play. He recalls humour was a big part of the Gibb family's life, which he believes they got from Hugh – similar to *The Goon Show*. 'Turps', as he was affectionately known, also participated in another of the family passions – making home movies. He distinctly remembered one called *The African Queen* was very funny.

Turpie, who lived with the Gibb family for a short time in 1962, also recalled the brothers working constantly, which he considered was 'quite interesting', as the child protection laws limiting children working were quite strict at the time, 'but they seemed to get around it'. He also remembered they were more of a comedy act in those days. Turpie, who would have an enduring and successful career hosting many television shows over the next 40 years, would meet up with the Gibb brothers again when he hosted *The Go!! Show* in Melbourne in the mid-1960s.

They were now working virtually every weekend, and making a reasonable living, enough to support a family of seven, but in their eyes, they weren't getting anywhere professionally. Hugh remembered, 'The boys wanted to go to Sydney, which was like going to New York. They wanted to get to the big time'.

A fortuitous meeting between the Gibb brothers and Australian pop star Col Joye and his brother Kevin Jacobsen occurred on 30 August 1962. Col recalls being at a party on the Gold Coast amidst his annual *Col Joye Spectacular* tour of Queensland with his band The Joy Boys and being asked to stay longer to cast his eye over a local singing trio. When the Gibbs did arrive and perform, Col was impressed – so much so that he asked their father Hugh to bring them to the St. John's Hall in the heart of Surfers Paradise the following day.

Barry's version of events is slightly different:

The hall where Col and his band were rehearsing happened to be no more than about one hundred yards from our house. We thought, 'This is the next step. If we can meet this guy, we can sell him a song and we're on our way'. We all talked about it, but nobody would go over and say 'Hello!'. So, I said, 'I'm going. It's the only chance we've got'. It ended up with me walking across the road to this hall, with Dad about one hundred yards behind with his date book. We got there and I said to this man that I would like to meet with Col Joye. What I didn't know was that I was speaking to Kevin Jacobsen, Col's brother. Kevin (The Joy Boys' pianist as well as their manager) replied, 'Hang around for a minute, Col is on his way out'. Col came through and I said, 'I'd like to sing you some of the songs we've written with a view to you recording them if possible'. He said, 'Oh sure'. I couldn't believe it.

Barry would also recall Col's arrival as like the archetypal pop star 'with sunglasses, like Presley. Everybody was a Presley in those days. He later came over to the house, and we sat down and played for him'.

Barry recalls that '(When) we played for him, he wasn't totally knocked out by the material as much as he was mesmerised by the way we were singing and harmonising at that age. He said, 'You've got to come to Sydney and make a record''. One song that Col especially liked was '(Underneath The) Starlight Of Love'. It impressed him enough that he would record it himself within a matter of months. According to Barry, 'It was the first solid sign we'd ever had that we might be going somewhere'.

The Jacobsen brothers knew talent when they saw it and were in a good position to assist and promote that talent. So impressed were they by the three brothers' performance, they were invited to travel to Sydney and audition, with the possibility of making a record. Col and Kevin promptly arranged to visit the family home and meet Hugh and Barbara and organised the boys' travel to Sydney for more auditions, this time at Festival Records' studios in the suburb of Pyrmont.

Within a few weeks, the three brothers arrived at the studios, where they recorded some demos under Col's watchful eye. Col remembers the day clearly: 'In come these three kids with their little shirts with these little felt badges that said 'BG'. I've still got the original tape where he says, 'My name is Barry Gibb, I live at 23 Cambridge Avenue, Surfer's Paradise. My first song is 'Let Me Love You'' … and they had these magic harmonies'.

Regardless of Barry's memory of 'shivering like leaves because he was such a big star', both Kevin and Col were again taken by the distinctive harmonies of the trio and were confident of their potential. It was strongly recommended that a permanent move to Sydney would be in the group's best interests for a greater chance of success. Kevin also offered to manage them and try to get the trio a recording contract.

While it wasn't the first time relocation to Sydney had been suggested for the Gibbs, coming with the offer of management from Kevin, and supported by Col, this time there was a ready-made incentive to make the move. Hugh was in full agreement but later spoke highly of his sons' time on the Gold Coast: 'Today, getting to the top is a catch-as-catch-can affair. The business forces youngsters to walk before they can crawl. When my boys were at Surfers Paradise, they played to some of the most diverse audiences you'd find in Australia. If they failed, they weren't going to drop into obscurity. They had the opportunity to learn from their successes and to gain strength from them. But there, you can go so far in the entertainment world and no further'.

When the 1962 school year finished in mid-December, and with Robin and Maurice just a week short of their thirteenth birthday, the twins left school for the last time. Although the legal age for leaving school was fifteen, the education authorities were possibly of the belief that they were a year older based on press cuttings from this period. Maurice recalls: 'We actually did fill some forms out and passed some tests and left at thirteen. The school said, 'They can't concentrate – they're too involved in show business''.

From this point on, they would join elder brother Barry in becoming full-time entertainers, devoting most of their spare time to learning their craft. In 1999, Robin summarised their school years: 'As for my academic work, I was only good at the things I was interested in. I loved natural history and social history. I wasn't too interested in military history, but I was fascinated by how wars were caused. We weren't particularly creative at school, you see. We were just normal schoolkids – all the singing went on outside. A lot of the kids simply could not understand our obsession with music. We lived in a world that kids don't normally visit – a creative kind of world. We took it very seriously. They were into playing football, and we were in the basement writing songs. Because of this, we didn't have that many close friends'.

1963

Before the family moved to Sydney in early 1963, the brothers completed all their local commitments, including another appearance at the Grand Hotel on Southport. Again, with great foresight, The Bee Gees were billed as 'Famous Stars of National Radio and TV'.

Kevin Jacobsen, with his usual effectiveness, wasted no time in advocating for his new protégés. He first arranged for The Bee Gees to appear at a Chubby Checker concert on Saturday 19 January at the Sydney Stadium – before the family had moved from Queensland. Robin remembers the excitement of the phone call they received from Col Joye with the invitation a few months earlier: "Would you be interested in doing a show with me and Chubby Checker at Sydney Stadium because we don't have a fill-in act?'. Chubby Checker was very, very big at this time. He was very hot and we were very young'.

How the Bee Gees – at that point, an unknown act in Sydney and one more suited to clubs – came to be included on a bill of established acts that included heavyweights like Johnny O'Keefe, Col Joye and The Joy Boys (who backed all of the artists), Warren Williams, Judy Stone and Little Sammy Gaha, can only be attributed to Kevin's persuasion skills.

However, if the three brothers expected to be introduced to the Sydney rock 'n' roll community as an opening act, they were in for a big surprise. Backed by The Joy Boys, the trio went on stage as the act between Johnny O'Keefe and Chubby Checker, who closed the show. Barry would recall: 'It was totally mind-blowing for us. It was the first time we had worked with – in terms of what was going on in Australia at the time – an overseas star. You had a crowd of screaming teenagers and these three kids – us – playing this stadium, sandwiched between Johnny O'Keefe and Chubby Checker. We protested that we were unknown and would be murdered, but we were stuck with it. It was a complete nightmare!'.

Barry would later remember the experience – for which they were paid £15 – as 'Incredible! For that time, it was amazing! Thousands of screaming kids, not screaming at us, but it was a sight for us to see, to be part of it. Chubby Checker was the American star of the moment, and he closed the show. Johnny O'Keefe was the Australian rock star of the moment, and he was on third-to-last. Somebody decided to put The Bee Gees in between ... We sang some rock 'n' roll songs, but we weren't a rock 'n' roll group. Then we sang things like 'Alexander's Ragtime Band' – enough to get us into deep trouble. We just didn't know what kids wanted. We'd worked in nightclubs. We didn't think anybody was ever going to thrust us on kids. As much as we wanted it, we didn't think it was ever going to happen to us'.

Following the show, the brothers returned to Queensland to help their family pack, and the nomadic Gibb family made the (then) twelve-hour drive south to Sydney. After living with the Jacobsen family for a short while, they settled at 23 Colin Street, Lakemba, about seven miles southwest of Sydney's central business district. Within a few weeks, The Bee Gees – as they were now more occasionally billed – already had a regular spot performing at the Three Swallows Hotel in Bankstown, in southwestern Sydney.

Whilst their appearance on the Chubby Checker 'Spectacular' didn't receive any media attention, it did assist in getting what they had aimed for from their inception: a recording contract. Robin remembers, the contract 'came as a direct result of the Chubby Checker concert in Sydney. Now in Sydney, that's where all the labels are – you don't get signed up anywhere else but Sydney. So, Festival Records approached us with a contract'. Whilst this quote from Robin is not quite accurate – as the other Australian states all had their own record companies – they were in fact signing with one of the biggest record companies in the land: Festival Records Pty. Ltd.

Festival Records' Managing Director Fred Marks had heard a tape of the Gibb brothers' audition from the previous year (provided by Kevin Jacobsen) and was possibly in the audience for the Sydney Stadium concert. Initially, though, he was not at all impressed: 'Vocal groups don't sell', he would proclaim. Kevin Jacobsen – never a man to be put off easily – demonstrated his confidence in his trio's potential by offering to drop one of his own recording acts from his artist management list. The artist Kevin suggested he would delist was Judy Cannon; but in reality, this was but a clever ruse, as the young singer was going overseas shortly anyway. Marks, if not impressed by Kevin's offer, was entertained by Kevin's desperation, and agreed to sign the brothers to a contract – albeit one that would allow the trio's records to be released on the Leedon label, which was a Festival subsidiary.

The Leedon record label had been established in 1958 by Lee Gordon and his Australian general manager Alan Heffernan, as an offshoot of their *Big Shows* concept. Gordon was a Florida-born entrepreneur and promoter whose business gall and brash showbiz style had already made him a celebrity in his own right in Australia. By 1963, Gordon's business, and health, were in disarray, and Festival had taken over Leedon records.

Whilst plans were being made to make their first record, the Gibbs kept on working. On 16 February, they made their first appearance on Australia's most popular TV music show *Bandstand*, presented by Brian Henderson. With their first record still in the production stage and not ready to promote, the trio performed two of their club favourites: 'Alexander's Ragtime Band' and 'My Old Man's A Dustman'. Footage of both performances still exists and has since been released on *Bandstand* DVD box sets. Lonnie Donegan's version of 'My Old Man's A Dustman' had been a number 1 hit in Australia just three years prior. 'Alexander's Ragtime Band' – the 1911 Irving Berlin standard – would continue to be included as part of their acoustic concert set as late as 1974.

The Bee Gees' first official recordings were made at Festival Records studios at 223-229 Harris Street, Pyrmont, in Sydney. Col Joye had offered to produce them rather than use Festival's in-house engineer, Robert Iredale – the term 'producer' was not commonly used in the early-1960s.

The group were very fortunate to have their mentor at the helm, as all artists were very much at the mercy of the engineer. If, for example, the drums played well all the way through the song together with the keyboards and/or guitars, but the bass had one bad note, it was not uncommon for that bad note to be left in if the allotted recording time was up. Recordings of that time were on a pre-stereo two-track mono machine. The drums, bass, keyboard and rhythm guitar parts usually went down on the first track. Then that track was played back while the lead vocal, the harmonies, percussion and lead guitar were recorded on the other track. The two tracks were mixed together and that became the finished mono recording. Assisting Col at the session sitting behind the control room glass, was Hal Sanders as the assistant engineer. Hugh Gibb was also there, observing his sons' performance and the recording process. Col used his group The Joy Boys for the backing, including a string bass, drums, and what sounds like either a damped guitar or a ukulele: possibly played by guitarist Norm Day.

The session produced the trio's first ever record: 'The Battle Of The Blue And The Grey', backed with 'The Three Kisses Of Love': both original compositions penned by Barry.

'The Battle Of The Blue And The Grey' (Barry Gibb)
Recorded at Festival Studios, Sydney: circa February 1963
The Bee Gees' very first single was released on 22 March 1963 on the Leedon label in Australia. The record label had a hyphenated version of

the group's name – The Bee-Gees – and was the only record they would release on the black and silver 'boomerang' Leedon label design.

In retrospect, it's difficult to ponder what sort of record should have been expected from the young teen group, but this is certainly a song that would have defied most expectations. It's a fast track, remarkable in its maturity bearing in mind that Barry was merely sixteen when he wrote it. It's written from the perspective of an old soldier reminiscing about the American Civil War – the colours refer to the uniforms worn by the Union and Confederate armies. It has a distinctive country flavour, perhaps inspired at least in part by skiffle music. Lonnie Donegan's 1957 hit 'Jack O'Diamonds' is a reasonably close prototype.

Ironically, although 'The Battle Of The Blue And The Grey' was a country and western song, in essence, The Bee Gees in 1963 were certainly not a country act. That music, however, was an integral part of their live performance repertoire. In particular, on their many TV appearances over the next few years in Australia, they would be required to sing songs in the genre, of various qualities.

While they were in Australia, The Bee Gees were generalists – they had to be to survive. Like most acts at the bottom of the showbiz ladder, their act needed to span genres and age groups. Their song list prepared them for audiences at schools, fêtes, dances, clubs and RSL halls – both in the city and in the bush.

The single had a nine-week run on Sydney radio station 2SM's National Top 100 chart, making its first appearance at number 92 on 12 April 1963, peaking at 50 for two weeks commencing 17 May 1963. They performed the song during their appearance on *Bandstand* on 4 April 1963 and again live on *The Country and Western Hour* in February 1964. The latter, which featured a studio house band, added something that was missing in their pre-recorded *Bandstand* performance.

'The Three Kisses Of Love' (Barry Gibb)
Recorded at Festival Studios, Sydney: circa February 1963

The first single's B-side was, in comparison with its A-side, an adolescent love song with a simple but pretty melody, giving the young brothers a good platform to showcase their harmonies.

Perhaps influenced by The Everly Brothers, 'The Three Kisses Of Love' is not dissimilar to another Barry Gibb composition, 'Let Me Love You', which predated it by three years. According to Barry, 'The Three Kisses Of Love' got more plays than the A-side at the time.

Strangely, when they made their first appearance on Channel Seven's *Sing, Sing, Sing* on 6 April, just two weeks after the release of their single, rather than promoting the record, The Bee Gees performed 'All I Have To Do Is Dream' – a 1958 hit for the Everly Brothers – and Patsy Cline's 'Tra Le La Le La Triangle', which was also covered by Heather McKean in Australia.

Undoubtedly more pleasing to their record company, the group did perform both sides of their single when they made their second appearance on *Bandstand* on 24 April.

Other television appearances made to promote the new record at the time, included *Saturday Date* (presented by Jimmy Hannan), in addition to appearances at various clubs, all secured through the Jacobsens' management agency, ATA. They also appeared on another Channel Seven music program, called *Surfsound*: compered by Rob E.G., a very popular local Sydney artist fresh from his own hit single '55 Days At Peking'. With the increased television work and live performances, The Bee Gees were at least earning enough to meet the family's bills. Reputedly, the trio were being paid £15-£20 for anything up to five hours work: a reasonable pay-packet in the early-1960s. However, the boys' own weekly share of that was somewhat meagre, as they were now assuming the responsibility of being the breadwinners for their family of seven.

In retrospect, the role seems entirely reasonable, considering the three boys' career had now taken over the whole Gibb family's lives – with Hugh as roadie, chauffeur and road manager, Barbara assigned to wardrobe management, and elder sister Lesley contributing by overseeing the fan club. Only five-year-old Andy was left to his own devices. On the subject, many years later, Maurice was quite clear on the matter: 'We don't find it embarrassing at all to say we supported our family. We did for many years. Our father put in as many years as we put in. And my mum did just as much, always looking after our clothes and getting us together. We always looked after our family 'cause they looked after us'.

When their first single failed to set the world alight, by Robin's account, they weren't perturbed at all: 'It bombed. It didn't matter to us; we just wanted to see our name on a record. We didn't care if it was a hit or not. It was very hot with one guy at 2SM in Sydney, and he was playing it all the time, but it didn't do anything'. The guy Robin was referring to was Bob Rogers – one of the most popular disc jockeys in Sydney; and by some accounts, the record wasn't the abject failure that Robin said it was: creeping into the top twenty of one local Sydney chart for at least one week.

The Bee Gees made their first appearances at the annual Sydney Royal Easter Show, which was held from 5-16 April at the Sydney Showground. Amongst their fellow performers were many of their fellow *Bandstand* performers, and country music star Chad Morgan.

There wasn't much time before the next milestone was achieved. Col Joye recorded one of the very first songs he'd heard Barry play the previous year in the church hall on the Gold Coast. Col's version of Barry's '(Underneath The) Starlight Of Love' – which was released as the B-side to his single 'Put 'Em Down' in the last week of April – gave him the distinction of being the first-ever artist to cover a Barry Gibb song.

The song – the lyrics of which may have sounded dated even then – remains a bright, cleverly produced, extremely commercial track. It remains a fine testament to an emerging, but still young, songwriter. Undoubtedly, it would have been a proud moment for sixteen-year-old Barry Gibb, to have one of the country's top performers record his composition.

'Put 'Em Down' achieved some chart success, peaking at number 31 on the Victoria state chart and 64 on Sydney's 2SM radio station chart. Unusually, however, '(Underneath The) Starlight Of Love' took on a life of its own at 2SM and charted in its own right, peaking at 61 in the fourth week of a six-week run.

This was the first of what would become some six decades later, a catalogue of over 7,000 cover versions of songs written by various combinations of Barry, Robin, and Maurice Gibb – performed by more than 2,500 artists. Of course, the list is continually expanding.

The current total of covers of their Australian compositions alone is over 500, including nearly 300 sung in languages other than English. A brief overview includes Chinese, Danish, Finnish, French, German, Hungarian, Italian, Norwegian, Spanish and Welsh. Approximately 20% of the Australian cover versions are instrumentals. On their return to the UK in 1967, even before they had success themselves, well-known British and European singers were lining up to cover their songs

One of the great ironies of The Bee Gees' time in Australia in particular, is the high demand from collectors and completists today, not just for the group's recordings, but also for early covers of Gibb compositions. In addition, any recordings on which the Gibb brothers' vocals were present – or even if they were rumoured to have assisted in the studio – achieve high prices in those circles.

The 6 May edition of the popular national weekly magazine *Woman's Day*, featured a story about The Bee Gees titled 'Manx Cats Come to

Town', with two accompanying photos: one with the whole Gibb family – including Lesley's then-fiancé Alan Curtis in front of their recently installed 'Swinging House' sign – and another with the three boys singing into a reel-to-reel tape recorder.

In what was another huge accomplishment for the group and their management's PR work, they appeared on the front cover of the *Teenagers Weekly* supplement to *The Australian Women's Weekly*'s 15 May edition. Photographed wearing their now-almost-trademark tartan waistcoats, their exposure in Australia's biggest-selling magazine would have done their pursuit of a greater national profile, no harm at all.

On 8 June, The Bee Gees made their third appearance on *Bandstand*, this time performing 'Little Band Of Gold' – which had been a top five hit for its composer James Gilreath just three months previously – and The Beatles' first Australian single 'Please Please Me', which although released some four months earlier on 21 February, had been treated with some indifference locally, despite making number 2 in England.

On 29 June, The Bee Gees made their second appearance on a country-and-western-themed episode of *Sing, Sing, Sing,* performing 'Abilene': a number 1 US country music hit for George Hamilton IV. In 1998, The Bee Gees' cover of the song which was pre-recorded for the *Sing, Sing, Sing* show and was still in Festival's archives, was almost included in the *Brilliant From Birth* collection of the group's recordings from their Australian era. Only the lack of disc space thwarted its inclusion. It presently remains unreleased. Other guests on the show included John Laws, Judy Cannon, Warren and Denis Williams, Laurel Lea, Barry Stanton, Arthur Blanche and Tommy Spencer. Host Johnny O'Keefe led the cast, including The Bee Gees, in a performance of 'Once A Year Day', which was originally performed by John Raitt and Doris Day in the movie *The Pajama Game*.

The following Monday, the trio went back into the studio to record their follow-up single. This time, Festival's in-house engineer and producer Robert Iredale was in charge. Iredale – an urbane, bespectacled gentleman in his early thirties – had learned his producer skills working for Coronet Records in the 1950s and was well-regarded as a wonderful improviser with Festival's limited studio technology. Iredale would oversee many important recordings of the era, using groundbreaking techniques to make up for the primitive recording equipment: then limited to a one-track Ampex tape machine, later to be updated to two-track equipment.

However, before the second Bee Gees single saw daylight, a four-man group from Liverpool would change the course of popular music forever. The Beatles – who would inspire the Brothers Gibb like no other act – exploded on the Australian charts, as they had already in England and Europe and would do so about twelve months later in America. 'From Me To You' was the first Beatles single to chart in Australia, peaking at number 3 in July 1963. It would be followed by four more singles within the next five months, including two which topped the chart. The Beatles' appeal to The Bee Gees was obvious – a harmony singing group writing and recording their own songs, whose members were near their own age. The Beatles had grown up in a working-class neighbourhood in Liverpool, not unlike where the Gibbs had lived in Manchester, and not too far away geographically.

With their unique sibling harmonies, The Bee Gees were also beginning to be sought-after as backing vocalists, and the first of these sessions was with Sydney-born pop and country singer Judy Stone. On 22 July, she released 'It Takes A Lot (To Make Me Cry)'. The track – which featured The Bee Gees' vocals prominently – was produced by Robert Iredale and made the top twenty in most Australian states. This was the follow-up single to her national top ten record '4,003,221 Tears From Now'.

Another appearance on *Sing, Sing, Sing* followed on 27 July, with The Bee Gees this time performing 'Surfin' Hootenanny': a surf pop/rock song written by Lee Hazlewood, and a current hit for Al Casey.

With the fresh, innovative music that was now coming out of Britain making a massive impact in Australia, The Bee Gees' second single 'Timber!'/'Take Hold Of That Star' – released on 29 July – seemed suddenly out of date. One suspects that Barry Gibb, already a keen observer of musical trends, must have known immediately that his writing was going to have to adapt – and quickly – if The Bee Gees were to be successful.

'Timber!' (Barry Gibb)
Recorded at Festival Studios, Sydney: circa June 1963
The track was very short at just 1:46, but this was not unusual for popular songs at that time. The record label boasts an 'orchestral' backing to the song – in all likelihood just a single violin and some fancy studio trickery from producer Robert Iredale – which makes this sound like it's more from the late-1950s than 1963. But it did feature some more

contemporary Beatles-like 'yeah, yeah, yeahs' amongst the otherwise rather adolescent lyrics. The single failed commercially. Later, Robin amusingly stated that it 'did exactly what the title suggested!'.

This single was the first time the group's name would appear on record in the form to which we are now accustomed – The Bee Gees – without the hyphen that had appeared on the first single's label. Their new 'brand' would serve the three brothers well, lasting to the end of the century and beyond, taking the brothers into musical history.

'Timber!' was later issued as the lead track on an EP issued by Leedon, simply titled *The Bee Gees*. It was their first record to be released in a picture sleeve. Its B-side 'Take Hold Of That Star' was included, with 'The Battle Of The Blue And The Grey' and 'The Three Kisses Of Love' comprising the EP's second side.

'Take Hold Of That Star' (Barry Gibb)

Recorded at Festival Studios, Sydney: circa June 1963

This was the B-side of 'Timber!'. Incredibly, Barry was still only sixteen when this was released, and his amazing versatility as a songwriter was already showing with this impressive ballad.

The accompaniment consists of Barry's strummed guitar, a lounge-style piano, double bass and drums, which give this quite a 1950s feel. The young trio's harmonies are to the fore for the majority of the song, but the bridge is Barry's solo spot: the maturity of his voice and delivery is incredible for one so young.

5 August 1963 saw the release of 'I'd Like To Leave If I May', recorded by Lonnie Lee, who, like The Bee Gees, recorded on the Leedon label. It was the second Barry Gibb composition to be covered. Lee, who was a very successful pop singer at the time, placed Barry's song as the B-Side of his single 'Acres Of Everything But Love'. Lee was looking for new songs to record, particularly homegrown material, and was given a tape of several Gibb songs. Lee was impressed by the demo, noting Barry's unusual guitar sound and exceptional voice. Lee recalled: 'Even then, you could see he was destined for great things'.

On 19 August, when The Bee Gees made their fourth appearance on *Bandstand,* possibly conceding that 'Timber!' was beyond saving commercially, they took the opportunity to promote the B-Side 'Take Hold Of That Star'. As was the show's format, they also performed their version of Bob Dylan's folk staple 'Blowin' In The Wind'.

Performing the bizarre country song 'Hilly Billy Ding Dong Choo Choo' and 'I Want You To Want Me', the group made another appearance on *Bandstand* on 7 September. The former, silly, gimmicky song was performed first by Soupy Sales in America, but it was The Appalachians' version that was better-known in Australia. Fraternal duo Denis and Warren Williams also did their penance when they performed the song on *Sing, Sing, Sing* a month earlier. 'I Want You To Want Me' was a vocal number by the well-known English group The Shadows, who were better known as an instrumental group. It was the B-side of their hit single 'Atlantis'.

Two days later, on 2 September, The Bee Gees performed for their biggest crowd to date at the first Sydney 2UW Radio Spectacular at Lane Cove National Park. With over 40,000 music fans in attendance, the other artists performing at the four-hour concert included Col Joye and The Joy Boys, Noeleen Batley, The De Kroo Brothers, and The Echomen, who also backed The Bee Gees. The press reported that the concert was so crowded, the performers had to be rowed in across the river to get to the stage.

In September, The Bee Gees made their first appearance on a long-playing record. Festival Records' *National Top 100 Hits* featured a smattering of Australian artists, including Col Joye, Dig Richards and Rob E.G., and also well-known international acts Ray Charles, George McCurn, and The Four Seasons. Rather oddly, it was 'The Three Kisses Of Love' – the B-side of The Bee Gees first single – which appeared on this compilation.

With no new single of their own to promote, the group was forced to cover other artists' hits again when they made their next appearance on *Bandstand* – their sixth in less than eight months. For the 19 October show, they performed The Crystals' 'Da Doo Ron Ron' and The Searchers' big hit 'Sweets For My Sweet'. Singing other artists' hits may have been somewhat bittersweet for the three ambitious Bee Gees. While they enjoyed singing these songs – particularly those by other harmony groups like The Searchers – the trio's lack of chart success may have started to frustrate them. Ironically, in 1973, the tables would be turned when The Searchers covered The Bee Gees' 'Spicks And Specks' in their own quest for a new hit.

Singer Tony Brady – whose day job was working for Barry's music publishing company Belinda – worked hard to promote Barry's songwriting abilities, so it seemed only reasonable that he should record a Barry Gibb song also. Barry wrote 'Let's Stomp, Australia Way' with New Zealand rock export Johnny Devlin. It was a fairly average song, aimed to cash in on the new Australian dance craze The Stomp. The single, released by RCA in October 1963, was the first-ever to contain covers of two Gibb compositions – the reverse side was 'Lucky Me'. At one second shy of two minutes, it's one of the shortest Barry Gibb compositions, and apart from that fact, it's a completely unremarkable song. Despite a television tour around Australia to promote the single, it failed to make the charts.

'The Stomp', referred to in the song, evolved out of the booming surf culture that was sweeping Australia at the time with its own music and preferred artists like The Delltones, Little Pattie and Australia's first big guitar band, The Atlantics. Their classic 'Bombora' was an Australian number 1 in August 1963. It charted all over the world and was chosen by America's *Cashbox* magazine as its Record of the Week.

New Zealander Johnny Devlin was the next artist to use The Bee Gees as backing vocalists on his Festival single 'Stomp The Tumbarumba', which was released on 14 October. It became a top five hit for the Kiwi, now an Australian resident – and significantly, it was The Bee Gees' first-ever appearance on a genuine hit single. It also became the brothers' first showing on a record in Europe when it was released in Scandinavia on the Olga label. Quite what the appeal of Tumbarumba – a town in northern New South Wales – was in Scandinavia, has never been explained.

The three fresh-faced lads from Manchester may not have been ones to *hang five* on a surfboard, but they *were* on board for the craze. In November – tying in nicely with the trend – Barry's new composition 'Let's Stomp Australia Way' was assigned copyright, and The Bee Gees appeared at several surf and stomp dances, including the 1963 *Surf Spectacular* at Sydney Stadium on 15 November with Kevin Todd, Laurel Lea, The Atlantics, Paul Wayne and Del Juliana; and at Stomp City, Taylor Square, Darlinghurst, Sydney on 22 November: the day of US President Kennedy's assassination in Dallas, Texas. The next day, The Bee Gees performed their first show in the Australian capital, Canberra, at the Hotel Ainslie Rex.

In November, another Festival recording artist, Sydney-born Noeleen Batley – who was nicknamed Australia's Little Miss Sweetheart – released the first of four songs that Barry would write specifically for her. She recalls: 'The songs that Barry wrote were especially for me. Barry played many songs to me, which I wasn't really impressed with at the time. So, we made another appointment, and he came up with 'Surfer Boy', my first recording by him. I loved it'. 'Surfer Boy' is a sweet ballad with a mature sound but with lyrics all about teenage angst. It was the B-side to her 'Forgive Me' single, which peaked at number 34 in New South Wales. The A-side was a Burt Bacharach and Hal David song, so Barry's songs were at least keeping good company. Batley would remain a lifelong friend of the Gibb family, even appearing at an official Bee Gees fan club gathering in Miami in 1994. When attendees participated in a karaoke contest singing covers of Bee Gees songs, she joined in with her take on their 1968 hit 'I've Gotta Get A Message To You'.

On 2 December – in the same week that *TV Week* hailed The Bee Gees as 'The best vocal group since The Delltones' – the trio provided uncredited backing vocals on the single 'Beach Ball'/'You Gotta Have Love' by Sydney entertainer and television host Jimmy Hannan. The record was the first release on the RG label, owned by television entrepreneur Reg Grundy. Festival Records distributed the single and it was a substantial hit in Australia, peaking at number 3 in Sydney and number 8 in Brisbane.

Following the single's success, the record was also released in the United States, on the Atlantic label in August 1964 – the first time the world's biggest popular music market was exposed to The Bee Gees' distinctive vocal sound, which is very evident on both sides of the single.

Meanwhile, the group kept busy with various live performances. One of their shows that December was at the Wentworthville Leagues Club, seventeen miles west of Sydney, where Barry met his future wife Maureen Bates, through their respective parents. As both families were relatively recent migrants from the UK to Australia, the Bates' were invited to visit the Gibb family home, and Maureen and her younger brother Tony accompanied them. An enduring friendship between the two families developed from that point forward.

The Christmas edition of *Sing, Sing, Sing* on 14 December blended traditional Christmas music with current pop favourites, performed by host Johnny O'Keefe and guests Sharon O'Brien, Al Lane, The Flanagans, Tommy Spencer and Pam & Ade. The Bee Gees performed 'The Girl Sang The Blues' (The Everly Brothers) and 'Midnight Mary' (Joey Powers). More than 120 adults and children appeared in the finale, which included fifteen girls of different nationalities dressed in their national costumes, saying 'Merry Christmas' in their native languages.

The Bee Gees' final TV appearance of 1963 was on *Sing, Sing, Sing* a week later on 21 December. They performed more covers: 'I Wanna Hold Your Hand' (The Beatles), and 'Glad All Over' (Dave Clark Five), which was performed as a duet of sorts with the show's host Johnny O'Keefe.

The group would begin a month-long season at the Sydney restaurant/nightclub *Spellsons,* beginning on Boxing Day. Although they'd previously aimed at the teenage market, they had a sophisticated stage act lined up for their club opening. It included comedy numbers and new arrangements of oldies such as 'Alexander's Ragtime Band', which were popular with adult audiences.

1964

1964 got off to a promising start when The Bee Gees appeared at the second *2UW Spectacular* in front of 45,000 people at Lane Cove National Park, Sydney, on 2 January. Also on the bill were Warren Williams, Johnny Rebb, Judy Stone, Noeleen Batley, The Atlantics, The Dave Bridge Trio, The Denvermen, Johnny Devlin and Digger Revell. As a testament to their growing respect within Sydney's pop music industry, the three brothers had already recorded, or soon would be, with three of these acts.

In February, Barry achieved his biggest songwriting success to date with renowned country-pop singer Jimmy Little's cover of 'One Road'. A follow-up to Little's number 1 hit 'Royal Telephone' from a few months before, 'One Road' became a top ten record across the country. Barry changed it from a love song to a religious theme to suit the gospel style of Little's previous single.

'Peace Of Mind' (Barry Gibb)
Recorded at Festival Studios, Sydney: circa February 1964

The Bee Gees third single, 'Peace Of Mind', was released on 10 February 1964; unfortunately suffering the same fate as its predecessor by failing to make any impression on the Australian charts. As Robin succinctly joked in later years, 'We went back to the studio to record a follow-up, 'Peace Of Mind', which didn't give us any when it flopped!'.

This was something of a shame, as the brisk Merseybeat-influenced 'Peace Of Mind' deserved to be appreciated by a wider audience. With the Gibbs sounding a little less like children on the arrangement, it had a looser, more adult feel – highlighted by a couple of screams not dissimilar to those heard on some Beatles songs of that period. A lead guitar augmented the now-usual Barry on rhythm guitar, along with a double bass and drums.

By this time, The Beatles' sound had well and truly hit Australia; and while The Bee Gees' unique harmonies had actually predated their idols, the success of the Liverpool band certainly gave the brothers the impetus and confidence to use their own harmonies in a more R&B style.

'Don't Say Goodbye' (Barry Gibb)
Recorded at Festival Studios, Sydney: circa February 1964

The B-side of 'Peace Of Mind' was 'Don't Say Goodbye'. It's a slower, almost country-style song with Barry taking the lead vocal.

On 1 February, The Bee Gees travelled to Adelaide to make their first appearance on the NWS Nine television show *The Country and Western Hour,* compered by Roger Cardwell. Backed by a traditional country band made up of fiddle, upright bass, banjo, guitars and even a piano accordion, they performed 'The Battle Of The Blue And Grey' and 'Don't Say Goodbye'. The trio were most impressive. In particular, their performance of the former song added something that was missing in their pre-recorded performances of that song on *Bandstand* and *Sing, Sing, Sing.* This time wearing black short-sleeved polo shirts – in contrast to their usual tartan waistcoats or suits and ties – the trio seemed well-matched to the country music format.

The group made another appearance on *Sing, Sing, Sing* on 1 March, with guests including Johnny Devlin, comedian Reg Quartly, and Trevor Gordon: another friend from their Queensland days. The main attraction, however, was Earl Grant: an American pianist, organist, singer and dancer who had his first and biggest hit with 'The End' in 1957.

This was followed by an appearance on *Surfsound* compered by Rob E.G., with guests Noeleen Batley, and Kenny Shane & The Silhouettes. Said to be earning £150 per week now for their regular slots on *Bandstand* and *Sing, Sing, Sing,* The Bee Gees' performances of their respective new singles were usually accompanied by their covers of various hits of the day, including The Beatles' 'From Me to You' and 'Please Please Me'; Chad and Jeremy's 'Yesterday's Gone'; The Dave Clarke Five's 'Can't You See That She's Mine' and The Hollies' 'Just One Look', to name a few. These covers were particularly well regarded, and The Bee Gees' version of Skeeter Davis' 1963 hit 'The End Of The World' – and even the relatively bland 'Little Band Of Gold' – are classic.

On 17 March, Barry, Robin, and Maurice were in the audience at the *Macquarie Tunetable Awards* at the Macquarie Auditorium in Sydney. As one of 25 acts that were 'introduced to records in 1963', The Bee Gees were eligible for the *Outstanding Newcomer Award.* Although they didn't win, they may have influenced the result with their harmonies evident on the 'Beach Ball' single for which Jimmy Hannan won. Johnny Devlin won *Composer of the Year* for 'Stomp The Tumbarumba': another single for which The Bee Gees had provided background vocals; and Jimmy Little – for whom Barry had written songs – won the *Best Male Vocalist Award* for his 'Royal Telephone' single. When a compilation album commemorating the event – *Macquarie Tunetable Awards 1964* – was released later in the year, The Bee Gees' vocals were on five of the twelve tracks, and Barry and Robin were clearly visible in the audience photo on the cover. Surreptitiously it seems, The Bee Gees were slowly becoming omnipresent in Sydney's pop music scene.

In Sydney's *Sunday Telegraph* of 22 March, in an article headed 'Bee Gee Singer Finds Success in New Role – Top Songwriter At 17', Belinda Music's promotions manager Tony Brady was quoted praising Barry's songwriting prowess: 'I'd go so far as to say he could become the first Australian songwriter to make a living from composer's royalties alone'. Continuing, Brady said that Barry 'had become truly professional in his field, and between September 1963 and March 1964, he had twelve of his compositions recorded by other artists. This makes him one of the few songwriters in Sydney who has material constantly recorded. He has the greatest potential of any songwriter in Australia. Barry is one of the few songwriters in Sydney who can satisfy this great demand from the record companies'. Brady also revealed that Barry's composition 'One Road' – covered with some success by Jimmy Little the previous month – was being reviewed by 19 record companies in America, 'and we expect it to be recorded by at least three or four companies. If the song becomes a hit in the States, Barry could earn up to £2,000 from this song alone'.

Whilst this did not entirely come to fruition, when a Christian vocal group called The Gospelaires – from Ballarat in the Central Highlands of Victoria – heard 'One Road' on the radio, they were inspired to record it themselves. They pressed a limited run of just 50 copies in a picture sleeve later in the year. They obviously liked the song enough to keep it in their repertoire for a number of years, and recorded another version in 1968, initially pressing 200 copies in a more elaborate laminated card sleeve. A further run of 200 copies was made a year later. Although sheet music for Jimmy Little's version does exist, the group worked out the arrangement themselves by ear. It would appear they didn't actually own a copy of the record either, as their own version appeared under the title 'One Road to Happiness' on both releases.

Meanwhile, in November, a group from the Netherlands called The Happy Four released a Dutch-language version of the song as the literal translation 'Een Weg'. While on the face of it this doesn't appear to be particularly noteworthy, it is in fact a hugely significant event for Barry Gibb as a songwriter, as this was the first of his songs to be released outside Australia, and also the first to be translated into another language.

With most of the *Sunday Telegraph* attention centred on their elder brother, how the twins felt about it is not known. But Barry remained resolute in keeping The Bee Gees together: 'The two careers are equally necessary to me. Without either one, I would be dissatisfied'. In the article, Barry divulged, 'I have been composing pop songs since I was ten, and only occasionally have I had any urge to change the type of song I write. I find it easier to write a song when I know the performer and can adapt the song to his style and talent. Once the type of song I have to write is clear, then the actual tune and words come easily, mostly when I'm walking down the road – I suppose the beat of my feet on the pavement has something to do with it'. No matter how creative his mind, he certainly could never have imagined that precise concept serving as the opening sequence of *Saturday Night Fever*, as their career-defining hit 'Stayin' Alive' pulsed in sync with John Travolta's now-legendary strut down a Brooklyn sidewalk well over a decade later.

The Bee Gees provided backing vocals once again, for both sides of an obscure single by Syd Wayne: a Queenslander about whom very little is known. While it's thought that he may have been more a TV performer than a club or a pop singer, Festival Records' signing of the Brisbane-based artist was mentioned in the US' *Billboard* magazine of 25 April 1964. The brothers' appearance has never been confirmed, though their unique vocals are clearly heard on both sides of the single, which appeared on the Leedon label and was released on 23 March 1964. The A-side 'Where's Old Charlie Gone' was a cover of a song written by Noel Richards, while the B-side 'She's Apples' was written by American cabaret singer Ruth Wallis.

The Bee Gees also provided backing vocals for the follow-up to Jimmy Hannan's big hit 'Beach Ball'. 'Hokey Pokey Stomp'/'You Make Me Happy' was released at the end of March, and while it wasn't as successful as its predecessor, it still made number 21 on the Sydney charts.

Completing what had been a very busy month for the brothers, they returned for a twelve-day engagement commencing on 20 March at the Sydney Showgrounds for Sydney's Royal Easter Show: one of Australia's largest annual events, attracting approximately 700,000 visitors over its duration. The group's fellow performers were other *Bandstand* regulars, including Judy Stone, Bryan Davies and Col Joye.

April 1964 saw The Bee Gees appearing in a half-hour television special on Brisbane's Channel Nine, produced by American Nat Kipner: a man with whom the trio would have greater associations in a few years. Although plans to turn the special into a weekly series did not eventuate, Kipner – who was also the talent coordinator and producer of the *Saturday Date* TV show, and an emerging songwriter himself – was impressed: 'They played me what they had. At the time, even though I was a writer, his (Barry's) songs were so unique, that I thought no point trying to get in on that deal. Barry had some ordinary songs too, but every so often, he'd come up with an unusual method like 'Spicks And Specks'. Their harmonies were amazing, and everything was different, so I thought this is going to be a great group if they can get out of Australia. Australia is a great place, but it's limited as far as sales are concerned, and a big wheel here is nothing overseas. I was very tempted to go with them when they asked me to go, but I thought, 'Well, I've got all this happening here', I didn't want to pick up and leave. Unfortunately, that was a big mistake, a huge mistake'.

From Brisbane, the Gibb family travelled to Adelaide again to appear on 16 April on the long-running NWS Channel Nine nightly variety show *In Adelaide Tonight*, compered by Ernie Sigley. Appearing with The Bee Gees were Sydney comic (Ugly) Dave Gray (also a former native of Manchester), and singers Beverly Hay and Johnny Cole.

The 1 May edition of *Australian Cash Box* magazine reported, 'When The Bee Gees arrived back from their recent visit to Adelaide, they met the stars of the 'Liverpool Show' at Mascot airport before their departure from Sydney. Gene Pitney – who had heard so much about the songwriting success of young Barry Gibb, lead singer of The Bee Gees – arranged to take some of Barry's material back to America with him with a view to recording some of his compositions in the future'. In the same edition, a full-page article included more than a little hype, claiming that 'The Bee Gees, who are one of the most popular groups in Australia, have an International fan club which receives about 500 letters per week'.

The next evening, The Bee Gees performed at the St. Clair Club, Woodville, in the local community recreation centre – a popular venue for teenage dances at the time – emceed by vocalist Terry Brooker. Although the group had enjoyed no chart success at this point, their television fame ensured that they were the show's headline act. The Del-Aires, Chessmen and Marlene Richards were the support acts.

New Zealand-born vocalist Del Juliana was next to record a Barry Gibb composition, with 'Never Like This' released in early July. Produced by Johnny Devlin, it was a typical song of the era, with a strong melody that mirrored The Beach Boys' Phil Spector-era production. The song was only one of a number of Barry Gibb songs that RCA suggested to Del, and she remembers that she recorded another one – the surf-sound-influenced

'Boy On The Board' – at the same session. Sadly, no copies of the latter song exist.

Del has gone down in Australian music folklore as the singer who almost supported The Beatles on their Australian tour. Initially, the sole female amongst the support acts, she later received a telegram withdrawing the offer, but in April, it was extended again. Frustrated by the confusion, she made her complaint public to a press hungry for any Beatles-related news, saying, 'The fee is ridiculous and I have to provide my own accommodation. I would lose money on the tour, so after a talk with mum, I have said no. Naturally, I am bitter, but there is a principle involved, so I'm not even going to see The Beatles'. Ironically, Del's place on the tour was taken by fellow Kiwi expatriate – and her producer – Johnny Devlin.

The trio appeared on *Sing, Sing, Sing* on 7 June, sharing the bill with Billy Thorpe – another former Mancunian – and his band The Aztecs, which at the time included lead guitarist Vince Melouney: 'In Australia at the time, I think there were a couple of music shows, and we were on one particular show, which was a very popular show, called *Sing, Sing, Sing*, hosted by legendary Australian rock 'n' roller Johnny O'Keefe', Vince remembers. 'And on that particular night, I was there with the group that I was in, which was called Billy Thorpe & The Aztecs, and also The Bee Gees were there. We all did a song, which I think was probably for the finale of the show. We sang The Beatles song 'Money'. And so, that's where I got to meet The Bee Gees. More than likely, we probably did some other TV shows'. The significance of this meeting cannot be overstated, as three years later, Vince Melouney would become a full-time member of The Bee Gees.

The show's finale was indeed a rousing version of 'Money (That's What I Want)' – a song written by Berry Gordy and Janie Bradford, originally released by Barrett Strong in 1959, but popularised by The Beatles on their second album *With The Beatles*.

Johnny Devlin called on The Bee Gees for a second time to contribute backing vocals on both sides of his June 1964 release 'Whole Lotta Shakin' Goin' On'/'Blue Suede Shoes'. The single was rush-released to capitalise on the announcement that Devlin and his band The Devils would be supporting The Beatles on their 1964 Australian tour. Johnny was honest enough to admit the Gibbs were not his first choice for these recordings. 'I remember, at the time we wanted The Delltones, who were big back then', he confessed, 'but they were unavailable, so we settled for what we thought was second-best: The Bee Gees! How times have changed'. The A-side was a fine cover of the 1957 Jerry Lee Lewis classic, with The Bee Gees vocals presenting prominently. The B-side stayed true to Elvis Presley's cover of Carl Perkins' 1955 standard.

Also in June, The Bee Gees' music made another LP appearance when their earlier single 'Peace Of Mind' was included on the *Leedon Hit Parade* album – this was to be their second song included on the long-playing format. Indicating that even their own record company was still struggling with their group name, 'Peace Of Mind' was credited to the now-archaic 'The B.G's' on the actual record label, though the album cover used what was now the preferred name: The Bee Gees. 'Peace Of Mind' had been released way back in February and was the album's oldest single – the others being from April, May and June 1964.

The biggest event on Australia's 1964 rock 'n' roll calendar kicked off early In The Morning of 11 June, when The Beatles' BOAC Boeing 707 from Hong Kong landed in Australia. Despite the early arrival time of 2:53 a.m., over 400 fans greeted them during a brief stopover in remote Darwin. The Beatles' plane then flew on to Sydney's Kingsford-Smith International Airport, commencing a ten-day tour of Australia before moving on to New Zealand. In Australia, The Beatles would play sold-out concerts in Adelaide, Melbourne, Sydney and Brisbane. In Adelaide, some 300,000 fans – approximately half the city's population at the time – crowded outside the Southern Australia Hotel to await their arrival. On the journey from the airport to the city, John, Paul, George and replacement drummer Jimmy Nicol (Ringo Starr missed the first part of the tour due to illness) were received by masses of fans saturating both sides of the roads, cheering them on.

Once the Beatlemania had subsided, The Bee Gees and their local counterparts were back to work. In July – as if to cement their own names as part of Australian pop music's so-called 'establishment' – the three brothers appeared in *Everybody's* magazine, in an MGM-styled double-page colour spread of 60 of the most popular recording artists in Australia at the time.

Country and western singer Reg Lindsay revealed that 'Barry Gibb of The Bee Gees has penned several numbers for me to record' in the 1 May edition of *Australian Cash Box* magazine. He was aiming for an American sound with his new single, distinct from his old Australian sound. When the record was released in early July, the A-side was 'Lonely Road' written by Joe Halford, while the B-side was Barry's 'Scared Of Losing You'.

Lindsay's record company, Columbia, was trying to organise the release of the record in Memphis, Tennessee.

In early August, The Bee Gees made an appearance at the Penshurst RSL Club to the south of Sydney. By the time they made their next appearance on *Sing, Sing, Sing* on 14 August, they had a new single to promote.

'Claustrophobia' (Barry Gibb)
Recorded at Festival Studios, Sydney: circa July 1964

The fourth single, 'Claustrophobia', was released on 17 August 1964. Once again, unfortunately, it failed to chart.

The song has a fuller sound than previous releases due to the presence of The Delawares – a Sydney band comprising Bruce Davis (guitar), Leith Ryan (guitar), Bill Swindells (bass) and Laurie Wardman (drums), who made their recording debut on this record.

In those days, recording session details could be decidedly casual. In this instance, the uncredited Delawares' support came about after the Gibbs had seen the band play at a dance in Wollongong. The band would also support The Bee Gees on television shows like *Saturday Date*, *In Melbourne Tonight*, *In Brisbane Tonight*, *Seventeeners*, and *Sunnyside Up* while promoting the single. Barry would return the favour the following year by writing two songs for the group, fronted by lead vocalist Denis Williams: 'Bad Girl' and 'They Say'.

Robin also makes his instrumental debut on this song, playing a melodica: a hybrid keyboard-recorder instrument that sounds similar to a harmonica.

The song has clever lyrical imagery, with the protagonist telling the object of his desire that he gets 'claustrophobia 'cause there's too many boys in your heart'. Robin would later recall: 'We started our experimental stage because The Beatles were happening, and we thought, 'Let's get some inspiration from this group that are doing so well overseas. It's a British group – we're British, living in Australia, so surely we can do something, so let's experiment''.

The tight, youthful harmonies are wonderfully typical of The Bee Gees' Australian era, and in many ways, 'Claustrophobia' remains a fine snapshot of the group's ongoing development.

'Could It Be' (Barry Gibb)
Recorded at Festival Studios, Sydney: circa July 1964

The B-side 'Could It Be' again featured The Delawares providing the accompaniment. Barry once again kept close to the beat blueprint, possibly under pressure to replicate The Beatles' mode rather than follow his own style within the new sound as he would later. Overall, it's a great rocking track with strong harmonies from the brothers, and was probably the nearest thing to rock 'n' roll that they'd attempted up to that point.

Despite the promotion and positive reviews – one of which predicted, 'The local group will crash every chart in Australia with 'Claustrophobia', their best release to date' – and imploring the local disc jockeys: 'DJs don't be frightened to spin this one – would like to see both sides have the acid test in 'The Battle of the Sounds', the single didn't garner much radio airplay and subsequently failed to sell in enough volume to break into any charts of the day. Their music publisher Tony Brady would recall that selling The Bee Gees' songs to the radio programmers was difficult because their material was too close in sound to The Beatles: an attitude he described as 'stupid'.

On 26 August, *Australian Women's Weekly* reported, 'There is talk that The Bee Gees soon will be touring New Zealand. They've been so busy lately with Australian club work, television appearances and tours, that they've had to refuse some offers, including a tour with Screaming Lord Sutch'.

More shows to promote The Bee Gees' now-faltering single, continued, including another appearance on *Sing, Sing, Sing* on 25 September, with other guests including Bryan Davies, Little Pattie, and The Epics. Despite their many television appearances, according to Kevin Jacobsen, getting the trio on screen was not always easy: 'It was dreadfully difficult getting them on television for a while, because they were considered cheeky young upstarts. It was almost impossible to get *Bandstand* to take them. Robin was such an extrovert; he frightened people'.

Their regular appearances on the very conservative *Bandstand*, along with various adult variety shows and clubs of the era, may have contributed to The Bee Gees' inability to find a consistent audience in Australia. The contrasting images they presented possibly contributed to the group's inability to score hit records. When they performed to adults, their act more resembled one you would see in a cabaret, complete with comedy, impressions, and songs from bygone eras. While Festival Records tried to promote them as a teenage group performing original and contemporary material, the television shows for which they were booked insisted on them performing variety-style material that ranged from country to musical theatre. Only occasionally did The Bee Gees get to feature their own songs. Moreover, *Bandstand*'s producers stipulated that their studio audience attend in semi-formal dress, and the performers had to fall in line. The besuited, clean-cut Gibbs catering to mature audiences, didn't give them much room to express themselves as young, hip hitmakers like their pop peers of the period.

'Turn Around, Look At Me' (Jerry Capehart)
Recorded at Festival Studios, Sydney: circa September 1964

The continued commercial Australian-chart failure of Bee Gees singles written by Barry Gibb, led to a change of record-company strategy. Despite Barry's songs being successfully marketed to other artists, The Bee Gees were impelled to record material by other writers.

'Turn Around, Look At Me' was therefore chosen as their fifth single, released on 12 October 1964. It was a ballad written by American composer Jerry Capehart – co-writer of 'Summertime Blues' and 'C'mon Everybody', which were hits for rock 'n' roll singer Eddie Cochran, who he also managed. It has been suggested The Bee Gees' cover may have even been a ploy to draw the attention of Capehart, who had impressive overseas contacts.

The song was first released by Glen Campbell in 1961 and was his first chart hit, peaking at 62 on the *Billboard* Hot 100. The Lettermen followed with their rendition in 1962, which peaked at number 5. The song had a pedigree, and Festival sensed that it could be a hit. It would therefore be nice to think the label had invested some money in the production, as there are strings and a choir in the accompaniment. But we would not be remiss in theorising that the orchestration might've been a pre-recorded backing tape.

This could also explain the origins of some strange song choices that appeared on the 1970 *Inception/Nostalgia* LP that showcased many Bee Gees' recordings from the period. Were the songs 'The End', 'Hallelujah, I Love Her So', 'I Love You Because', 'Somewhere', The Twelfth Of Never', 'You're The Reason' and 'You're Nobody Till Somebody Loves You' merely audition tapes to help Festival choose a song to release as a single?

Perhaps as a consolation for not releasing one of his own compositions – or possibly to try to boost sales of the single by trying to cash in on Barry's growing popularity with young teenage girls, and also to reflect his status as the leader of the group – the new release was the first to credit the group as 'Barry Gibb and The Bee-Gees'. It also saw the hyphen return to the group's name.

Unfortunately, despite Festival's best efforts, 'Turn Around, Look At Me' suffered the same fate as its predecessors and was not a success. As for The Bee Gees' performance, it was actually a strong vehicle for their ensemble singing.

'Theme From Jaimie McPheeters' (Jerry Winn, Leigh Harline)
Recorded at Festival Studios, Sydney: circa September 1964

The B-side belonged to an American TV show called *The Travels of Jaimie McPheeters*, which ran for a single season on the ABC network in 1963-1964. The series was based on the Robert Lewis Taylor novel, which won him the Pulitzer Prize for Fiction in 1959. The TV adventure series debuted on 15 September 1963 and ran for a total of 26 episodes: the final one airing on 15 March 1964. It starred twelve-year-old actor Kurt Russell in the title role of Jaimie McPheeters, Dan O'Herlihy as his father 'Doc' Sardius McPheeters, and Charles Bronson as the wagon master Linc Murdock. The very young Osmond Brothers – Alan, Jay, Merrill and Wayne – appeared as the Kissel Brothers in nine episodes and sang the theme song over the closing titles.

The songwriters Jerry Winn and Leigh Harline were both prolific composers – Winn probably best-known for 'Angel', which was recorded by Eddie Cochran, and 'Three Stars Will Shine Tonight' by Richard Chamberlain: better known as the theme tune for *Doctor Kildare*. Harline wrote more than 50 songs for projects associated with The Walt Disney Company, and composed the score to the movie *Pinocchio*, which includes his best-known song 'When You Wish Upon A Star'.

The Bee Gees' version of the song remains fairly close to The Osmonds' with its simple arrangement of guitar, bass and martial drum rhythms. But as a stand-alone song – and as a theme for a TV show that likely wasn't seen broadly across Australia – it was a very strange choice.

In October, the group departed for another four-town tour of country Victoria, with stops in Cohuna, St Arnaud, Kyabram and Bendigo. During this time, eight new Barry Gibb songs were assigned for copyright. Four of them – 'Baby I'm Losing You', 'I Will Love You', 'Walkin' Talkin' Teardrop' and 'Tribute To An Unknown Love' – had already been, or would shortly be, recorded by four different artists. The others – 'I'm In The Middle Of A Dream', 'Leave The Lovin' To The Boy', 'Since I Lost You' and 'This Is The End', would not be heard of again.

Also in October, another young Sydney singer Bryan Davies (who, like the Gibbs had emigrated from Manchester as a child) recorded two new Barry Gibb songs – 'I Don't Like To Be Alone' and 'Love And Money' – for his next single on the HMV label. Whilst not a huge hit, it did reach the top 40 in several state charts and number 22 in New South Wales.

The New Zealand band The Pleasers were sufficiently impressed by Bryan Davies' version to record their own cover – albeit with the slightly amended title 'I Just Don't Like To Be Alone' – for their album *Let's Go*, released on their native Red Rooster label in 1965. Formed in 1964, the group were unashamedly inspired by The Beatles, and covering Barry's Beatles-like 'I Don't Like To Be Alone' seemed totally appropriate.

November was quieter for The Bee Gees, with another appearance on *Sing, Sing, Sing*, where they were joined by guests Colin Cook and Brian Withers. The break in their busy touring schedule allowed Barry to devote himself to his writing, and by month's end, six more original songs – 'Boy With A Broken Heart', 'Hey Jennie', 'Mr. Mod Man', 'My Baby Can', 'The One That I Love' and 'You Were Made (For Me)' – had been assigned for copyright, although no recordings of any of the songs are known.

Following a concert tour of Australia, the 23 December edition of the *Australian Women's Weekly* magazine reported 'Wayne Newton, the American singer, took eight (Barry Gibb) numbers back to the States to show Bobby Darin'. It was later reported – in the 25 May 1966 edition of *Everybody's* magazine – that Newton was so impressed, that he was willing to sponsor the entire Gibb family's removal to the United States, but too much was against it … the threat of conscription being one.

As Christmas approached, The Bee Gees made their final television appearance for the year on *Sing, Sing, Sing* with artists including Lucky Starr and Paul Wayne. The show also featured a film clip of Ray Charles: possibly some footage from his Australian concert tour earlier in the year.

In retrospect, 1964 was another year of forward movement for The Bee Gees, and in particular for Barry, as he wrote his first significant hits for other artists, and his composition portfolio continued to grow. The Bee Gees' regular TV appearances had grown immensely throughout the past twelve months, and there were now regular calls for shows in other states outside of New South Wales and Queensland. However, the five successive singles' failure to crack the charts was becoming embarrassing. The Beatles, who had inspired the trio so much, had done so fourteen times by now.

Brilliant From Birth

Australia release date: 1998

Disc 1: 1. 'The Battle Of The Blue And The Grey' 2. 'The Three Kisses Of Love' 3. 'Timber!' 4. 'Take Hold Of That Star' 5. 'Peace Of Mind' 6. 'Don't Say Goodbye' 7. 'Claustrophobia' 8. 'Could It Be' 9. 'Turn Around, Look At Me' 10. 'Theme From Jaimie McPheeters' 11. 'Every Day I Have To Cry' 12. 'You Wouldn't Know' 13. 'Wine And Women' 14. 'Follow The Wind' 15. 'I Was A Lover, A Leader Of Men' 16. 'And The Children Laughing' 17. 'I Don't Think It's Funny' 18. 'How Love Was True' 19. 'To Be Or Not To Be' 20. 'Cherry Red' 21. 'I Want Home' 22. 'The End' 23. 'Hallelujah, I Love Her So' 24. 'I Love You Because' 25. 'Somewhere' 26. 'The Twelfth Of Never' 27. 'You're The Reason' 28. 'You're Nobody 'Til Somebody Loves You' 29. 'All By Myself' 30. 'Butterfly' 31. 'Can't You See That She's Mine' 32. 'From Me To You'

Disc 2: 1. 'Monday's Rain' 2. 'All Of My Life' 3. 'Where Are You' 4. 'Playdown' 5. 'Big Chance' 6. 'Glass House' 7. 'How Many Birds' 8. 'Second Hand People' 9. 'I Don't Know Why I Bother With Myself' 10. 'Jingle Jangle' 11. 'Tint Of Blue' 12. 'Born A Man' 13. 'Spicks And Specks' 14. 'I Am The World' 15. 'Daydream' 16. 'Forever' 17. 'Coalman' 18. 'Exit Stage Right' 19. 'Paperback Writer' 20. 'I'll Know What To Do' 21. 'In The Morning' 22. 'Like Nobody Else' 23. 'Lonely Winter' 24. 'Lum-Dee-Loo' 25. 'Storm' 26. 'Terrible Way To Treat Your Baby' 27. 'Yesterday's Gone' 28. 'You Won't See Me' 29. 'Top Hat' 30. 'Just One Look' 31. 'Ticket To Ride'

In 1998, Festival Records released *Brilliant From Birth*: the first curated collection of all 35 Australian-era Bee Gees songs originally released between 1963 and 1966. It also contains other tracks which remained unreleased until they appeared on the extremely rare *Inception/ Nostalgia* set in 1970 and the Australian *Birth Of Brilliance* LP in 1978.

Brilliant From Birth is included at this point for the purpose of highlighting the four tracks from 1964 included in the project that had never been released before. They were recordings the very young Gibb brothers made especially for use on television only. The *National Film and Sound Archive* in the Australian capital Canberra, digitally remastered the material used, and it's obvious that this two-CD set can easily be called the ultimate collection of Australian-era Bee Gees recordings, rendering the hundreds of other miscellaneous compilations obsolete. It's a true must-have for any dedicated Bee Gees fan anywhere in the world.

The rare recordings were found by chance in October 1983. Sydney resident Bill McSorley discovered a batch of canisters containing some oddly-labelled records at a garage sale in suburban Rushcutters Bay. After doing some local checking, he took them to renowned rock historian Glenn A. Baker for his advice. What Mr. McSorley had found were the original acetates of these exceptionally rare recordings.

The songs 'Can't You See That She's Mine', 'From Me To You', 'Yesterday's Gone' and 'Just One Look' had never been released in any shape or form previously – or for that matter, after the release of this album. These four recordings were made at the Festival Records studios in 1964, solely for the Australian television show *Sing, Sing, Sing*, which was hosted by Australian rock 'n' roll legend Johnny O'Keefe. They were never intended for release. As was the arrangement then, the artists would go into the studio to record the hits of the day a few days before filming, then miming – or to bring the term up to date, 'lip-syncing' – the songs on the TV show.

While a lot of time and care was spent on sharpening up the sound of the old Bee Gees classics for *Brilliant From Birth*, all the songs – with the exception of the four newly-discovered ones – had been released previously in other parts of the world.

Also on the acetates was The Bee Gees' previously-mentioned superb version of George Hamilton IV's 1963 hit single 'Abilene', which, due to time constraints, did not make it onto the album.

Festival Records' promotion of the album made much of the fact that the tapes were hidden in their vaults – which was not quite true, as Mr. McSorley had them the entire time.

The artwork for this release was by Louise Cook and was in keeping with Festival Records' other reissue collections at this time. The main photograph of The Bee Gees was from a 1963 appearance on *Bandstand*, while smaller photos scattered around it were used on the sheet music of 'Peace Of Mind' in 1964 and the *Wine And Women* EP in 1965. The fourth photograph is of the very young brothers in about 1961 with Peter Allen of the popular cabaret act The Allen Brothers. Peter was to later marry and divorce actress/singer Liza Minelli and have his own international success.

Sleeve notes were by Australian rock historian Glenn A. Baker, with additional notes by renowned Bee Gees expert Mark Byfield.

The album's songwriting credits are rather sloppy, as are the publishing company details, but the responsibility here lay with the record company to ensure that mechanical royalties were paid to the correct people.

'Can't You See That She's Mine' (Dave Clark, Mike Smith)
Recorded at Festival Studios, Sydney: circa June 1964

Incorrectly credited on the album to Dave Clarke (with an 'e'), this song was a big hit for The Dave Clark Five in 1964. Both writers were members of the group – Mike Smith was the lead vocalist and keyboard player, and Dave Clark was the drummer. Released in May 1964, it peaked at number 10 on the UK charts, and, importantly, at number 13 in Australia.

It's a jumpy little track, and the version by the very young Bee Gees is good fun.

'From Me To You' (John Lennon, Paul McCartney)
Recorded at Festival Studios, Sydney: circa June 1964

The Beatles' song, of course. 'From Me To You' was their third UK single, released in April 1963. Significantly for them, it was their first chart-topper in their home country. With the help of a Bee Gees performance of the song on television in Australia, it peaked at number 9.

The young Gibbs turn in a fine cover of the song, and it's a real album highlight.

'Yesterday's Gone' (Chad Stuart, Wendy Kidd)
Recorded at Festival Studios, Sydney: circa June 1964

This was a 1963 hit single for Chad and Jeremy. Although the English duo would have a string of successful records in the United States through the mid-1960s, this was their only hit in their native land.

The song was written in 1962 by group member Chad Stuart, and Wendy Kidd: the manager of a band Stuart belonged to at the time. According to Stuart, Kidd was given the songwriting credit in return for allowing him to compose the song on her piano. It remained unrecorded until Stuart and his colleague Jeremy Clyde began performing as a duo, eventually committing 'Yesterday's Gone' to tape in July 1963 during a session at Abbey Road Studios.

The single reached an unremarkable summit of number 37. It fared a little better in the United States, peaking at 21. In Australia, it was issued on the Festival label in February 1964 but flopped. But the song's American success occasioned an Australian re-release, where it charted over the summer of 1964, eventually reaching number 26. It was probably helped on its way by the excellent Bee Gees version – which doesn't stray far from the original arrangement – when they performed it on *Sing, Sing, Sing*.

'Just One Look' (Doris Payne, Gregory Carroll)
Recorded at Festival Studios, Sydney: circa June 1964

Incorrectly credited on the album as being written by The Hollies' lead guitarist Tony Hicks and singer Allan Clarke, 'Just One Look' was in fact written by American R&B singers Doris Payne and Gregory Carroll. The original recording was by Doris Troy, which was Payne's stage name, and was a hit in the United States in 1963.

The song became a UK hit for The Hollies, who reached number 2 with it. It's that version upon which The Bee Gees' cover is based. More significantly, it was a minor hit, peaking at 29 on the Australian charts: the reason the song was recorded for performance on the popular music show, *Sing, Sing, Sing*.

The similarity between the harmonies of The Hollies and The Bee Gees is not surprising, considering both groups have roots in Manchester.

1965

Following what had been a momentous year in popular music, Australia – like most of the western world – was undergoing great cultural change in 1965. Popular music there shifted with the times. The Beatles' now-ubiquitous impact went beyond music, exciting everyone below the age of 30 and seemingly frightening everyone older. Suddenly hundreds – if not thousands – of new Australian beat groups were being formed.

Lennon and McCartney's songwriting success had also inspired more Australian artists to write their own songs rather than cover overseas material. Also, The Beatles' prominence as pioneering pop vocalists had forced a number of instrumental surf bands to include lead singers to have any chance of getting live work and recording contracts. Aussie jazz bands, though dismissive of the new 'beat' sound, were also changing their format. The highly regarded The Loved Ones were formed in Melbourne from a trad jazz group – The Red Onion Jazz Band – and they were soon one of the most popular acts going. Just to add to the mix, teenagers everywhere were forming their own three, four or five-piece groups.

If the scene wasn't competitive for The Bee Gees before, it certainly was now. As *Everybody's* magazine columnist Maggie Makeig cautioned, 'The beat field is crowded and unwieldy, with no definite trends cornering the market. There are now 2,000 pop groups with registered names, and our population is simply not big enough to support that number'.

In Sydney, in particular, established local artists such as Col Joye, Little Pattie, Lucky Star, Judy Stone, Bryan Davies, Lonnie Lee, Sandy Scott and Noeleen Batley were all struggling to keep their place in the new order. Some, like Stone, Lee and Dig Richards, would forge successful careers in country music. Others, like Little Pattie and Sandy Scott, would move successfully into the club circuit. Col Joye would also move more to country music with only occasional forays into the pop world. Johnny O'Keefe – who had never fit into the clean-cut middle-of-the-road style anyway – continued to have hits, though his health problems didn't help his career prospects. The major injuries he sustained in a devastating 1960 accident in which his car hit a gravel truck and almost killed him and his passengers, didn't help matters.

While surfing as a sport would continue to grow in popularity in Australia, its accompanying musical soundtrack championing artists like American duo Jan and Dean, and locals including The Delltones and The

Atlantics, would diminish. Only The Beach Boys would thrive, and then only through the brilliance and innovation of their leader Brian Wilson. Popular music had just been revolutionised.

The Bee Gees were back in the studio at the tail end of 1964, but things were a little different. This time, hoping to gain some return on their investment, Festival Records united The Bee Gees with another Leedon artist to record two of Barry's most recent compositions.

'House Without Windows' (Barry Gibb)
Recorded at Festival Studios, Sydney: circa December 1964

The Gibb brothers had known Trevor Gordon since their days in Brisbane, where young Trevor – who was about two years younger than Barry – had hosted a children's television show for a short time. Trevor and The Bee Gees had a few things in common: they were all English migrants, signed to the Leedon label, chasing their first hit records. The result of the sessions was 'House Without Windows' and 'And I'll Be Happy', which were released under the banner Trevor Gordon and The Bee Gees.

Born Trevor Gordon Grunnill on 5 May 1948 in Skegness, Lincolnshire, England, he was already a good friend of the Gibb brothers. He recalls that he 'first met The Bee Gees after I emigrated to Australia with my parents in 1961. We were both sort of novelty acts as we were so young, and used to meet on the Johnny O'Keefe Show *Sing, Sing, Sing* (which was like) Australia's *Top of the Pops*'.

'House Without Windows', released on 18 January 1965, was the sixth Bee Gees single. The style was a bit dissimilar to their previous releases, and whilst the famous Gibb brothers' harmonies are present, they certainly weren't being used to their full potential. The lyric concept is quite interesting and almost a companion piece to Lennon/McCartney's 'A World Without Love', which would be a huge global hit for UK duo Peter and Gordon a month or two later. Trevor Gordon had a pleasant enough voice, but it wasn't particularly remarkable. Nonetheless, he carried the song reasonably well.

Trevor eventually returned to Britain, ahead of his friends the Gibbs, in 1966, when he was signed to Pye Records and released the single 'Love Comes And Goes' under the slightly more hip moniker, Trev Gordon.

A couple of years later, he was reunited with The Bee Gees when he and his cousin Graham Bonnet formed a group called The Marbles. The Bee Gees wrote five songs especially for them, including the hit singles 'Only One Woman' and 'The Walls Fell Down'.

'And I'll Be Happy' (Barry Gibb)

Recorded at Festival Studios, Sydney: circa December 1964

The B-side of 'House Without Windows' was unlike any Barry Gibb song up to that point: it lacked a catchy chorus – instead, reprising just the title phrase at the end of each verse. 'And I'll Be Happy' is a pretty tune, but the trite lyrics make it sound rather dated now.

This single marks the only time during the Australian era that the group would split performing credits on a record, although there were many instances of *silent* partnerships where they provided backing vocals for other artists, including big-name stars like Jimmy Hannan and Johnny Devlin.

Sadly, this single went the same way as its predecessors, and the songs were consigned to obscurity until being reissued on the *Assault the Vaults: Rare Cover Versions of the Brothers Gibb* compilation in 1998.

Early 1965 saw a couple of solo artists come back for second helpings of Barry Gibb songs. Bryan Davies was first, with the February release of 'Watch What You Say' as a single A-side. Like his previous Gibb covers, it's very Beatlesque. Davies' vocal style is uncannily similar to John Lennon's, which may have been intentional given Beatlemania was in full swing in Australia at the time. Davies, like the brothers Gibb, was born in Manchester and emigrated to Australia with his family in 1954.

Noeleen Batley did likewise with the release of her first single of 1965 on 15 March, with 'Baby I'm Losing You'. This mature-sounding song with a strong hook and robust production was a great showcase for her voice, but sadly, it failed to chart.

The Bee Gees themselves quickly tried again with yet another single; and for the second time, the A-side was a non-Gibb composition, again due to pressure from Festival.

'Every Day I Have To Cry' (Arthur Alexander)

Recorded at Festival Studios, Sydney: circa February 1965

The seventh Bee Gees single was again credited to Barry Gibb & The Bee Gees, although the hyphen was dropped again. Festival Records continued to make the group record songs other than Barry's. That formula wasn't working now either.

'Every Day I Have To Cry', released in March 1965, was written by American R&B singer Arthur Alexander in 1962. It was first recorded by Steve Alaimo that same year and became a minor hit for him, peaking at number 46 in the United States. Alexander himself did not record the song until 1975.

The Bee Gees version is probably the best example of their distinctive vocal sound up to this point in their career. Barry's lead vocal and the three-part harmonies are all used to good effect; and for the first time, Robin's soulful voice is able to assert itself on the closing ad-libs.

Sales were again disappointing: the seventh successive dud for the trio. As Barry put it some years later, 'Well, if we're going to have flops, we may as well have flops with our own songs'.

'You Wouldn't Know' (Barry Gibb)
Recorded at Festival Studios, Sydney: circa February 1965

The choice of the A-side as a single – although a quality song and a good recording – is a good example of how Festival Records was still out of touch with British beat music's growing influence on Australian pop. When Festival consented to Barry writing the B-side, he used the opportunity to show that he at least was keeping up with the times. 'You Wouldn't Know' is a real pacey R&B-influenced song with a real John Lennon sound to its lead vocal. Although not one of their best songs from the period, it's far more contemporary than the A-side. Once again, Robin and Maurice's harmonies add great support to Barry's lead vocal.

The identity of the engineer and producer on this single is uncertain, although it's about this time that Bill Shepherd replaced Robert Iredale in those roles at Festival, so it could very well be him. Shepherd came from England, and was not only an engineer, but he had more musical training than Iredale, already having released two accomplished jazz albums of his own: *Swingin' Shepherd* (1958) and *Shepherd & His Flock Swing* (1959). He began assisting The Bee Gees as their musical director.

Shepherd's rapport with the brothers, and his appreciation of their potential, had immediate positive results – on the records at least. Coincidentally, he had previously worked with showbiz entrepreneur and future Bee Gees manager Robert Stigwood. Perhaps it was the universe working in strange ways that just a couple of short years later, the three parties would be brought together halfway around the world to launch The Bee Gees' international career.

The 31 March edition of the *Australian Women's Weekly* reported that The Bee Gees and Trevor Gordon had entered into a business partnership and formed a company called Begore Pty Ltd. Aimed at promoting and helping new Australian talent, they occupied a small office in a Sydney city building, one floor above a musician's club and next door to a music publishing company. 'We wanted an office just as our own headquarters' said Barry, 'but we found so many other young acts who wanted a general meeting place for appointments, fan mail and so on, that we decided to go into business'.

Maurice continued, saying, 'We talked it over with our parents, and they said that if we thought we could do it and were prepared to use our own money, to go ahead'.

Trevor Gordon added, 'We want to try to find new artists and help them get started. We are all established enough to have contacts in the television and recording industries, so we can arrange auditions and introductions which are very difficult to get when you're an unknown'.

Rather sensibly, Barry stated, 'Of course, we're not going to neglect our own careers. We feel we can manage both jobs, and we have a girlfriend who is acting as secretary for us'.

Begore's headquarters would also serve as a place for artists to store instruments and for clients to change clothes before important appointments. Barry explained that 'As we have just started, we are moving slowly till we find our feet, but we're hoping to expand in the future; then maybe if it gets too big to handle, we might ask our father, who manages us, to become a partner'.

On the music front, Bryan Davies recorded his fourth Barry Gibb song – 'I Should Have Stayed In Bed' – for an April release, and he can recall Barry being in the studio for all four recording sessions: not only to provide backing vocals, but also to harmonise with Bryan's lead. For some reason, the songs that Barry gave to Davies all have a more distinctly rock feel than most Bee Gees songs of the time. 'I Should Have Stayed In Bed' is no different but has more narrative than any other Gibb song to this point.

Barry's publisher Belinda Music Ltd., was working hard to get his songs recorded by American artists, so Tony Brady contacted Wayne Newton while he was on tour in Australia in 1964, and offered him some of Barry's compositions. As a result, Newton – known today as a music legend in the US for his decades-long career as a Las Vegas performer – recorded the ballad 'They'll Never Know' on 5 November 1964, and it was released on his album *Red Roses For A Blue Lady* on 12 April 1965. The album entered the charts on 11 May and peaked at number 17 on the *Billboard* 200.

Newton is noted in some previous books about The Bee Gees as being the first international act to release a Barry Gibb song. But this is not correct, as the Dutch group The Happy Four had beaten him to the punch by releasing their single 'Een Weg' – a translation of Jimmy Little's hit 'One Road' – in November 1964. However, Newton's recording is still the first Barry Gibb composition to be released in the United States.

Although Trevor Gordon had shared the billing with The Bee Gees on his previous single, Leedon Records chose to promote Trevor solo when he released his next single on 18 April. 'Little Miss Rhythm And Blues' and 'Here I Am' – both of which were Barry Gibb songs – featured all three brothers on backing vocals. Robin's are particularly prominent on the A-side.

'Little Miss Rhythm And Blues' is a fast Chuck Berry-esque rocker, and was later covered by Steve & The Board, and New Zealander Judge Wayne. The B-side 'Here I Am' is a simple, if unimpressive, ballad. The A-side surfaced on a rare Australian compilation called *Ugly Things (Australian Rock Archives Vol. 1)* in 1980, and later, both sides appeared on *Assault the Vaults*.

May 1965 saw the release of The Bee Gees' first EP. Simply titled *The Bee Gees*, the disc featured the four songs from their first two singles. Considering both singles were two years old and rather unsuccessful, it was a curious choice on Festival's part, and In retrospect, a good example of their lack of thought and marketing awareness of their artists. The EP's picture sleeve is a 1963 photo of the three young brothers identically dressed in white shirts with dark ties, dark trousers, black winklepicker shoes, and tartan waistcoats with 'BG' lettering. It was precisely the image The Bee Gees were trying to move away from by mid-1965.

The EP is now one of the rarest Bee Gees records of all. Since only a few hundred copies were produced at the time, it's almost impossible to find.

In June 1965, two new Leedon label artists came knocking on Barry's door seeking songs, and he happily complied. Michelle Rae was presented with 'I Wanna Tell The World' and 'Everybody's Talkin'', which were released as a single. The A-side has an authentic gospel feel and suits her voice nicely, while the B-side is pure country-pop and features the brothers in the introduction. Michelle handles the singing on both tracks with ease, and impresses as an accomplished vocalist. All three brothers appear on the record – Barry on vocals and guitar, Robin on vocals and possibly organ, and Maurice on vocals and guitar. The producer was Bill Shepherd. The single was not a hit, and Michelle Rae quickly faded into obscurity.

Jenny Bradley was the other singer who released a pair of Barry Gibb songs in June 1965. Aged just ten at the time, her name was occasionally featured in the local entertainment media. Both Barry's songs – 'Who's Been Writing On The Wall Again' and 'Chubby' – were appropriate for the singer's age. The A-side has a childlike chant woven into a catchy melody. In its own way, it's one of Barry's cleverest songs from the Australian period. 'Chubby', the B-side, is far more basic and not particularly well-produced, nor sung for that matter.

Tony Brady, who was known locally as Australia's Sinatra, switched to the Parlophone label, and in May, attempted to relaunch his career with a bizarre novelty song – 'I'm Gonna Buy My Mother-In-Law A Block Of Land On Mars' – written by Nat Kipner, who would become a key figure in Maurice's writing development in the not-too-distant future. The B-side was another ballad from Barry, titled 'I Will Love You'. It's a reasonably good song and should have been the A-side, if only to give Brady a modicum of credibility. Needless to say, the single flopped badly.

Having just recovered from Beatlemania, Australia was now about to catch 'Easyfever'. Sydney group The Easybeats' second single 'She's So Fine' rocketed to number 1 in Sydney, then Melbourne, followed by the rest of the country in June 1965. They would have six more top ten singles over the next sixteen months, including three number 1s, before departing for the UK. Not only were The Easybeats based in The Emerald City like The Bee Gees, but its five members were from families who had migrated to Australia from Europe. In the wake of The Beatles' visit the previous year, the Australian music scene had been crying out for a local band to take full advantage of the opportunities The Beatles' success had demonstrated was possible. Frustratingly for the Gibb brothers, The Easybeats – formed barely a year before – were doing exactly what The Bee Gees aspired to.

Despite The Easybeats' line-up including three British expats, Barry at times felt that his family's English origins were a disadvantage: 'We didn't get much time in the studio. In fact, being an English group in Australia wasn't the thing to be, which is the weirdest thing. Even when The Beatles came up, still being an English group in Australia didn't do us any good at all. They tended to think of us as 'Pommies' and all that business, and you become second down the line as far as favours, or as far as help, or as far as getting a break anywhere'.

Wayne Newton's producer Terry Melcher was seemingly keen on the song Barry had penned for Newton, as Melcher also produced Jimmy Boyd's cover of the upbeat 'That's What I'll Give To You'. Boyd is best known for his hit record of 'I Saw Mommy Kissing Santa Claus', released in 1952 when he was only twelve. He later pursued an acting career

Barry's 'That What I'll Give To You' made the A-side of Boyd's single, with the B-side being 'My Hometown', written by Melcher, who was a successful songwriter in his own right, including several songs for his famous mother: actress and singer Doris Day. This was Boyd's first single for the Chicago-based Vee-Jay Records: the first company to release the early Beatles records in the United States. But disaster struck just as the single was released in August 1965, when the label went bankrupt after their license to issue and distribute The Beatles' works had expired and been turned over to Capitol Records. It was promoted on television on 14 July with an appearance on a high-profile *Hollywood A Go-Go* special filmed in Hawaii, titled *Aloha A Go-Go* – which also featured, among others, Jan and Dean. However, with poor distribution to support the single, it stood little chance of becoming a hit.

In July, The Bee Gees were back in the studio, this time using the energy and production skills of Festival Records' new house producer and arranger Bill Shepherd. With Shepherd in charge, the brothers were excited to try for chart success once again, as he was a producer with a far more engaging style than Iredale. The brothers would form a lifelong friendship with Shepherd, and a professional relationship that would continue when the brothers returned to the UK.

The results were the group's strongest recordings to date, and – at long last – a hit single: 'Wine And Women'/'Follow The Wind' – both written by Barry.

'Wine And Women' (Barry Gibb)
Recorded at Festival Studios, Sydney: circa August 1965

Rumours were rife that the Festival Records powers-that-be were tiring of The Bee Gees and their lacklustre commercial performance, even after changing strategy trying to score hits with other writers' songs for the previous two singles. They had one more chance to prove themselves, and were again allowed to record two of Barry's songs for both sides of their eighth single. This was make or break.

For the first time, Robin shared lead vocals with Barry, and their alternating yet contrasting styles would become one of their trademarks for years to come. Their harmonies had never sounded better, and Robin's distinctive voice suited the song beautifully. In terms of orchestration, Barry's rhythm guitar was highlighted more, as was the bass. It's unsure if Maurice was playing bass at this time, but whoever it was had certainly appropriated Paul McCartney's influence. However, it was the vocals that were the strength of this recording.

'Wine And Women' was later issued as the lead track on The Bee Gees' second EP in 1967 – also titled *Wine And Women* – which was attractively housed in a picture sleeve. The other tracks were the single B-side 'Follow The Wind' on side one, with 'Peace Of Mind' and 'Don't Say Goodbye' on side two.

'Follow The Wind' (Barry Gibb)
Recorded at Festival Studios, Sydney: circa August 1965

The B-side was a folk-hued composition. It's a song quite obviously influenced by Australian group The Seekers, who had just achieved their first of many successes in the UK. It has a beautiful melody with stunning harmonies on the chorus, and once again, Barry and Robin trade the lead vocal. The growth in Barry's writing and all three brothers' singing in the two years since they'd begun recording, was quite remarkable.

Another Australian folk group, The Flanagans, released their own version of this song as a single in December 1965, as did Australian actor Lionel Long on his album *Today* in 1967. In a strange quirk, original Seekers' member Keith Potger and his new group The New Seekers, recorded the song on their first album in 1970.

Some reviewers saw The Beatles' influence in both songs, but Carol Rogers' article in the *Sunday Telegraph* referred to them as 'commercial folk'. In an article headed 'Barry Boosts the Folk Cult', Rogers confirms 'Wine And Women' as a 'humdinger' and a 'quite extraordinary composition'. She continued by saying that it was a 'kind of gospel folk song done to oom-pah-pah in waltz time. Crazy, but it seems to work'. So, the critics liked it, but what of the radio stations and record-buying public?

Knowing their future was looking grim unless they scored a hit with 'Wine And Women', the boys were not going to leave anything to chance and rely on Festival's decidedly under-invested marketing department to promote such a critical release. The single was released on 18 September 1965, at which point the brothers decided to take matters into their own hands. The Gibbs' ingenuity led to their best commercial showing to date, and the single made Sydney radio station 2UE's top 40 chart.

It took a bit of research to understand how that particular chart was compiled, as Robin explained: 'We found out the shops of the radio station's survey, *Waltons*, *Woolworths* ... about six in all. That's all we needed. You didn't have to sell very many records to get on the actual Sydney charts'. The research was complete, and it was now time to put the plan into action. 'We arranged for our fan club to meet us on the steps of Sydney Town Hall', Robin recalled, adding sarcastically, 'It wasn't hard to rendezvous with them because there were only six of them'. Barry continued: 'We knew if we could sell 400 records on that Saturday afternoon, by the next Wednesday chart, we'd be at number 35. We only had £200, so it could be no higher than 35. Sure enough, the next week, the record was 35 with a bullet. We were going to get there eventually, but we had to find a way to make it happen, and we did. 'Wine And Women' charted mainly because we went out and bought it! You could do that in those days; you can't do it now'. Years later, Nat Kipner would hint that the 2UE chart 'caper' was Hugh Gibb's idea, and the cash to 'finance the deed' was provided by him.

No matter whose idea it was, it worked. As hoped, once the record entered the 2UE charts – eventually peaking at 19 – it also began to receive airplay from other stations. While it didn't crack the top ten, the single was a reasonable success on the New South Wales chart, reaching number 29, and may have even kept the testy Festival executives at bay for a while. Barry was adamant the subterfuge for the 'Wine And Women' single was worth it: 'It did an enormous amount for us. It made momentum for us in the country. Even if it was just one hit, it was something. After eight attempts, The Bee Gees had cracked the charts.

Encouraged by their first, albeit modest bout of commercial success, they were rushed back into the studio for a follow-up. However, if they thought Festival might give them more studio time as a reward for their accomplishment, they were sadly mistaken. Barry: 'We weren't what you might call priority. In those days, it was Normie Rowe, or it was Ray Brown & The Whispers. Normie Rowe was the king of Australian pop and Johnny O'Keefe was the king before him. It was like another world over there. There are big stars in Australia, but they remain inside Australian record boundaries'.

In an oft-told tale of one particular incident that he experienced, Maurice recalled: 'We'd done the backtrack and the (engineer) says 'Hurry up, the pub opens in six minutes – you've got the time to do the vocal in six minutes and that's it!'. In those days, (the record company) paid for the studios, they paid for the musicians, and if you wanted strings on it, they paid for it. And they would say, 'Who the hell do you think you are? Khrushchev?', and they wouldn't give you the strings, although it's obviously the opposite in England. We never knew that, but in Australia, when the pub is opening, and one's got to catch a train back to somewhere outside Sydney and he had to leave and six minutes we had. We did the vocal in six minutes, and double-tracked it!'.

Robin's recollections of recording in Australia weren't much more positive: 'I don't think there was anybody more frustrated. We were kids, and part of it *was* the fault of the record company. We all blame the record company, but part of it was in so much as the studio that we recorded at was at the label. We'd ring up and say, 'We'd like to make our new record next week – how much time can we have?', and if you didn't have a hit record or anything, then you'd get about an hour. An hour! Believe it or not, we'd cut a record in an hour. It's atrocious, but we did, and this was the way things were in Australia, and if we didn't do so well there, then this was one of the reasons'.

In October 1965, Sydney band Denis & The Delawares recorded two energetic Barry Gibb pop/rock songs for their single – 'They Say'/'Bad Girl' – which was released on the HMV label. The Bee Gees' former producer and engineer Robert Iredale was in the recording booth as producer. Barry helped to promote the single release by also attending its launch. Although 'They Say' was listed as the A-side, it was the B-side 'Bad Girl' that attracted some radio airplay. The Delawares had also backed The Bee Gees when they recorded their fourth single 'Claustrophobia'/'Could It Be' the previous year.

In October 1965, Noeleen Batley's third recording of a Barry Gibb song was 'Watching The Hours Go By' – the B-side to her 'Padre' single, a non-Gibb composition. It failed to chart. 'Watching The Hours Go By' lacked the impressive arrangements of Batley's earlier releases; on the other hand, it does have considerable accompaniment from The Bee Gees to restore the balance, and was at least another source of nice memories for Noeleen: 'The boys joined in and played their instruments', she recalled. 'I remember Maurice on the organ, working out all of the chords. Even then, at their young age, they were brilliant, and Barry was such a perfectionist, especially, rehearsing the song over and over again'. This was a penchant the eldest Gibb brother would demonstrate many times during his career.

With nine singles and an EP to their name, an album was the next natural progression for The Bee Gees. Despite Barry's rise as a popular young songwriter with songs recorded by a diverse range of artists (and a prolific pen able to write new songs very quickly), Festival Records decided to simply gather up eleven of the group's previously-issued single A and B-sides for the project, giving Barry room to add just three new songs. For all intents and purposes, their debut was a compilation.

It was, of course, disappointing, as the Gibbs had plenty of good songs available to record, and these were of sufficiently good quality for them to have been picked up by singer Bobby Darin's publishing company on a recent Australian visit. On the positive side, Festival's faith in the Gibbs had obviously been restored somewhat with the modest success of 'Wine and Women'. The brothers were thankful they were being kept on the roster.

The Bee Gee's Sing And Play 14 Barry Gibb Songs (1965)
Australia release date: November 1965
Side 1: 1. 'I Was a Lover, A Leader of Men' 2. 'I Don't Think It's Funny' 3. 'How Love Was True' 4. 'To Be Or Not to Be' 5. 'Timber!' 6. 'Claustrophobia' 7. 'Could It Be'
Side 2: 1. 'And The Children Laughing' 2. 'Wine And Women' 3. 'Don't Say Goodbye' 4. 'Peace Of Mind' 5. 'Take Hold Of That Star' 6. 'You Wouldn't Know' 7. 'Follow The Wind'

The fact that the album contained just five new songs shouldn't really come as a big surprise, as the company had always failed dismally to invest in The Bee Gees, both in terms of time and money. Collecting their previous recordings and adding a few new tracks gave them a new album to put in record store racks very cheaply.

Nowadays, the original release of *Sing And Play* on the Leedon label is one of the most sought-after Australian records of the era, selling for well into four figures when a copy surfaces in the used record marketplace. The 1968 reissue on the Festival subsidiary label Calendar, achieves prices in the high hundreds.

All the album's tracks, along with others from the period, have been recycled on countless *early days* compilations by budget record labels over the years. In 1998, Festival/Spin finally assembled a definitive remastered collection of The Bee Gees' Australian output – *Brilliant from Birth* – making all of them redundant.

The only other worthwhile set from the era is *The Festival Albums Collection 1965-67*, released in 2013. This contained straightforward issues of The Bee Gees' three Australian-era albums. True to form, budgetary constraints still seemed to be in force, with the collection's packaging cheaply made with the CDs housed in card sleeves within a flimsy slipcase. They deserved better.

Along with the woefully flavourless title *The Bee Gee's Sing and Play 14 Barry Gibb Songs,* cover art – complete with the obvious punctuation error – also suffered at the hands of Festival Records' less-than-stellar marketing department. By now, they should have figured out that the apostrophe was not required in the group name, but at least the hyphen didn't reappear.

The design was as flat as the album title, and did The Bee Gees no favours in terms of making them look hip and appeal to a teenage audience. It features a photograph of the brothers posing by a tree, smartly dressed in blue jackets with black collars, and black shoulder and cuff trim. Other photos from the shoot reveal light grey trousers and Barry and Robin wearing Beatle boots, while Maurice opted for cowboy boots. As released, the entire package made the Gibbs look more like a starchy gospel group than a band set to ride the next wave of the British Invasion in about eighteen months' time.

Jon Wadey took the photos (for David Hewison Photography) at various locations in Sydney's Centennial Park, including the historic stone stairway leading to the No. 1 Reservoir near the Reservoir Fields; and one of the two Crimean War cannons located in the park area known as Bryan's Backyard.

The back cover shows a photo of a *Farfisa Portable Electronic Organ* with the subtext 'which is featured on this album'. Perhaps Festival, in their usual subtle way, arranged the product placement to recoup what little money they incurred in releasing the album.

The 1968 reissue on the Calendar imprint, retained the same cover as the original issue, but with the original Leedon logo covered by a Calendar label sticker. The back cover, except for the tracklisting, was dedicated entirely to listing other Calendar releases.

'I Was A Lover, A Leader Of Men' (Barry Gibb)
Recorded at Festival Studios, Sydney: circa October 1965

The ninth single was released on 18 December 1965 but made its first appearance on record as the first album's opening track a few weeks earlier. At more than double the length of their shortest song so far – clocking in at 3:35 – it was the longest recording The Bee Gees had ever made. It was built around a strong chugging rhythm guitar, much like that on 'Wine And 'Women'. Barry obviously felt that this could be part of a successful formula for writing another hit single. Vocally, the group was maturing quickly, and this was their strongest collective performance yet. If their promotional appearances on *Be Our Guest* and *Bandstand* are an accurate replication of the studio session, Maurice played the brief guitar solo.

If the group and record company were expecting a repeat of the 'Wine And Women' success, they must have been frustrated that the new single only charted in Adelaide, where it peaked at number 9 during a thirteen-week run.

There was, however, one positive that came from the song. Barry received his first-ever award, from Adelaide radio station 5KA, for 'Composer of the Year', proving that the music industry as a whole likely thought more of him than his own record label did. This did not diminish his pride in accepting it. 'That was a very big moment for us. That told us we were going somewhere. We knew not where, but we were going somewhere'.

Now formally recognised as one of Australia's leading songwriters, Barry conceded that one unique aspect of his composing set him apart from the others. 'The words come fairly easily. Whenever I think of a tune, I record it on tape and pay someone to write it down for me. It would probably make things a lot easier if I did learn how to write music. Anyway, I've still managed to write hundreds of songs one way or another'.

'I Don't Think It's Funny' (Barry Gibb)
Recorded at Festival Studios, Sydney: circa October 1965
First released on this LP, 'I Don't Think It's Funny' is notable for being the first Bee Gees song on which Barry did not take a lead vocal role. Instead, Robin was given the opportunity to showcase his unique vocal style on this very pretty song with an outstanding melody, mirroring the timbre of an old folk song with some nice acoustic guitar-playing. The lyric is a bit of a letdown in comparison, with some occasionally banal lines – particularly the trite rhymes on 'funny'.

'How Love Was True' (Barry Gibb)
Recorded at Festival Studios, Sydney: circa October 1965
Another of the album's new songs was 'How Love Was True' – another excellent composition, and one of the most mature-sounding products of their Australian recording years. The song is rather short, but what it lacks in length, it makes up for in quality. Robin again turned in an excellent lead vocal.

'To Be Or Not To Be' (Barry Gibb)
Recorded at Festival Studios, Sydney: circa October 1965
'To Be Or Not To Be' is a raucous rock 'n' roll song very much in the vein of Jerry Lee Lewis. For the first and only time on any Bee Gees song

before or since, the song has not one, but two instrumental breaks, both featuring some wonderfully boisterous piano. It's unknown who played it, though it certainly doesn't sound like Maurice at this stage.

'And The Children Laughing' (Barry Gibb)
Recorded at Festival Studios, Sydney: circa October 1965

Making its first appearance on the album, but also released as the B-side to 'I Was A Lover, A Leader Of Men' a few weeks later, 'And The Children Laughing' is one of just a few examples ever of a Bee Gees song written with a blatantly obvious social message. Without a doubt, this was the first.

Barry drew stylistic influence from Bob Dylan's protest songs, but there is a clear sonic parallel to American singer-songwriter Barry McGuire's 'Eve Of Destruction', which had been a US number 1 hit and a top five single in the UK and Australia in September 1965. While 'And The Children Laughing' is rather lyrically naïve, it is essentially a very reflective, if somewhat overly-optimistic, song from a nineteen-year-old who was very conscious of what was going on in the world.

The song is unusual in that Barry broke what was already his golden rule when writing songs; that the melody should never be interrupted to suit the lyrics. In 1997 Barry explained his songwriting process: 'At some point, we establish exactly what the melody is, note for note, and then when we do our lyrics, we don't detract from that melody. We don't change the melody to go with certain words we may like; we really make the words fit the melody we have pre-established'.

To close the year, The Bee Gees made an appearance on *Bandstand* on 18 December, performing their hit single 'Wine And Women', coupled with their current offering 'I Was A Lover, A Leader Of Men'.

1966

1966 would be the eighth and final year of the Gibb family's stay in Australia. It would also prove to be the most productive and successful year to date for The Bee Gees.

13 January saw the year's first Gibb-related record release, from accomplished television singer Lynne Fletcher. The powerful cabaret-style ballad 'You Do Your Loving With Me' was penned by Barry as the A-side to Lynne's new single. The song, which suited her voice well, was sent to her by HMV, but Lynne already knew the Gibbs from her Brisbane days and even dated Barry for a short period.

Although The Beatles would continue to dominate the Australian charts throughout 1966, the Merseybeat era was in decline, replaced quickly by a new, edgier rock sound from overseas by the likes of The Spencer Davis Group and The Yardbirds. New Australian bands were now eclipsing former chart stalwarts like Tony Worsley and fellow Sydneysiders Ray Brown & the Whispers, who would have their final hits that year before fading away. Sydney – once the epicentre of Australian pop that had coaxed the Gibb family away from Queensland in 1963 – was no longer as influential. Melbourne, some 550 miles away, was where two of the country's rising music TV shows – *The Go!! Show* and *Kommotion* – were filmed. It was also home to *Go-Set*, Australia's newest and most popular magazine for the 'teens and twenties'.

Whilst The Bee Gees' popularity was expanding all the time, their live shows still had a vaudevillian aspect that included impressions of other acts, from Rudy Vallee to Elvis Presley. Considering that their send-up of local songstress Little Pattie involved one of the twins wearing a blonde wig, it's not difficult to understand the confusion among Australian audiences regarding The Bee Gees' identity: were they a pop group or a variety act? Whatever they were, the bookings were still coming in. And as popular as they were on stage, they had yet to score a legitimate big hit record.

It was at this point The Bee Gees began to contemplate the possibility of a move back to England, believing they'd exhausted their potential as performers and recording artists in Australia, and longing to be a part of the burgeoning rock music scene that had created explosive success for the bands they idolised: The Beatles, The Rolling Stones, The Hollies and The Kinks, among others. Hugh and Barbara flatly refused the idea at first, remembering the constant struggles they encountered before emigrating nearly a decade earlier. However, their sons' ambitions eventually won out, and plans were made for their return to Britain in early 1967.

The Bee Gees also seriously considered another major career move. On 27 February, Sydney's *Sunday Telegraph* newspaper reported, 'After eight years of being known as one thing, they have decided that what their image really needs is a name change! So, from Monday on, it won't be The Bee Gees any more. They want to be known as Rupert's World'. The group explained that 'it's a different sort of name, and to us, it symbolises the different sort of music we'll be playing'. In an article on the front page of *Go-Set* magazine on 26 October, the Gibbs restated their intention to adopt their revised moniker when they arrived in England.

The mysterious, abstract name was pretty much in tune with the times, though it isn't known why they specifically chose it. All of the hullabaloo, however, was for nothing, and the change never came to fruition. There was a British psychedelic group that released a number of singles in 1967-1968 called Rupert's People, and this may have been influential in the decision not to make the name change.

March saw the release of The Bee Gees' next single, 'I Want Home'/'Cherry Red', which was to be the group's final appearance on the Leedon label. It was the first record produced using the new four-track facilities at Festival Studios, although everything was mixed down to mono for release. Barry would recall the frustration of having the new equipment in the studio for some time before it was actually in working order: 'They didn't have anyone who knew how to use it'. Nat Kipner also remembered when Festival obtained the four-track technology: 'I heard about this and went up to see it and couldn't believe my eyes or ears, and it boggled my mind to think that such technology could exist'. The Gibb brothers didn't have to be asked twice whether they would like to be the first to use the new equipment, and they quickly went to work on a new single.

'I Want Home' (Barry Gibb)
Recorded at Festival Studios, Sydney: circa February 1966

'I Want Home' is a great pounding rock track, somewhat derivative of The Beatles' work of two years prior, with unusual shifts in the melody and some nice guitar riffs. It was the most straightforward rock song The Bee Gees had recorded to date.

From the promotional material for this single, it appears Festival were undecided as to which song should be the A-side, asking radio

DJs to play both at their leisure. While it's possible the label was trying to pave the way for a Bee Gees hit in any way they could, in hindsight, Festival seemed to be out of ideas – and likely, enthusiasm – in terms of promoting The Bee Gees' music.

Historically, 'Cherry Red' is usually acknowledged as the A-side, but 'I Want Home' is listed first on the record company's promotional flyer for the single, describing it as 'Right up to standard with the driving exciting vocal sounds which have placed The Bee Gees up and apart from the majority of vocal groups, whilst 'Cherry Red' is a big sounding high-quality ballad'.

The single's matrix number – which appears in smaller print below the record catalogue number – also points to 'I Want Home' as the A-side with MX19819, and the B-side 'Cherry Red' as MX19820. The lower number is indicative of the lead side of the single.

Bill Shepherd departed Festival Records and left for England ahead of The Bee Gees in early 1966. It's widely believed this single was the last work he did for the label before his exit; however, both 'I Want Home' and 'Cherry Red' were actually produced by former EMI producer Joe Halford, who was familiar with four-track recording equipment. Shepherd and the Gibbs would reunite a year later on English soil with much more favourable results.

'Cherry Red' (Barry Gibb)
Recorded at Festival Studios, Sydney: circa February 1966

'Cherry Red' is a slow ballad with some fine harmony singing, in some ways a return to their old ballad format. The song's length of 3:07 indicated some maturity in Barry's writing, but its slow pace may have only turned off fans wanting uncomplicated pop music they could dance to.

Future Bee Gees drummer Colin Petersen (then with Steve & The Board) may have played drums on both sides of this single.

Neither side of the record made any noise at radio or retail, and with essentially no fanfare, The Bee Gees' Festival era came to a close.

Kiwi country singer John Hore included his cover of Barry's 'Tribute To An Unknown Love' on his album *Hit The Trail* in March 1966. Hore – one of New Zealand's best-known country artists – met the Gibb brothers in 1964 while touring Australia. Following the meeting, tapes of four Barry songs were sent to him when he returned to New Zealand. Unfortunately, the tapes and the master of *Hit The Trail* were lost in a fire at EMI's studios some years later.

Before the month was out, Festival also released The Bee Gees' second EP *Wine And Women*, which combined both sides of that single, plus their February 1964 release 'Peace Of Mind'/'Don't Say Goodbye'. The EP's picture sleeve showing the three brothers in suits, ties, and slicked-back hair, was once again more befitting the late-1950s than the mid-1960s.

While the release of *The Bee Gees Sing And Play 14 Barry Gibb Songs* the previous year finally gave the Gibbs their long-awaited debut on the long-play format, it did little else to further their commercial success or to save their fracturing relationship with Festival. Hugh Gibb – still the group's manager at the time – was by all accounts livid, blaming Festival's consistently poor promotion and lack of support in the studio for the group's chart failures. As had been hinted at in the newspapers, the three brothers may have been preparing for a fresh new start with a different record company, which only exacerbated the tension. However, despite Hugh Gibb's angry threats, Festival Records boss Fred Marks was never a man to be taken lightly, and through the support of local industry heavyweight and long-time Bee Gees fan Nat Kipner, a compromise was reached.

Following that fallout, The Bee Gees moved to Spin Records: owned by Australian Consolidated Press (ACP) and managed by ACP's Clyde Packer. By no coincidence, Kipner was a partner in Spin, and also its artist and repertoire (A&R) chief. Spin, although a new label, had just enjoyed some big hits, including 'Giggle Eyed Goo' by Steve & The Board, and 'Someday' by former Aztec member Tony Barber.

The big catch of The Bee Gees' transfer to Spin Records was that Festival would gain the exclusive distribution rights for all Spin releases in perpetuity. It was a deal that would make all parties, particularly Festival Records, a lot of money over the next forty-plus years, well beyond all of their wildest imaginations at that point. All three parties would have been content with the arrangement.

Not only had Marks rid himself of all his Bee-Gees-associated issues, and their angry father, he'd also secured an extension of their distribution rights into the mid-1970s, ensuring that no matter where The Bee Gees might live at the time, revenue from their Australian releases would still filter back to Festival. The Gibbs, for their part, were simply glad to be free of Festival. Kipner was also content, confident he could do something with the talented brothers whom he knew from their Brisbane days. Forty years later, Kipner was still an unabashed fan of the Gibb brothers: 'The Bee Gees were the most talented group in the world after The Beatles.

They were so different. Somewhere along the road, somebody would have recognised this thing, but fortunately, I was there at the time, and I was lucky to be associated with them. A hundred years from now, someone, somewhere, will still be playing some Bee Gees songs, that's for sure'.

As part of the enticement to come to Spin, Kipner had promised The Bee Gees as much studio time as they wanted. He knew of a local recording studio; though it didn't have the new four-track recording facilities, it did offer two mono recorders: technology comparable to the other small studios in Sydney at the time. It was also significantly cheaper than the other studios, as Kipner recalled: 'I'd heard about this studio out in Hurstville, so I went out there and met the owner Ossie Byrne. It was nothing but a garage. You opened the door and bazoo! – there's microphones everywhere and bits and pieces, and obviously, he'd had some experience in this. Finally, we recorded 'Spicks And Specks' there. Studios at the time were two mono tape recorders; everything was miked, so you had to get it perfect the first time. You didn't have a million tracks; you didn't have a drum machine, you had nothing'.

Ossie Byrne, the studio owner and self-taught producer, was then 40 years old. He would play a big part in The Bee Gees' future over the next two years. Byrne, who had lost an eye serving with the RAAF in New Guinea during World War II, established St. Clair Studios in an old butcher's shop at 56 Queens Road, some ten miles outside of Sydney proper. He made full use of the former shop space and storerooms as singer Jon Blanchfield recalled: 'The old coolroom was the control room with the two-track player'.

The beauty of Ossie's St. Clair Studio was that, unlike its peer facilities in the area, the visiting artists were also not limited to strict two-hour sessions like The Bee Gees had experienced at Festival Studios. By this time, Byrne was an excellent sound engineer and producer, renowned for making the most out of the limited recording technology available to him. In addition, he was eager to put his studio to its full use, taping demos and master recordings – not only for Spin Records' artists, but for other clients.

In Byrne, The Bee Gees also found a friend, and more importantly, someone who believed in them, telling them he felt they were the most original band in Australia. Robin recalled that Byrne 'had always been a fan of ours, but thought that we should have been handled a bit better; so he said, 'Come to my studio, you can have all the time you want'. And we were in there day and night, and we could experiment for the first time. We felt great, wrote all our own music. It was like a whole new door had been opened'. Byrne told 19-year-old Barry and the 16-year-old twins to keep recording, to keep writing songs, to persist. Between live performances, the brothers made the St. Clair Studio their second home. Unlike some artists, all three Gibb brothers loved the recording process, and with Byrne producing long sessions that sometimes ran well into the night – often with Nat Kipner present – they found a willing and patient teacher. Importantly, Byrne got along well with Hugh and agreed to help him manage his sons' careers. Unlike with Robert Iredale, the age difference between Byrne and the Gibb brothers did not create problems, and the boys saw him as more of a friendly mentor than a supervisor. Soon, The Bee Gees were given free run of the studio when it was not being used, allowing them to experiment with sound effects and overdubs, and to learn how to make the best of the simple equipment in front of them.

Barry remembered the creative freedom and positive relationship with Byrne was what they had always hoped for: 'It was what we wanted. He was like a spirit guide, sent to make sure that what we wanted to do happened. He wanted to help us develop'. Robin concurred: 'Ossie said, 'Your greatest enemy has been that no one has ever given you studio time', so we said, 'All we want is to go in there for two months. If we put time in the studio, we can bring out a number one record'. We knew that, so we went in there and did it'. Encouraged by both Byrne and Kipner, Maurice and Robin also began composing songs at this time. Maurice in particular took to the challenge with relish, occasionally co-writing with Kipner, who, like Barry, was a prodigious songwriter and always on the lookout for ideas for new compositions.

'Neither Rich Nor Poor' – another Barry song – was released in May 1966. While the label attributed the recording to The Richard Wright Group, the song was actually cut by Wright solo, prior to the group's formation. The record was produced by David Mackay, who was a very successful record maker in Australia – coincidentally, he had served his apprenticeship under The Bee Gees' former producer Robert Iredale.

Also, in May, Judge Wayne replicated Trevor Gordon's 1965 single, covering both 'Little Miss Rhythm And Blues' and 'Here I Am'. Originally part of a band – Judge Wayne & The Convicts – this single was Wayne Harrison's first solo outing. His cover is without a doubt the best version of 'Little Miss Rhythm And Blues', with some solid guitar and piano work.

The 25 May edition of *Everybody's* magazine featured an article titled 'Bee Gees for UK', hinting that the group were 'shortly to embark on a Far East tour which would wind up in England' – though the latter part of the adventure didn't materialise until The Bee Gees finally visited Japan, Hong Kong, Malaysia, Indonesia and Singapore in 1972.

On 30 June, The Bee Gees' new single 'Monday's Rain'/'All Of My Life' was released. Both songs were Barry compositions, and the record was produced by Kipner and Byrne. However, if The Bee Gees and their management were expecting a positive reaction for their first release on their new label, they were in for a shock. Melbourne newspaper *The Sun* wrote, 'Sydney's Bee Gees should stop trying to sound so much like The Beatles. Sydney's *Sun-Herald* heard other influences: 'The Bee Gees sound like The Righteous Brothers on Barry Gibb's 'Monday's Rain''. In the *Sunday Telegraph*, Carol Rodgers' Under 21 column reported on the brothers' growing disenchantment with Australia, writing that The Bee Gees 'have been feeling unhappy with the way the pop business is treating them. Maybe they have been around too long to be news anymore. They certainly feel that there just isn't the opportunity here as there is overseas – and they could be right'.

Unfortunately for all concerned, and despite Spin's best endeavours, radio stations certainly weren't playing 'Monday's Rain' or 'All Of My Life' – adding to the band's growing list of commercial failures.

'Monday's Rain' (Barry Gibb)
Recorded at St. Clair Studio, Hurstville: circa April 1966

The Bee Gees' first single for the Spin label was initially proposed for release in May 1966, backed with 'Play Down', and was chosen as the title track for their second album. That plan was scrapped, but the single was eventually released a month later with 'All Of My Life' as the B-side.

This track was indeed the first real evidence of the long-promised 'new Bee Gees sound', and the most experimental Barry Gibb composition to date. Unfortunately, it wasn't particularly good.

Robin and Barry alternate lead vocals in the verses, and both sing deeper than heard before on record. Robin's vibrato-laden vocal, in particular, seems to be in too deep a register and sounds like a cross between Roy Orbison and Scott Walker. For the first time, we hear Barry's breathy vocal, a style that would become one of the eldest brother's trademarks. The production is clumsy, with annoying wave-crashing cymbals, which would have been better suited to a surf instrumental. In retrospect, it's obvious the teenage trio were absorbing various influences and understandably were being encouraged to stretch themselves – but here, it doesn't quite work.

'Monday's Rain' was perhaps the most soulful and musically innovative song they'd recorded to date. The version that would eventually appear on the *Spicks And Specks* album, is different from the single, with Robin slightly altering the lyrics and Barry varying his pacing. The single version is a bit more elusive, but it can be heard on the 1978 Infinity Records compilation *Birth Of Brilliance*, and on 1998's *Brilliant From Birth* collection.

'All Of My Life' (Barry Gibb)
Recorded at St. Clair Studio, Hurstville: circa April 1966
Released as the B-side of 'Monday's Rain', this was initially intended as the opening track on side two of the *Monday's Rain* LP, but It was ultimately not used for the eventually-issued *Spicks And Specks* album. This very commercial song is one of the best examples of how The Bee Gees could sound like The Beatles when they wanted to. But the downside was that radio didn't want to play it because it sounded *too much* like The Beatles.

However, it's a fine song and could have fitted nicely on The Beatles' 1965 *Rubber Soul* album, with Barry doing an excellent John Lennon imitation in his lead vocal. The Bee Gees had been hearing comparisons with The Beatles for over two years now, usually unfavourably. But to have one of their singles supposedly blocked because of it, the issue was now becoming serious.

Perhaps the brothers consoled themselves by thinking that previously radio programmers didn't play their songs because they didn't like their music, and at least now there was a reason they could understand, even if they didn't agree. The fact that they'd been recording as long as The Beatles, and performing even longer, was irrelevant. As Barry has said, 'The Beatles got there first'.

In July, The Bee Gees played at the Wagga Wagga Police Citizens' Boys Club. The journey to Wagga Wagga – some 280 miles southwest of Sydney – was not without its problems, when the group's transportation – a Volkswagen Kombi van, later made famous on the cover of their final album *This Is Where I Came In* – broke down. While rehearsing for their show that night at the club, Barry wrote possibly the finest song of his Australian output: 'In The Morning' – later known as 'Morning Of My Life'.

From about mid-July 1966, the Gibb brothers worked non-stop at St. Clair Studios, even sleeping overnight there at times. This access also made them available to contribute to many recordings by other local artists. A number of Gibb-related releases would appear on the short-lived Downunder label, formed by Ossie Byrne and Nat Kipner for the express purpose of issuing recordings made at the studio. The label existed for a mere five months from June to October 1966 and was responsible for producing just thirteen singles, all of which were manufactured and distributed by Festival Records.

The first Downunder single of interest was released in July, and is an extremely obscure record that is the only known release by an artist known as Wee Liz: a teenage singer from Wollongong whose real name was Elizabeth Reed. The A-side was 'Tiny Little Pebble', but it's solely the B-side 'Lonesome 409' which has any relationship to The Bee Gees – Robin played the triangle which mimicked the ringing of a telephone, while Barry and Maurice were in another room. It was reported at the time that only four copies of the record were sold.

The first Downunder single with the Gibbs' involvement as writers was 'Hey'/'Young Man's Fancy' by Bip Addison, which was released in August. Both songs were co-written by Maurice Gibb and Nat Kipner. This was the first song written by Maurice to ever be recorded. He also played bass, piano, harmonica and maracas in addition to providing vocals on the A-side. Barry was featured on guitar, and drums were by future Bee Gee Colin Petersen. 'Young Man's Fancy' features all three Gibbs on backing vocals, whilst Maurice played a solid electric 12-string guitar line to achieve the desired Byrds-like effect.

Another Downunder release in August was Sandy Summers' 'Messin' Round'/'A Girl Needs To Love'. 'Messin' Round', at just 1:45, was a very short Maurice Gibb/Nat Kipner composition. Maurice sang backing vocals on the up-tempo song and played piano and bass, while Barry played guitar. Drums were again probably played by Colin Petersen. 'A Girl Needs To Love' was a Barry composition, and is one of the more mature songs he'd written to this point. Barry can clearly be heard singing along with virtually all of Sandy's lead vocal, while the twins provide the backgrounds.

August also saw an ingenious bit of experimentation from Maurice on the penultimate single by M.P.D. Ltd. – a band who had a short but meteoric career in the Australian rock and roll scene. The Bee Gees provided backing vocals on both sides of the single. Guitarist Mike Brady confirms that 'on 'Absence Makes The Heart Grow Fonder', Maurice Gibb played the solo by plucking the strings of an open piano like a guitar. All The Bee Gees were in the studio for that one – they all helped out, which was terrific'. Released on the Go!! Label as the B-side to the band's 'I Am What I Am', the record was also issued on the Ariola label in Germany. The Gibb brothers' coincidental connection to the group's bass guitarist Pete Watson, went back to 1958 when he emigrated to Australia from the UK on the *Fairsea*, on the same voyage as the Gibb family.

On Monday 22 August, Barry married his girlfriend, Maureen Elaine Bates at Holy Trinity Church in the Sydney suburb of Kingsford. Maureen, also aged just nineteen, had migrated from Yorkshire with her family in 1958 on the *Fairsea* – the same ship, but not the same voyage that had brought the Gibbs from overseas. The couple had been dating steadily since the age of sixteen. Their relationship dissolved quickly as The Bee Gees' career prospects continued to escalate, finally ending in divorce in July 1970 after a long separation.

Barry's 20th birthday on 1 September saw the release of three records with The Bee Gees' involvement: two of which would fade into obscurity. The third would finally give them the big hit they'd always sought that had so far evaded them.

The first was another Downunder release: 'Talk To Me'/'I Miss You' by Anne Shelton. 'Talk To Me' was written by Maurice with Nat Kipner, and The Bee Gees provide quite dominant background vocal support. 'I Miss You' is a Nat Kipner and Ossie Byrne composition. Again, The Bee Gees furnish backing vocals, including a verse that they sing on their own with Shelton speaking over them.

The second release was by The Mystics, who had a one-off record contract as a result of winning a local 'Best Band' competition. Sadly, 'Don't You Go, I Need Your Love' – another Maurice Gibb and Nat Kipner composition released on the Downunder label – failed to launch The Mystics' career. Lead singer Ron Watford remembered Maurice's amazing ability to notice little details, Maurice telling Ron that his guitar's G-string was flat, from behind the recording console. He also has clear memories of the Hurstville studio toilet having its doorway bricked in, with recordings being played in and then back out of the room to achieve an echo chamber effect.

The third record was The Bee Gees' own single 'Spicks And Specks'/'I Am The World'. After so many tribulations, it took just one hastily-recorded two-minute and fifty-two-second studio cut to change their entire path forever.

'Spicks And Specks' (Barry Gibb)

Recorded at St. Clair Studio, Hurstville: circa June/July 1966
Chart positions: New Zealand: 1, Netherlands: 3, Australia: 4, West Germany: 28, Japan: 56

Over the years, the brothers and many others have perpetuated the myth that 'Spicks And Specks' was their first number1 hit in Australia, and that they received word of it after leaving the country while en route to England on board the ship *Fairsky*. This, however, is not correct, as the single's peak placement on the *Go-Set* magazine chart – which was Australia's national singles survey at the time – was number 4 on 9 November 1966. The only evidence of it reaching the top spot anywhere in the country, is on a regional chart in Canberra on 23 November. The song *was,* however, a genuine number 1 single in New Zealand, but even that wasn't until the week of 19 May 1967, when the Gibbs were already back in England and finishing work in the studio for *Bee Gees' 1st.* The news they *did* actually receive aboard ship was that 'Spicks And Specks' had won *Go-Set* magazine's *Best Record of the Year* award.

The song was composed very quickly at St. Clair Studio while singer Jon Blanchfield was there recording a couple of the Gibbs' songs: 'Town Of Tuxley Toymaker Part 1' and 'Upstairs, Downstairs'.

Maurice was messing about on the piano, heading in no particular direction, when Barry heard something he liked and immediately picked up his guitar and developed it into a melody. The title 'Spicks And Specks' came from a name the boys dreamed up for an imaginary pop group, and in little more than an hour, the song was finished.

Local musician Geoff Grant was brought in to play the trumpet solo – and also for 'I Am The World'. Russell Barnsley played drums, and Nat Kipner's son Steve – who would become a successful songwriter and musician in his own right – added some backing vocals.

The single was promoted with appearances on prominent new and popular music television shows like *The Go!! Show* and *It's All Happening* – the latter on which they gave a stunning live performance, followed by a cover of the Rolling Stones' 'Out Of Time'. A fun promotional film for the single was also made, at Bankstown airport in Western Sydney.

The Bee Gees had finally notched the major hit that had eluded them for over four years of working in Australia, just in time to bid their adopted home farewell. When they arrived back in England, they signed a management deal with Robert Stigwood within a matter of weeks, along with a recording contract with Polydor Records. 'Spicks And Specks' was the first single release on their new label, on 24 February 1967, before they had even had the opportunity to record any new material. It was issued in many European countries, and although it bombed in the UK, it fared well in the Netherlands and West Germany.

In March 2015, the song made a shocking appearance at the end of a fifth-season episode of the acclaimed US drama series *The Walking Dead* for the AMC network. It was an especially strange choice given that it's surely not known by most North American audiences, but perhaps its obscurity and the surprise for viewers who later discovered who sang the song, was part of the appeal for the show's producers.

'I Am The World' (Robin Gibb)

Recorded at St. Clair Studio, Hurstville: circa June/July 1966

A very important song for Robin, giving him his first solo songwriting credit on a Bee Gees record. Released as the B-side to 'Spicks And Specks', it's a very fine song in its own right. The dramatic chorus showcases his incomparable vocal power and vibrato: a foreshadow of his signature performance on 'I Started A Joke' two years later.

Notably, 'I Am The World' was covered by two Australian artists – Johnny Young, as the B-side to his version of the Bee Gees song 'Craise Finton Kirk Royal Academy of Arts' in 1967; and Bev Harrell, as the B-side of 'One Way Ticket' in 1968. Harrell's version was produced by David Mackay, who would eventually work directly with The Bee Gees in the UK in the 1980s during recording of tracks for The Bunburys project.

Robin revisited the song himself, recording a new version in 2009, although this would not see a release until 2014, on his posthumous solo album *50 St. Catherine's Drive*.

For the remainder of the year, until they left Australia in early January 1967, The Bee Gees were frantically busy, touring, writing and producing for themselves and other artists. The output would keep Festival's record presses, and radio stations playlists, occupied for some months.

Vince Melouney spent periods as lead guitarist with Billy Thorpe and The Aztecs, Vince & Tony's Two, and Tony Worsley and The Fabulous Blue Jays, but tired of correcting the spelling of his name for journalists, he conceded by calling his next group The Vince Maloney Sect. After releasing two singles and an EP, they split, and Vince released a solo single in September – 'I Need Your Lovin' Tonight'/'Mystery Train' – with backing vocals by The Bee Gees.

Vince explained, 'There was an Australian record producer called Nat Kipner, and he said The Bee Gees were doing some recording and they asked whether I would play guitar on a couple of their songs, which I of course agreed, and in return, they would sing backing vocals on a couple of my songs, which they did. So, we went out and we did the recordings. It was a really fun day and it was good to be with the guys'.

What may have been seen as opportunist at the time, would ultimately be life-changing for Vince, as he recalls: 'That time I was there, I said to Maurice – he and I are about the same size – and I said I was selling all my stage clothes because I was going to England with my wife and we needed to get together as much money as possible. And so, he said he was interested. So, I came back sometime later and he tried the clothes on and he took them, but he was short of a few dollars. And he said, 'Well, you know, we'll be going to England as well. So, we'll catch up with you there and I'll give you the money'. So, you know, there's 60 million people in England ... I really liked his optimism! But anyway, that's what happened'. Whether or not Maurice eventually paid Vince is unknown, but the two would have a rather ceremonious reunion in London in a matter of months.

Two further releases on the Downunder label appeared in October. The first was Barrington Davis' 'Dear Lady'/'Complicated Riddle'. Barrington himself is unsure whether The Bee Gees contributed to the recordings, both written by Nat Kipner and Ossie Byrne. However, he recalls being in the studio when The Bee Gees recorded 'Spicks And Specks' at about the same time; and as they lent themselves to so many other releases on the Downunder label, it's not unreasonable to assume that they provided uncredited backing on these two songs.

Also in October, April Byron's 'He's A Thief'/'A Long Time Ago' was the final single released by the Downunder label. Best known in Australia for her 1964 hit 'Make The World Go Away', April would retain a lifelong friendship with the brothers until her death in 2019. Whilst the Maurice Gibb/Nat Kipner collaboration 'He's A Thief' was the A-side, it's the B-side – Barry's 'A Long Time Ago' – that is the superior song. It's a dark, atmospheric recording. All three brothers sang backing vocals on both tracks. They also supplied superb background harmonies on Ray Brown and the Whispers' single 'Too Late To Come Home'. Released in October 1966, it was the final single from the band, who had achieved substantial success in Australia over the previous two years.

Another artist who recorded at the Hurstville studio was singer-songwriter Tony Barber. A fellow English emigrant, Barber had previously been a guitarist in Billy Thorpe and The Aztecs with future Bee Gees member Vince Melouney. Fresh from the success of his debut solo single 'Someday', which was a top ten hit across Australia, Barber said 'I used The Bee Gees on quite a few of those tracks' on his album *Someday ... Now!*, but this is highly unlikely as it was recorded entirely at Festival Studios and concluded in March, which makes it too early for any Bee Gees involvement. However, his memory may have faded slightly, and he may have confused the album tracks with the songs he recorded at St. Clair, which he recalled 'was a great little studio'. The songs recorded were released as the singles 'Wondrous Place'/'No, No, No' (July 1966), 'Lookin' For A Better Day'/'I Don't Want You Like That' (November 1966) and 'Woman Of Stone'/'Bird's Eye View' (April 1967). While there are no vocal clues to The Bee Gees' involvement, it's entirely possible they were involved in an instrumental capacity. Barber also joined with Maurice to produce singer/dancer Denise Drysdale's debut single 'Sunshine Shadows'/'Rescue Me', which was released on the Melbourne-based Phono Vox label in October. Best known then as a prominent go-go dancer on the music show *Kommotion*, sixteen-year-old Denise would go on to become one of Australia's national treasures, with a long television career. The record label erroneously credits Maurice as M. Gibbs.

On 27 November, The Bee Gees' long-awaited second album *Spicks And Specks* was released. It received varied reviews. *Everybody's* magazine awarded it three stars, but was relatively passive in its praise: 'There are some second-rate songs sprinkled amidst a strong collection of melodious, original sounds from The Bee Gees'.

Sydney's *Sun Herald* wrote:

The Bee Gees have been writing and performing some exceptional pop tunes. The lyrics are good, and the intonation, if somewhat in a Beatles bag, is unique and confident. The LP takes its title from the unusually good pop song 'Spicks And Specks'. The words have the simplicity of rustic blues, and the melody is a framework of strong repetitive chords which allow a buildup of tension. There are other songs on the LP almost as good – 'Glass House', 'Monday's Rain', 'Tint Of Blue' and 'How Many Birds'. Barry, Maurice and Robin Gibb, members of the trio, appear to provide all of the backings themselves: a multi-instrumental feat. The LP is a most exciting, original performance by a young group.

The reviewer's assumption of the brothers providing their own accompaniment was not entirely correct. While they did play much of it themselves, there are a number of uncredited musicians on the album. They include Roger Felice of The Soul Agents (drums); Russell Barnsley and Dennis D. Wilson of Kevin Bible & The Book on drums and guitar respectively; Mal Clarke of The Blue Jays (guitar); John Robinson of Monday's Children (guitar); Eugene Brancourt of The Tremors, along with future Bee Gees member Colin Petersen of Steve & The Board (drums) and Vince Melouney (guitar).

In retrospect, the *Spicks And Specks* LP was where The Bee Gees first became a truly cohesive outfit, rather than Robin and Maurice serving as Barry's background vocalists. All three contributed songs and lead vocals. On a few tracks, Barry and Robin shared lead vocals: an interplay that would become one of their most valuable assets over the years. Barry's voice no longer dominated all of the tracks, although his characteristic rhythm guitar was very prominent. Robin's distinctive vocal sound was now well to the fore, and he also played melodica on some songs. Maurice played piano, lead guitar, bass and 12-string guitar – of which Steve Kipner also remembers: 'Maurice got an amazing electric guitar sound by plugging it into a record player with a speaker in it'.

Barry's recollection of the album nearly 50 years later in 2013 was that the songs 'weren't that fantastic. When I hear the really early songs, I can hear the learning process going on and the absorbing of how a good song should be and how you have to reach someone's heart with a song. It's all the different elements that make a great song, and the X factor, of course'.

Spicks And Specks (1966)

Personnel:
Barry Gibb: vocal, guitar
Robin Gibb: vocal, melodica
Maurice Gibb: vocal, guitar, bass, piano
Additional Personnel:
Recording engineer: Ossie Byrne
Producer: Nat Kipner
Recording dates: April and May 1966 – St. Clair Studio, Hurstville
Australia release date: November 1966

The *Spicks And Specks* album was originally titled *Monday's Rain*, after the single released in June 1966. However, when the innovative and somewhat experimental 'Monday's Rain' failed commercially, the album title was changed to the title of the single that was racing up the Australian charts.

In terms of maturity and confidence, *Spicks And Specks*' sonic arc feels miles ahead of what they'd released even a year prior. On some tracks, it's easy to hear how their singing and songwriting would evolve into the pop classics they crafted for *Bee Gees' 1st*.

However, in the haste to get the renamed set into the shops to cash in on the success of the hit single, some early editions of the album were pressed and sold with the original title – *Monday's Rain* – printed on the LP's side two labels, making those copies particularly collectible nowadays.

Despite 'Spicks And Specks' generating some good reviews and the group's biggest hit up to that point, the album was only a moderate seller. It was deleted from print in late 1967 after The Bee Gees' new material from England proved more attractive to Australian record buyers.

Two years after its original release, the *Spicks And Specks* album was repackaged, electronically reprocessed into stereo, retitled *Rare, Precious & Beautiful* and released globally. Such was The Bee Gees' rapidly-expanding success in the US, the album eventually made it to number 53 on the *Cashbox* chart in 1968. Ironically, considering their lack of success in Australia up to late in 1966, this chart placing made it the most successful Australian-produced album to date in the US.

In terms of design quality, the album cover was streets ahead of *The Bee Gee's Sing And Play 14 Barry Gibb Songs* – some thought was actually put into combining the title with the artwork. A trendy pair of chequered patterned glasses – evidently representing the 'spec(k)s' – and a random selection of colourful, fashionable earrings adorn the front cover. These items were supplied by *The In Shop* at the Imperial Arcade located at 168 Pitt Street in Sydney. Individual black and white photographs of each brother were strategically inserted, with Robin and Maurice in place of lenses in the glasses, and Barry in one of the earrings. The album title stood boldly in red above the glasses, and the group name below in magenta.

The back cover was pure text, including sleeve notes by Nat Kipner: Spin Records' owner and the album's producer. The twelve songs are listed, but writing credits appear only on the record label.

'Monday's Rain' (Barry Gibb)

See the entry for the single.

'How Many Birds' (Barry Gibb)

Recorded at St. Clair Studio, Hurstville: circa April/May 1966

The album's second track is incredibly short – clocking in at just 1:57 – but it has a superb vocal by Barry and an irresistible rock feel. By now, Barry was beginning to write songs that didn't sound like anything else on the scene.

'Play Down' (Barry Gibb)

Recorded at St. Clair Studio, Hurstville: circa April/May 1966

'Play Down' is a slow song, with Barry and Robin doubling the lead vocal in the verses, joined by Maurice for added punch in the chorus harmonies. The middle-eight could have been better with an instrumental solo rather than Robin's strange wailing.

The Festival Albums Collection 1965-67 and the compilation album *Morning Of My Life – The Best Of 1965-66* surprised aficionados when Warner Music's Festival label released them in 2013 to coincide with Barry Gibb's first-ever solo tour of Australia. The version of 'Play Down' included on these albums was different to the previously-released version, notably in the middle-eight where Robin enters with 'bom-bom-bom' vocal fills – the jury is still out on whether this was better or worse than the original take.

As 'Play Down' was the intended original B-side of the 'Monday's Rain' single and two versions also exist of that song, it would be reasonable to surmise that this alternate version was intended for that release.

Barry surprised Australian concert audiences on his 2013 *Mythology* tour when he included 'Play Down' in his set along with 'In The Morning' and 'Spicks And Specks', both of which made regular appearances in Bee Gees' setlists over the years. Recalling St. Clair Studio's former glory as a butcher's shop, Barry introduced the song at the Melbourne stop on his road trip, by humorously quipping, 'We recorded this song with the smell of steak wafting into the studio'.

'Second Hand People' (Barry Gibb)

Recorded at St. Clair Studio, Hurstville: circa April/May 1966

Another example of a rare Bee Gees attempt at direct social commentary, 'Second Hand People', although snappily-titled, suffers from some rather feeble poetic licence in its rhyming lines. Musically, however, it's strong, and benefits massively from Ossie Byrne's engineering skills which focused on the fat guitar sound and Maurice's fine McCartney-inspired bass-playing. Australian pop star Mike Furber released a cover version in 1967 as the B-side to his single 'Where Are You' – another *Spicks And Specks* track, which was penned by Maurice.

'I Don't Know Why I Bother With Myself' (Robin Gibb)
Recorded at St. Clair Studio, Hurstville: circa April/May 1966

This, the second recorded instance of Robin's songwriting is a simple but pleasant song quite becoming of its time. With Robin taking the lead vocal – double-tracked in places – it broadens The Bee Gees' canvas and we begin to see new possibilities with their already unique sound.

Whereas many songs from this era don't fade out, this one does; and strangely and prematurely so, with Robin still in full flow with at least the final line of the second verse to conclude.

'Big Chance' (Barry Gibb)
Recorded at St. Clair Studio, Hurstville: circa April/May 1966

'Big Chance' appeared as the B-side to The Bee Gees' final Australian-era single 'Born A Man', issued in February 1967. This is one of the early examples of Barry and Robin equitably sharing lead vocals on a song: in this instance, Robin on the first verse and Barry on the second.

'Spicks And Specks' (Barry Gibb)
See the entry for the single.

'Jingle Jangle' (Barry Gibb)
Recorded at St. Clair Studio, Hurstville: circa April/May 1966

Whilst Robin takes the lead vocal for this hauntingly beautiful song, it's the harmonies that make this slow melodic number so special. This is apparently the song that caught the ear of Robert Stigwood some months later in London when he heard the discs that Hugh Gibb had submitted to NEMS on their behalf.

The Gibbs themselves must have regarded it highly, as it was one of only four songs from their pre-*Bee Gees' 1st* period to be performed internationally in their future stage shows. 'Jingle Jangle' was included in their 1971 tour setlist as part of a medley with 'Morning Of My Life (In The Morning)'.

'Tint Of Blue' (Barry Gibb, Robin Gibb)
Recorded at St. Clair Studio, Hurstville: circa April/May 1966

As well as splitting the lead vocals on 'Tint Of Blue' – a Beatlesque song that draws some melodic and rhythmic parallels to 'Help!' – Barry and Robin also share writing credits for the first time: a compositional partnership that would eventually turn out some of the group's most iconic tracks.

'Where Are You' (Maurice Gibb)

Recorded at St. Clair Studio, Hurstville: circa April/May 1966

A huge milestone for Maurice, 'Where Are You' is his first Bee-Gees-recorded composition, and his debut lead vocal. Aged just sixteen when he wrote this, it's quite an accomplished song, with lots of overlapping vocal lines that show the early development of his arranging skills.

'Where Are You' drew Nat Kipner's attention to Maurice's potential as a more-than-competent songwriter, although, by his own admission, Maurice felt more comfortable writing the music than the words. Kipner spent much of the 1966 Australian winter collaborating with him. Nine of their songs were given to other artists for release on his Downunder record label: 'Hey' and 'Young Man's Fancy' for Bip Addison; 'Messin' 'Round' for Sandy Summers; 'Talk To Me' for Anne Shelton; 'Don't You Go, I Need Your Love' for The Mystics; 'He's A Thief' for April Byron; 'As Fast As I Can' and 'Raining Teardrops' for Barrington Davis, and 'So Long Boy' for Jenene Watson.

'Born A Man' (Barry Gibb)

Recorded at St. Clair Studio, Hurstville: circa April/May 1966

The Bee Gees' final Australian-only single – 'Born A Man' – was released as the follow-up to 'Spicks And Specks' in February 1967 when the brothers had arrived back in England in search of their international break. It's not known whether they approved, or even knew of its release at the time.

It's another good example of the trio attempting different styles, although not very successfully in this instance, but all credit to them for attempting what is almost a blues style. The frantic breakdown in the middle features Robin's forced tenor vocal, which was to appear a number of times later in their career on stronger songs such as 'I Can't See Nobody'. The song's ending is interesting but not particularly good, concluding with a chaotic call-and-answer vocal with Barry and Robin rapidly shouting ad-libs at one another. It's an interesting experiment, but the result is messy.

'Glass House' (Barry Gibb, Robin Gibb)

Recorded at St. Clair Studio, Hurstville: circa April/May 1966

The album's final song is another joint writing effort from Barry and

Robin. It features a fine lead vocal from Robin on the verses, and tight harmonies from all three brothers on the slower choruses.

As the Gibb family's return journey to the UK loomed closer, Hugh, by all accounts, had second thoughts about leaving, and attempted to convince his three eldest sons that a good living could be made in Australia's club scene, particularly with a hit single behind them. On the subject of convincing their parents to go back to England, Barry recalled in 2012:

> I think they got a sniff of it; I think they saw that we were watching The Easybeats and The Seekers both go back to England and having great success. The Beatles were an influence, yes, yes, but The Hollies more – we loved The Hollies; and The Fortunes – they were probably the best vocal group I ever heard, they did that song 'You've Got Your Troubles' and things like that. Anyway, it was The Hollies, The Fortunes and The Beatles that convinced us we could do it, we could do the harmonies, and we could go back there and we could take a shot. Sort of what we did, and typical of the whole journey, we were told along the way we couldn't make it: 'Don't worry about it boys, you just need to get a job, don't worry about it', and we wanted to be discovered – we didn't know what it meant, but we wanted to be discovered.

With previous Australian pop artists and groups travelling to the UK amid blazing media publicity predicting great success, only to return unsuccessful some months later, The Bee Gees and their management team opted to remain relatively quiet about their departure, commenting only that they were returning to their homeland.

Nat Kipner had relinquished his management contract with The Bee Gees without cost, to his later regret: 'When their records came out, I thought. 'I'm going to shoot myself, I let them go'. You know I gave them their contract back. The rest is history'.

The Bee Gees had much to celebrate as the year came to an end. They had finally achieved a genuine hit single with 'Spicks And Specks' – a song that *Go-Set* magazine awarded 'The Best Australian Record of 1966' a month or so later. As songwriters, they were more sought-after than ever, as the next few months would show; and after chasing the affections of a fickle audience for more than four years, they were now one of Australia's most popular groups.

However, for the enterprising Gibb brothers, it was a case of too little, too late. Success or no success, they'd made their decision to try their luck back in London. Singer Johnny Young was one contemporary who was very supportive of the move: 'The Bee Gees had a great education here in Australia, but they also had a rough time because they were seen as a novelty act. Little Robin with his buck teeth, and Maurice with his smiley little face, and Barry with his Elvis haircut. They had beautiful harmonies and they wrote fantastic songs, but no one would take them seriously'.

The success of 'Spicks And Specks' was confirmation that the return trip home was the right path. Barry affirmed 'We proved something to ourselves, that given the time and inspiration from other people, we were able to do a lot of things, but we had to get to England because it was the doorway to international success. Australia could not give us that'. Of the three brothers, it's possibly Robin who felt less positive about his time in Australia: 'We never had many highlights considering how The Bee Gees were treated at that time. If we would have had any highlights in our professional career, we may have even stayed. But the way we were treated, the only remedy for The Bee Gees was to leave Australia'.

The group eventually looked back on their time in Australia with more objectivity. Reminiscing in 2014, Barry told *Rolling Stone* magazine: 'It was 48 years (ago), so there were times since we had the times of our lives, but it was never as sweet and innocent as it was in 1966'.

Steve & The Board – another very popular Australian band that were beneficiaries of The Bee Gees' songs – was formed by Nat Kipner's son Steve, and included drummer and future Bee Gee Colin Petersen. They recorded a version of 'Little Miss Rhythm And Blues' on their only album *Steve & The Board ... and the Giggle Eyed Goo* in November 1966. The song also appeared on the equally bizarrely-titled EP *I Call My Woman 'Hinges' ... 'cause She's Something To Adore*. Their take on 'Little Miss Rhythm And Blues' was slower than Trevor Gordon's version, giving it – appropriately – a more R&B feel. By coincidence, when Petersen left Steve & The Board to travel to the UK and (eventually) join The Bee Gees, he was replaced by Geoff Bridgford, who would also become a future drummer for the Gibbs, in 1971-1972.

The Twilights, from Adelaide, were a six-piece who were fast becoming one of the best pop outfits in Australia. Watching the band with their two great lead singers record at the Hurstville studio, Barry offered to write a song for them. The resulting track 'Long Life' appeared on the band's eponymous debut album released in late 1966, produced by the aforementioned David Mackay. One of the band's front men – Glenn Shorrock – would later form The Little River Band, where he found international success in the late-1970s and early-1980s. As a songwriter, he also penned the American top ten hit 'Cool Change', and Australian chart-topper 'Help Is On Its Way'.

The sibling harmonies of Barry, Robin, and Maurice were also heard on the December release of 'Why Do I Cry' by Vyt – a song that was a hit for The Remains a few years earlier. Vyt is a shortened version of the Lithuanian singer's full name – reputed to be so long that they didn't have room to fit it on the record label itself – Vytautas Zvirzdinas. His backing group The World normally accompanied him, but except for guitarist Chris Egglestone, the instrumentation is from Steve & The Board. Australian singer Marty Rhone and The Bee Gees also supplied backing vocals and handclaps. CBS released the song as the B-side to 'I Haven't Got You', which has no Gibb involvement.

There's been much speculation about how the brothers came to sing on this particular occasion. Of all the records they contributed to in their Australian years, CBS is the only label that was not connected in some way to Festival Records. Although their contract presumably did not allow any of the Gibbs to involve themselves in unsanctioned collaborations with other label's artists, the fact this recording took place at Hurstville studios where they were ensconced at the time, was probably too much of a temptation for them. Maybe they thought they could sufficiently disguise their voices to escape detection, but the slightly out-of-time handclapping is unmistakably theirs.

In November, Python Lee Jackson – another newly-signed CBS group – also came to St. Clair to record with Nat Kipner in the producer's chair. On this occasion, Maurice acted as the engineer – normally Ossie Byrne's job. The session produced their first single which was released in December – a catchy version of Curtis Mayfield's 'Um-Um-Um-Um', with 'Big City Lights' by Memphis songwriting team Stan Kesler and Stacey Davidson, on the B-side.

In 2010, Python Lee Jackson's lead singer Malcolm McGee recalled The Bee Gees as one of the few artists who approached music as a career, not just as a fun thing to do: 'While other bands were smoking pot, they were combing Brylcreem through their hair'. McGee had some misgivings as to how The Bee Gees were promoted in Australia: 'They were not a rock/pop act. They were an RSL/cabaret act and were completely behind the times

– completely dated in the type of music they were recording. They had to get out of Australia to achieve, because so many leeches had them boxed in Sydney and completely restricted their progress. They were fantastic – The Bee Gees leave The Beatles for dead in every aspect!'.

Another December release was from Spin labelmate Marty Rhone (real name Karel Lawrence van Rhoon), also recorded at St. Clair. The Gibb brothers provided harmonies on his fourth single 'She Is Mine'/'Village Tapestry'. Although it was not a hit, the B-side – which Rhone wrote – is highly regarded among 1960s enthusiasts. In Iain McIntyre's book, *Tomorrow Is Today: Australia in the Psychedelic Era, 1966-1970*, the track was listed as one of the 'Top 7 Proto-Psychedelic Australian Tracks from 1966'.

The final Gibb-related release of 1966 was 'Coalman'/'All The King's Horses' by 20-year-old singer Ronnie Burns. It was his third single and his biggest hit up to that point, making a very respectable top ten position in all Australian states. Both sides of the single were written by all three Gibb brothers, and it was the first hit they'd written collectively for another artist. For both songs, Ronnie essentially sang over Bee Gees demos featuring Bee Gees vocals, Barry's guitar, Maurice's piano and bass and Colin Petersen on drums. The brothers were assigned to write a whole album of material for Burns' forthcoming debut, and the late-December single release followed the work the Gibbs had completed with him in Sydney.

'All The King's Horses' was also later recorded by the British group The Peppermint Circus, released as a single A-side on the Olga label in the UK on 19 April 1968.

Inception/Nostalgia was a double album set released in 1970 on Polydor, the label to which The Bee Gees would be signed upon returning to England in 1967. It's prudent to mention here, as it collects the product of The Bee Gees' 1966 sessions at Ossie Byrne's St. Clair Studio that weren't properly released on other singles or LPs shortly after they were recorded. A mixed collection of 24 self-penned compositions and cover versions, it's presumably the follow-up to the *Rare, Precious and Beautiful* album series released in 1968/1969, and the first set on Polydor's budget labels: Karussell in Germany and Triumph in France. It was only available for a short time in these territories but received a further release on Polydor in Japan, as *Inception and Nostalgia*, in July 1972 following their successful first tour there in March. Many similar compilations appeared in later years, with varying selections of songs from the original release scattered amongst them.

Inception/Nostalgia (1970)

Personnel:
Barry Gibb: vocal, guitar
Robin Gibb: vocal
Maurice Gibb: vocal, guitar, bass guitar, piano
Recording dates: 1966 at St. Clair Studio, Hurstville
Release date: Germany: 1970, France: 1970, Japan: 1972

How and why exactly this compilation was conceived is unknown. Indeed, the Gibb brothers themselves were unaware of its existence until Maurice, Ringo Starr and their wives went on a skiing holiday to Switzerland, and Ringo chanced upon the album in a shop. Pointing it out to Maurice, Ringo commented that he'd never seen that one before. Up until that moment, neither had Maurice.

The included material was presumed to be covered under a licensing agreement between Polydor and Festival Records in Australia, but questions arise as to why Polydor in England didn't release it, or for that matter, Festival themselves, despite cutting actetates of the set which showed some intent to do so.

The new songs – written either individually or collectively by the brothers – were all composed and recorded during or shortly after the recording of the *Spicks And Specks* album at St. Clair. Those twelve songs could have made up the contents of a future Bee Gees album. An acetate produced at Advision Studios in London exists with the following track listing:

Side 1: 'All the King's Horses', 'Top Hat', 'Coalman', 'I'll Know What To Do', 'In The Morning', 'All By Myself'
Side 2: 'Exit Stage Right', 'Butterfly', 'House Of Lords', 'Terrible Way To Treat Your Baby', 'Lum De Loo', 'Like Nobody Else'

All of these tracks – except for 'All The King's Horses' and 'House Of Lords', which remain unreleased – appear on *Inception/Nostalgia*. The version of 'House Of Lords' that appears on the 2006 *The Studio Albums 1967-1968* box set, was a quite different later recording.

These tracks were ultimately used as demos for other artists, including Ronnie Burns, who promptly used eight of the songs for his 1967 debut album *Ronnie*, including 'All The King's Horses'. In fact, Burns used the original Bee Gees backing tracks for all of the songs he included on the album, except for 'In The Morning', which was completely re-recorded with a Melbourne band called The Strangers.

The album's cover versions remain the greatest puzzle. Some of the more contemporary songs – including the Beatles and Lovin' Spoonful tracks – would have most likely been recordings that The Bee Gees might lip-sync to on TV shows. Two other songs from this batch are known to exist – The Walker Brothers' 'Another Tear Falls', and the Beatles song 'If I Needed Someone', but these remain unreleased.

The most peculiar songs were seven renditions of pop hits with an orchestra: six by Barry and one by Robin. Again, they seem to be tracks which The Bee Gees would mime to on the small screen, but it appears other artists also used them. This theory seems sound when listening to the backing track for 'I Love You Because' and discovering that it is identical to the one used for Johnny O'Keefe's performance of the song on the 5 April 1963 edition of his television show *Sing, Sing, Sing*.

Another theory is that they could have been used as audition tapes to choose The Bee Gees' fifth single during their tenure with Festival, for which they were made to eschew Barry's compositions in favour of covering another popular song of the period in the hope of finally scoring a hit. This would eventually yield the selection 'Turn Around, Look At Me'. The orchestral and choral backing on that song and 'You're Nobody 'Til Somebody Loves You', is remarkably similar. Of course, these theories and assumptions may be over-thinking the purpose of these recordings, and perhaps they just added their vocals for fun with no intention of releasing them.

Inception/Nostalgia attained legendary status among collectors as one of the rarest Bee Gees albums and was highly desirable because the songs could be found on no other releases at the time. Within a few years, used copies were changing hands for several hundred pounds. It's generally accepted that the French edition is the rarest, followed by the German issue. The Japanese release is more common and, unusually, is less expensive than the others – although, in its heyday, it was still making well into three figures.

The German edition features an uncredited painting of a brightly-coloured fantasy bird on both the front and back covers, the only difference being that the front cover was adorned with the title *Inception*, and the back, *Nostalgia*. The French edition is exactly the same but with bolder record company identifiers. The 1972 Japanese edition front cover uses a group photograph from the *2 Years On* photo session, while the inner gatefold has song lyrics, and photographs from the group's recently completed Japanese tour.

'In The Morning' (Barry Gibb)

Recorded at St. Clair Studio, Hurstville: circa June/July 1966

Barry recalls, 'This song was written at Wagga Wagga Police Boys Club circa 1966. We used to play all over Australia in those days. The main entertainment circuit was the RSLs, or returned soldiers clubs. Working those places gave us priceless experience and many humorous insights on life itself'.

Most certainly one of the best songs written by Barry during his time in Australia, it shows how his songwriting skills had matured, although he was still only 19 when it was composed.

This is the first of two versions of the song by The Bee Gees, the second being the 1971 re-recording for the soundtrack of the movie *Melody*, which had a full orchestral backing. This original version here is much faster and has minimal accompaniment of acoustic guitars and low-key drums.

It's unfair to compare the two versions in this way. What's important is the quality of the song, and testament to this is the fact it has been covered well over 100 times, making it the most-covered Gibb composition of the Australian era. Most notable is a version by Esther & Abi Ofarim, which was a number 2 hit in Germany in late 1967. Other artists to cover the song include Mary Hopkin – who did versions in both English and Welsh – Paper Lace, Lulu, Nina Simone, and John Holt with his feelgood 1973 reggae version.

English folk-rock singer David Gray included a live take of the song on his 2007 album *A Thousand Miles Behind*. He's performed it regularly in his live shows over the years, sometimes sharing vocal duties with guest artists like Ray LaMontagne and KT Tunstall.

Barry recorded a superb solo version for his 2019 album *Greenfields*. It only appeared on special editions of the album, which is a great pity, as it deserved a wider audience.

'Like Nobody Else' (Barry Gibb, Robin Gibb, Maurice Gibb)

Recorded at St. Clair Studio, Hurstville: circa June/July 1966

Written by all three brothers, 'Like Nobody Else' is a screamer of an R&B track with Barry and Robin alternating on lead vocals. The R&B

influence heard here would become more and more prevalent in their later work.

As with many of the album's songs, The Bee Gees' own version was not released until after being covered by other artists. Australian singer Ronnie Burns placed it on the B-side of his hit single 'Exit Stage Right', while Los Bravos released it as an A-side in both English and their native Spanish. The mysterious Lord Sitar – long rumoured to be George Harrison – released it on his eponymous 1968 album. Lord Sitar was, in fact, James George Tomkins: a British session musician known professionally as Big Jim Sullivan.

'Daydream' (John B. Sebastian)
Recorded at St. Clair Studio, Hurstville: circa June/July 1966

The original hit for The Lovin' Spoonful in early 1966, performed well on the charts globally, peaking at number 2 in both the UK and US, and more importantly, at 13 in Australia, where it would have been heard by The Bee Gees.

This version has a laid-back groove, and Barry's vocal fits it quite well. It seems likely that the whistling heard here is part of the backing track and not Barry.

'Lonely Winter' (Carl Keats)
Recorded at St. Clair Studio, Hurstville: circa June/July 1966

'Lonely Winter' was written by Carl Keats, bass player of Steve & The Board – a group that had numerous associations with The Bee Gees over the years. The two groups struck up a deal where they each recorded one of the other's songs. The Bee Gees took on 'Lonely Winter', while The Board re-worked Barry's composition 'Little Miss Rhythm And Blues'.

Maurice puts in a plaintive lead vocal performance, and the production lends the song just the right desolate atmosphere.

Keats, under his real name Carl Groszman, later went on to write songs such as 'A Dose Of Rock And Roll' for Ringo Starr, 'Being On The Losing End' for Olivia Newton-John and Status Quo's big hit 'Down The Dustpipe'.

'You're The Reason I'm Living' (Bobby Darin)
Recording location and date could be Festival Studios, Sydney in 1963/1964, or St. Clair Studio, Hurstville 1966

This track is incorrectly identified on *Inception/Nostalgia* and all subsequent appearances of it, as 'You're The Reason' composed by the songwriting team Bobby Edwards, Mildred Imes, Fred Henley and Terry Fell – originally recorded in 1961 by co-writer Bobby Edwards. It was later released by American singer Johnny Burnette on his 1962 LP *Hits and Other Favorites*.

The song The Bee Gees *actually* recorded – and veritably what is heard when one spins the *Inception/Nostalgia* wax – is 'You're The Reason I'm Living', which was written and recorded by Bobby Darin in 1962 and covered numerous times by a number of high-profile artists including Brenda Lee, Esther Phillips, Don Cherry, Brook Benton and Elvis Presley.

Barry gets a chance to really exercise his vocals on this big production number with orchestra and backing singers – although they were pre-recorded – lifting the song to heights previously unimagined with the primitive studios the Bee Gees were used to up to this point.

'Coalman' (Barry Gibb)
Recorded at St. Clair Studio, Hurstville: circa June/July 1966
Side one closes with 'Coalman' – a Barry Gibb song that was a number 6 hit for Ronnie Burns in Australia in 1967. Ronnie's version actually consisted of the original Bee Gees master tape backing track, and Burns merely recorded his vocal over this.

The recording on *Inception/Nostalgia* is the same master tape with Barry's vocal left on. Both versions feature a tape played in reverse as a prologue to the song, adding an experimental and very-1960s feel.

'Butterfly' (Barry Gibb, Robin Gibb, Maurice Gibb)
Recorded at St. Clair Studio, Hurstville: circa June/July 1966
Side two opens with the group composition 'Butterfly'. Whilst there is a fine Barry Gibb solo lead here, there's also some tight unison singing which sounds like one voice but also sounds like each of the brothers at different points.

The British group Unit 4 + 2 – best known for their hit 'Concrete And Clay' – covered the song in June 1967, remaining faithful to The Bee Gees version. The Scottish band Marmalade failed to score a hit with their take in November 1969, despite orchestral embellishment and their superb harmony singing. But they *did* have a significant run of hits between 1969 and 1972, including 'Ob-La-Di, Ob-La-Da', 'Reflections Of My Life', 'Cousin Norman', and 'Radancer'.

Barry obviously has a soft spot for the song, resurrecting it for a collaboration with American artists Gillian Welch and David Rawlings for his 2021 duets album *Greenfields*. The album title came from the song's opening line. This new iteration also played during the closing credits of the Emmy-nominated Frank Marshall documentary *The Bee Gees: How Can You Mend A Broken Heart*, which premiered in December 2020.

'Storm' (Barry Gibb, Robin Gibb, Maurice Gibb)
Recorded at St. Clair Studio, Hurstville: circa June/July 1966
'Storm' was another group composition with Robin on lead vocal, and his voice suits the song perfectly.

British vocal group Family Dogg covered 'The Storm', as it was called on their 1967 MGM Records single. It's a truly spectacular version with superb vocal arrangements and harmonies.

'Lum-De-Loo' (Robin Gibb)
Recorded at St. Clair Studio, Hurstville: circa June/July 1966
Robin must have had his tongue firmly in cheek when he recorded 'Lum-De-Loo'. It's a nonsense song, with him experimenting and having fun with a track that was probably not supposed to be released.

'You're Nobody 'Til Somebody Loves You' (Russ Morgan, Larry Stock, James Cavanaugh)
Recording location and date could be Festival Studios, Sydney in 1963/1964, or St. Clair Studio, Hurstville 1966
Written in 1944, this was first recorded by co-writer Russ Morgan, and was a hit for him in 1946, reaching number 14 on the American charts. It has since been covered by numerous artists, but the best-known version is by Dean Martin, who spent nine weeks on the *Billboard* Hot 100, peaking at number 25; while reaching number 1 on *Billboard*'s Middle-Road Singles (sic) chart.

Barry delivers a killer vocal on this track, really putting his heart into it. He seems to really be enjoying the opportunity to sing with the support of an orchestra: a luxury they'd never been afforded up to this point. Within less than a year, those complex symphonic arrangements would be fixtures of The Bee Gees' recordings.

'You Won't See Me' (John Lennon, Paul McCartney)
Recorded at St. Clair Studio, Hurstville: circa June/July 1966

Side two's penultimate song is a workmanlike, if somewhat raw, version of The Beatles' 'You Won't See Me': originally recorded for their 1965 LP *Rubber Soul*. It was an unusual choice of song to cover, only to be left as an album track and not released as a single.

'The End' (Sid Jacobson, Jimmy Krondes)
Recording location and date could be Festival Studios, Sydney in 1963/1964, or St. Clair Studio, Hurstville 1966

The model for 'The End' was the original version recorded by Earl Grant, who scored a number 7 hit with it on the *Billboard* Hot 100 in September 1958. More importantly, it topped the charts in Australia, so the song would probably have been well known to the brothers.

This is another one where the origin of the backing track is unknown. It was probably used by somebody back in the day for a television appearance or live cabaret performance, and the track was left lying around on a studio shelf, leaving Barry to discover it and have some fun with it.

'I'll Know What To Do' (Barry Gibb, Robin Gibb, Maurice Gibb)
Recorded at St. Clair Studio, Hurstville: circa June/July 1966

On the second disc, we start again with some Gibb brothers originals. 'I'll Know What To Do' has an intriguing screamed opening from Barry, with a real R&B flavour. Once again, Barry and Robin's alternating lead vocals add to the song's edge. This was another of the songs Ronnie Burns recorded for his 1967 album *Ronnie*.

'All By Myself' (Maurice Gibb)
Recorded at St. Clair Studio, Hurstville: circa June/July 1966

One of Maurice's earliest solo compositions, he also takes the lead vocal, and does it well. 'All By Myself' has great rhythmic bounce that's quite infectious. Melbourne band The Brigade also covered this song as the B-side of their 1968 single 'Joan'.

'Ticket To Ride' (John Lennon, Paul McCartney)
Recorded at St. Clair Studio, Hurstville: circa June/July 1966

The Beatles single 'Ticket To Ride' was released in April 1965 and became their seventh consecutive number 1 hit in the United Kingdom, and their third consecutive number 1 in the United States. It similarly topped national charts in Canada, Australia and Ireland.

The brothers' version includes the classic opening guitar riff, although it lacks some of the clarity of the George Harrison original. The vocals, however, are good, and it's a worthy inclusion in this set.

'I Love You Because' (Leon Payne)
Recording location and date could be Festival Studios, Sydney in 1963/1964, or St. Clair Studio, Hurstville 1966

'I Love You Because' was written and recorded by country singer and songwriter Leon Payne in 1949. The song has been covered by several artists throughout the years, including hit versions by Al Martino and Jim Reeves. Martino's version was the most successful, peaking at number 3 on the *Billboard* Hot 100 in 1963, while Reeves' version stalled at number 54.

But the luscious, almost choral vocal support (which wouldn't have sounded out of place on Mitch Miller's classic television series *Sing Along with Mitch*) doesn't save Barry's cover. Sadly, it's rather dull.

'Paperback Writer' (John Lennon, Paul McCartney)
Recorded at St. Clair Studio, Hurstville: circa June/July 1966

This Beatles single was released in May 1966 and topped the charts in the UK, United States and Australia. A regular visitor to Ossie Byrne's studio at the time – guitarist Dennis Wilson – recalls hearing The Bee Gees' version only two days after The Beatles' single had come out.

'Somewhere' (Leonard Bernstein, Stephen Sondheim)
Recording location and date could be Festival Studios, Sydney in 1963/1964, or St. Clair Studio, Hurstville 1966

'Somewhere' is the classic song from the 1957 Broadway musical *West Side Story* that was made into a blockbuster film in 1961. The music was composed by Leonard Bernstein with lyrics by Stephen Sondheim.

American singer-songwriter P. J. Proby released his version of 'Somewhere' in 1964, reaching number 6 on the UK singles chart, and 7 in Australia. Proby's version is the model for the Bee Gees recording, where Robin takes the lead vocal and sings in a much deeper register than had ever been heard from him previously. It's an interesting interpretation, but whether it works is a matter of opinion.

Incidentally, P. J. Proby toured Australia in 1966 with Wayne Fontana, Eden Kane and Dinah Lee, performing a number of shows as part of the package. Local artists were also added to the bill for every show, and

Marty Rhone and His Soul Agents and The Bee Gees were chosen for the Sydney Stadium show on 29 September.

'The Twelfth Of Never' (Jerry Livingstone, Paul Webster)
Recording location and date could be Festival Studios, Sydney in 1963/1964, or St. Clair Studio, Hurstville 1966

'The Twelfth Of Never' was written in 1956 and was first recorded by Johnny Mathis. The title – a popular expression used as the date of a future occurrence that will never come to pass – here has the protagonist declaring their undying love to the object of their affection.

Mathis' original version reached number 9 in the United States in 1957, while a version by British singer Cliff Richard was released in 1964, reaching 8 in the UK.

Barry covers the song as the opening track on the final side of the LP set. It's a reasonable enough effort that doesn't differ that much from the original.

'Forever' (Barry Gibb, Robin Gibb, Maurice Gibb)
Recorded at St. Clair Studio, Hurstville: circa June/July 1966

This Barry, Robin, and Maurice composition is quite a standout and is the only Gibb original in this set featuring the benefit of orchestra and horns, so the recording must have some separate history. They might have recorded it for a television show that had a house orchestra. Otherwise, it's hard to explain who paid for it, given their modest means at the time.

British pop star Dave Berry picked up the song and released it as a single in August 1967.

'Top Hat' (Barry Gibb)
Recorded at St. Clair Studio, Hurstville: circa June/July 1966

Robin and Barry share lead vocals on 'Top Hat' – a generally unremarkable track apart from some amusing chit-chat from the brothers in the middle. It's another Gibb-penned song covered by Ronnie Burns and released not only on his 1967 *Ronnie* album, but also as a single.

'Hallelujah, I Love Her So' (Ray Charles)
Recording location and date could be Festival Studios, Sydney in 1963/1964, or St. Clair Studio, Hurstville 1966

This rhythm and blues song was written and released by Ray Charles in 1956. The song peaked at number 5 on the *Billboard* R&B chart.

Barry does a fine job on lead vocals on this one, and gets to emulate one of his heroes.

'Terrible Way To Treat Your Baby' (Barry Gibb, Robin Gibb, Maurice Gibb)
Recorded at St. Clair Studio, Hurstville: circa June/July 1966
A very strong composition from all three brothers. It's a dramatic song with bold production reminiscent of The Walker Brothers. Both Barry and Robin sing in deeper registers than they usually would.

This was also a big hit for Australian band The Vibrants in 1967.

'Exit Stage Right' (Barry Gibb, Robin Gibb, Maurice Gibb)
Recorded at St. Clair Studio, Hurstville: circa June/July 1966
The album's final song is the excellent 'Exit Stage Right', with Barry taking the lead vocal.

Similar to 'Coalman', the lead vocal was taken off the original demo and replaced with Ronnie Burns' lead, with the Gibb harmonies still very evident on his cover version, which was a top twenty hit in Australia in 1967.

1967

On Tuesday morning, 3 January 1967, the Gibb family – now including Barry's wife Maureen – boarded the *Fairsky* using the upper level of No. 21 Wharf, Pyrmont. Eldest sibling Lesley didn't join them. Recently married to musician Keith Evans, she elected to stay in Australia and raise her family there, which she would do very successfully. Also joining the Gibb family was their producer and now friend Ossie Byrne, who, like The Bee Gees, was about to try for fame and fortune in the UK. To fund his trip, Byrne had sold his studio to a religious organisation, and all demos and tapes were given to Festival Records. The *Fairsky* – by coincidence the sister ship to the *Fairsea* on which the Gibb family had travelled to Australia some eight years previously – departed Sydney harbour at 6 p.m. After stopping at Brisbane and Thursday Island, the ship commenced a circuitous route that visited Singapore, Ceylon (now Sri Lanka), Yemen and Italy.

During *Fairsky's* stopover in Sri Lanka, Maurice bought a sitar, apparently inspired by George Harrison, who had introduced the sitar to rock music on The Beatles' 1965 album *Rubber Soul*. Maurice recalled locals yelling 'George, Beatles!' as he carried the bulky musical instrument back to the ship: 'That day on the boat, we sat on a few cushions and we practised like mad. The sitar was the first thing I sold when we got back to England'.

As big brother Barry recalls, the sitar wasn't the only item purchased: 'We stopped off in the Middle East, the pyramids, and the things we discovered in back street bazaars! You could buy bottles of Dexedrine, every kind of stimulant, no questions asked. We were on a ship, but we flew all the way'.

Unlike the voyage out to Australia – during which the pre-teen brothers would spontaneously huddle on the ship's decks at night to sing for passers-by – the return trip found them performing regularly as part of the ship's formal entertainment program after Hugh had heard The Seekers had worked their way to England the same way. It was a lot cheaper than the fare.

The Bee Gees, with Hugh on drums, performed their first set in the ship's Grand Social Hall. With the vessel full of young Australians also travelling to the UK, they were a big hit. Their set included a Peter, Paul and Mary tribute, 'You Can't Do That' and 'Norwegian Wood' (The Beatles), 'Unchained Melody' (The Righteous Brothers), 'Women (Make You Feel Alright)' (The Easybeats), and their own song 'Spicks And Specks'. By some recollections, their set also included a magic act where Barry's wife Maureen obliged by becoming 'the disappearing woman'.

During the journey, while still in Australian waters, news reached the Gibbs that *Go-Set* magazine had awarded 'Spicks And Specks' its Best Record of the Year award. Barry recalls: 'We found out on the boat and we just couldn't believe it. We hadn't been able to get a solid hit record in that country since the moment we arrived, which was '58 in Queensland'.

Hugh wrote to *Go-Set* on behalf of the group to acknowledge the award, and it appeared on the magazine's *Postbox* page of the 25 January edition, with the headline 'Bee Gees Write From the High Seas':

C/v 'Fairsky'
From Hughie Gibb, manager
For The Bee Gees just
Approaching Thursday Island

Dear Go Set,

On behalf of The Bee Gees, I would like to thank you and your paper most sincerely for making their record 'Spicks And Specks' your choice as 'Best Record of the Year'. We are only sorry that we did not have time left to visit Melbourne again. I know that a lot of young fans think that the boys are heading for England on the strength of their current success, but I know you will appreciate the fact that our sailing arrangements were made as far back as August last year: some weeks before 'Spicks And Specks' was released. We purposely kept things quiet because there has been so much rubbish written about people going here and there and nobody moving. Therefore, we only vaguely hinted that we would be going in the new year.
Things are definitely progressing for the boys. We are expecting cables or mail at any of the ports we visit, so until we get the official news, we are keeping pretty quiet, but will contact you when things break. Once again, many thanks, and we wish you continued success with your paper.

Please give our fondest regards to all the gang at Go-Set.

Yours sincerely,
Hughie Gibb

During the brief stopover at Thursday Island, the brothers took the opportunity to send postcards to some Sydney DJs, as they believed many of them didn't realise the group had left the country. The message was allegedly brief: 'We're on our way to England'. Unlike many artists from Australia who had journeyed to the UK amidst great publicity and expectation of immediate success, only to fail, The Bee Gees had been determined to be quite circumspect about their imminent departure. Robin explained: 'Had we failed, we would have come back to Australia, but we went over there to find out whether we could make it or not, and we didn't broadcast it at all to anybody'.

Unbeknownst to the Gibb brothers, some of their songs and recordings made in their last few months at Ossie Byrne's studio were making an impact back in Australia. Ronnie Burns' cover of 'Coalman' released the previous year had finally broken into the charts. Eventually, it would reach number 6 on the national chart and spend twelve weeks in the top 40. It was his biggest hit to date.

Meanwhile, nine-year-old singer Lori Balmer released two Barry Gibb songs as her third single. The first was 'Who's Been Writing On The Wall Again' – a song that had been recorded by another child singer – Jenny Bradley – just a few months previously. The new song 'In Your World' was the B-side.

Born in Victoria to showbiz parents, Lori was working professionally by the age of six, and later explained that 'When I was living in Sydney, I was picked up by RCA at seven and was their youngest recording star'. She remembers that 'The house producer of RCA was Ron Wills, but Barry really produced under Ron's eye. We did the vocals, with the Gibbs providing the background vocals on one tape'.

Mike Furber recorded two Gibb songs – 'Where Are You' and 'Second Hand People' – for a single released on 9 January. The Bee Gees had already released both songs on their *Spicks And Specks* album. The A-side 'Where Are You' is a Maurice Gibb composition and is significant as being his first cover, despite it being erroneously credited to Barry on the record's label. Produced at Hurstville studios, both tracks feature The Bee Gees on backing vocals. The single is credited to Mike Furber as a solo artist, having parted ways with his group The Bowery Boys, though they are credited on the cover of a later-released EP containing both songs. It's understood that the New Zealand band Max Merritt & The Meteors provided the accompaniment.

Although The Bee Gees had recently won the 1966 National Radio 2UE Award for Best Group, their final single recorded in Australia – 'Born A Man'/'Big Chance' – barely attracted any attention in the press, and Australian radio ignored it when it was released in early February.

The A-side, in particular, sounds so rough and unfinished that it could well be a demo. Although bearing the influence of Stax artists like Otis Redding and Sam & Dave, it was not one of Barry's better songs, and was a bad choice as a follow-up to the engaging 'Spicks And Specks'. *The Sun-Herald* commented on the song in its review of the *Spicks And Specks* LP: "Born A Man' is a send-up of the Ray Charles type of performance – at least I presume it's a send-up – I don't think the grotesque features of this performance could be serious'. The B-side 'Big Chance' was a better song, but at only 1:40 in duration, it was perhaps too short to be considered for radio by 1967.

Jon Blanchfield's excellent recordings of 'Upstairs Downstairs'/'Town Of Tuxley Toymaker Part 1' were recorded in the final quarter of 1966 in Hurstville, and released as a single in February 1967 after The Bee Gees had returned to the UK. Like Ronnie Burns' 'Coalman' and a few other Gibb compositions, it seemed to infiltrate the Australian radio airwaves for some time, giving the impression that The Bee Gees, despite their physical absence, were omnipresent. The fast 'Upstairs Downstairs' is one of best Gibb covers from their Australian era. It's pure pop with a relentless driving beat throughout. A minor hit in Blanchfield's home state of Queensland, it deserved a better chart result. Apparently inspired by the melody of 'Matchmaker' from the 1964 musical *Fiddler on the Roof*, 'Town Of Tuxley Toymaker Part 1' is a very strong song in its own right. Both songs were written by all three brothers, and show their fast development as a songwriting team. In particular, Robin's propensity for unusual lyrics was having a positive influence.

After nearly five weeks of sea travel, the *Fairsky* arrived at Southampton docks on the evening of Monday 6 February. Disembarking on the following Tuesday morning, they were met by future Bee Gees drummer Colin Petersen with a hired van, and he drove them to what Maurice would describe as 'a crummy hotel in Hampstead'. Fortunately, Petersen – who had arrived in London some months prior – had been searching for more suitable accommodation. 'I had a letter from Hugh Gibb', Colin explained, 'and sorted out somewhere for them to stay, and they stored their equipment in my flat'. Accordingly, the family soon moved into a semi-detached house, as Hugh Gibb recalled: 'We arrived on a Tuesday, and by Friday we'd moved into a furnished house in Hendon'. Maurice even recalled his travel via the underground to Colin's flat while carrying his newly purchased sitar and receiving strange looks from bemused fellow passengers.

On arriving back in the UK, even before the family had fully unpacked, Hugh and Barry wasted no time in pursuing work, stopping first at the offices of staff agent Eddie Jarrett of the Grade Organisation, who was managing The Seekers at the time. As Hugh recalled, 'He painted a very black picture about the possibility of touring, but offered to put us into clubs to keep the boys working'.

Dejected, Barry and Hugh returned to the family's lodgings, where Barbara passed on the message that a 'Mr. Stickweed' had been ringing all day. 'Mr. Stickweed' was actually Robert Stigwood – a music promoter, manager and producer who just weeks earlier had merged his company with Brian Epstein's NEMS agency, which had been managing The Beatles since 1961. Stigwood's discovery of the freshly-repatriated Brothers Gibb seemed a bit of kismet, as twelve years earlier, he'd arrived in England from his native Australia in search of new opportunities. By 1966, he'd already signed and scored successes with actor/singers John Leyton, Mike Sarne, Mike Berry, blues rock outfit Junco Partners, and London rock supergroup Cream – which featured former Graham Bond Organisation drummer and bassist Ginger Baker and Jack Bruce respectively, and 21-year-old guitarist Eric Clapton.

NEMS was among a number of offices Hugh Gibb had sent records and acetates of The Bee Gees' recent material to prior to leaving Australia, hoping they would reach the desk of the infamous Mr. Epstein. Barry explained: 'We didn't know at the time that Brian didn't handle that side of the business', so they were instead passed to his newly-established business partner. He played them and liked them. 'He had our date of arrival in England and tried for days to contact us but couldn't find us. We tried every agency in the book, but none of them wanted to know us. Then Robert contacted us'.

Although Stigwood was already a well-established figurehead in the British music industry, when the parcel of Bee Gees recordings had arrived from Australia, he was fortuitously searching for a group he could mould in a similar way that Epstein had done for The Beatles. As Stigwood would later reminisce, he suspected immediately that he'd found his group. Once he'd made the fateful phone call to the Gibbs' temporary lodgings on Sunny Gardens Road in Hendon, he was determined to make that arrangement a reality. Hugh Gibb would later ponder, 'It's a funny thing, but not long before we left Australia, there was an article in one of the papers saying that Brian Epstein was looking for the new Beatles, and I thought at the time, 'You've got them here if you only knew it'. Then it happened – they were signed up by the Brian Epstein office within a week of arriving in England'.

'My gut instinct told me they would be sensational', Stigwood reflected in 2001, 'because you can't deny talent. And the talent was *so* obvious'.

The brothers were invited to a short audition at the Savile Theatre in Covent Garden before a reportedly hungover Stigwood. 'I've always felt to this day he was a little worse for wear when he came there', Barry quipped in the documentary *This Is Where I Came In – The Official Story of The Bee Gees*. 'But I'm being kind, Robert (*laughs*). He came in with his assistants and sat down and said, 'Okay. Sing. Show me what you do''.

'They claim I fell asleep, which is rubbish', Stigwood sparred. Still, the Gibbs recall their future manager's initial demeanour seemed less than enthusiastic. Robin: 'We didn't know how we were ... you know, getting across to him. We did about four or five songs. And he had two people next to him. He got up, nodded to them, and they all walked out! And that was it!'.

According to Barbara Gibb, the brothers returned to the house, deflated:

> They came home and they were really heartbroken. They said, 'It was just a waste of time'. They got home about five o'clock in the afternoon. At half-past eight, the phone rang, and it was Robert. He said, 'Bring them in tomorrow to sign the contracts'. Just as quick as that, you know. They didn't even think he'd heard them.

The result: a five-year management contract with NEMS, virtually unprecedented for a new group.

The following day, The Bee Gees signed with Polydor Records (established in Germany in 1913 before opening a British subsidiary in London in 1954). The company secured the rights to release the group's music in Britain, Europe, and eventually most of the record-buying world. Festival Records (through the Spin label) retained their rights for Australia; but the plans for the vast North American market had yet to be determined. Despite NEMS' close relationship with EMI and its US-based label Capitol – which carried The Beatles' releases – Stigwood negotiated a deal with his friend Ahmet Ertegun, head of Atlantic Records. Atlantic, long renowned for rhythm & blues and jazz music, wanted to move into the broader pop and rock market. Atlantic already had Cream on its roster courtesy of Stigwood, so they were keen to expand their stable with the Gibbs.

On 24 February, the Bee Gees' first Polydor single – 'Spicks And Specks' – was released in the UK and Europe. *New Musical Express* thought the single was 'a bit dated' but 'very good indeed'. Robin's vocal on the B-side 'I Am The World' was also given special mention. Alas, the record failed in the UK, though it would have some success in parts of Europe.

The Bee Gees quickly transformed from a trio to a four-piece when Colin Petersen was invited to join. Petersen, who knew the Gibb Brothers well from their days in Sydney, had already played on several Bee Gees recordings at Ossie Byrne's Hurstville studios.

On 4 March, they ventured back into a recording studio for the first time in about six months. The product of their first session was not for their own forthcoming releases but as backing vocalists for Billy J. Kramer's cover of their 1966 composition 'Town Of Tuxley Toymaker Part 1'. Other cover versions of this fine song were recorded by New Zealander Shane (Hales), Belgian band The Vipers, and Greek singer Vicky Leandros who, over her lengthy career, recorded it four times in three different languages – English and German, and two different versions in her native Greek.

Back in Australia, yet more Gibb material written the previous year was being released. 20-year-old Jenene Watson had been singing and performing since she was a child, and was best known as a presenter on ABC's television program *Crackerjack*. Her first single, 'So Long Boy'/'Don't Say No' released in March 1967 on the Spin label, was another product of the Maurice Gibb/Nat Kipner writing team, and was recorded with Ossie Byrne at Hurstville Studios in the summer of 1966. 'So Long Boy' was a big, bold and brassy jazz song, and one of their better productions; 'Don't Say No' was a strong ballad requiring a big vocal, which Ms. Watson provided with ease.

Another Barry Gibb song released in early 1967 was Jimmy Little's cover of 'Walkin' Talkin' Teardrops', which was written back in 1964. The song appeared on the album *New Songs from Jimmy*. Little's silky smooth vocals influenced by American singers Nat King Cole and Jim Reeves are to the fore in this quite traditional country song.

On 7 March, Barry, Robin, Maurice and Colin began recording sessions for The Bee Gees' first British album at London's Polydor Studios, including 'I Can't See Nobody', 'Red Chair Fade Away' and 'Turn Of The Century'.

One of the visitors to one of the early UK sessions was Australian musician and guitarist Vince Melouney. Vince remembers:

Right: The Bee Gees: Barry, Robin, and Maurice sing one of their songs to their sister, Lesley. (*Teenager's Weekly* – 29 June 1960)

Left: Redcliffe Speedway was where the boys were discovered by promoter Bill Goode and DJ Bill Gates. They performed on this day. (*Redcliffe Herald* – January 1960)

SPEEDWAY
REDCLIFFE SHOWGROUNDS
THIS SATURDAY NIGHT
JANUARY 9 — 8 P.M.

SEE ALL YOUR FAVOURITE SPEEDWAY STARS IN ACTION

FREE PARKING ... BAR OPEN
ADULTS 5/- — CHILDREN 1/-

Below left: 31 August 1962 – the life-changing day the brothers met Col Joye. (*Gold Coast Advisor* – 23 August 1962)

Below: The Bee Gees performing at the Hotel Grande's Palm Lounge in Coolangatta in July 1962, with vocalist Barbara Faulds and their father, Hugh Gibb. (*Unknown*)

On behalf of A. A. Artists' Agency, Max Moore presents—

THE FABULOUS
COL JOYE
'62 SPECTACULAR
Starring in person
COL JOYE
Together with the Nation's No. 1 Instrumental Group
☆ "The Joyboys"
☆ Judy Stone
☆ Frankie Davidson
☆ The De Kroos Bros.
☆ Vicky Simms
at St. John's Hall, Surfers Paradise
FRIDAY, 31st AUGUST
— BOOKINGS: —
12/6 at Malpas Jewellers
SURFERS PARADISE

Top: Recording at Festival
Studios in Sydney, January 1963.
(*Michael Giuliano*)

Above: The Bee Gees' first
single, released on 22 March
1963. (*Leedon Records*)

Left: 1963 promotional
photograph. (*Festival Records*)

THE
BATTLE OF THE
BLUE AND THE GREY
(Barry Gibb) (Australian Comp.)
(2.05)

JOYE
PUBLISHING
CO.

45

Leedon

THE BEE-GEES
VOCAL WITH ORCHESTRA

LK-346
MX12435

"THE BEE GEES"

Right: 1963 – Extremely rare Coca-Cola bottle tops featuring The Bee Gees. (*Mark Crohan*)

Left: The first of hundreds of front cover features. (*Teenager's Weekly – 15 May 1963*)

Right: At the *Bandstand* studio. (*TV Week – 7 December 1963*)

Left: Photo shoot at Centennial Park in Sydney. Barry with his Maton Capitol K10 guitar. (*Teenager's Weekly – 29 January 1964*)

Below: One of the rarest Bee Gees records – their first EP. (*Leedon Records*)

LX-10747

the

B
E
E
G
E
S

VOCAL WITH ORCHESTRA

✳ THE BATTLE OF THE BLUE AND THE GREY   ✳ TAKE HOLD OF THAT STAR
✳ THE THREE KISSES OF LOVE   ✳ TIMBER

Above: A gathering of stars at Sydney radio station 2GB. Back row (L-R): Lonnie Lee, Johnny Devlin, Theo Penglis (The Atlantics), Johnny Rebb, Vicki Forrest, Barry Gibb, Bosco Bosonac (The Atlantics), Jim Skaithitis (The Atlantics), Tony Brady, Leo De Kroo, Phil Bower (Digger Revell & The Denvermen). Front row: 2GB DJ Ward 'Pally' Austin, Little Pattie, Robin Gibb, Maurice Gibb. (*Wayne Mac*)

Five variations of the group's name

The Telegraph (Brisbane) – 9 April 1964

The Telegraph (Brisbane) – 10 April 1964

The Advertiser (Adelaide) – 17 April 1964

Above: Looking dapper and adopting a classic Napoleonic pose. (*TV Week* – 30 May 1964)

The Telegraph (Brisbane) – 8 December 1964

The Telegraph (Brisbane) – 12 December 1964

Above: The Bee Gees in their Volkswagen Kombi van. (*Australian Women's Weekly* – 23 December 1964)

Above: The Bee Gees with Trevor Gordon and Barry's future wife, Maureen Bates, promoting their new business partnership, Begore Pty. Ltd. (*Australian Women's Weekly* – 31 March 1965)

HOUSE WITHOUT WINDOWS
(B. Gibb (Aust. Comp.)

Leedon *Leedon*

45

LK-829
MX17091
(2.32)

TREVOR GORDON AND THE BEE GEES

Above: The Bee Gees' only shared credit on an Australian-era single, January 1965. (*Leedon Records*)

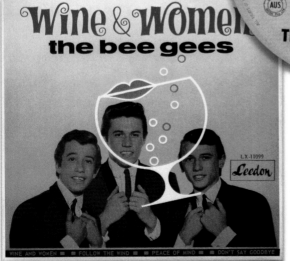

Wine & Women
the bee gees

LX-11099

Leedon

WINE AND WOMEN ■ ■ FOLLOW THE WIND ■ ■ PEACE OF MIND ■ ■ DON'T SAY GOODBYE

Left: The Bee Gees' second EP – *Wine And Women*. (*Leedon Records*)

Right: Performing at the Central Coast Leagues Club, Gosford, NSW on 20 February 1965. (*Les Allen*)

Left: *The Bee Gee's Sing & Play 14 Barry Gibb Songs* album cover – November 1965. (*Leedon Records*)

Right: Performing 'Little White Bull' on *The Barry Crocker Show*. (*Barry Crocker*)

Left: Image change! Name change? Rupert's World ... maybe not! (*Everybody's* – 25 May 1966)

Right: *Spicks And Specks* album cover, November 1966. (*Spin Records*)

Below: Individual photos for a *Go-Set* magazine photo shoot. (*Go-Set* – 26 November 1966)

Right: A Group photo for *Go-Set* magazine. (*Go-Set* – 26 November 1966)

Left: The Bee Gees' third EP – 'Spicks And Specks'. (*Spin Records*)

Right: The Bee Gees' first appearance on *The Go!! Show* with presenter Johnny Young on 17 October, 1966. He would later go on to record four songs written by the Gibbs. (*ATV-0 Melbourne*)

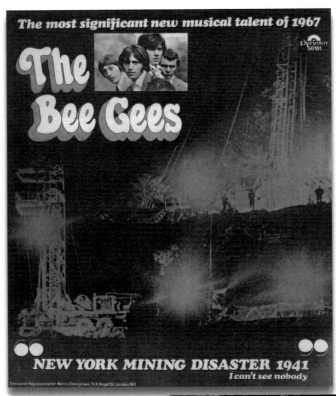

Left: The advertisement placed by Robert Stigwood in the British music press to herald the release of 'New York Mining Disaster 1941'. (*Disc & Music Echo* – 15 April 1967)

Right: *Bee Gees' 1st* UK album cover with artwork by Klaus Voormann – July 1967. (*Polydor Records*)

Right: *Bee Gees' 1st* Japanese album cover – February 1968. (*Polydor Records*)

Left: West German picture sleeve for 'Massachusetts', The Bee Gees' first international number 1 hit – September 1967. (*Polydor Records*)

Right: Released in late 1967, *Turn Around … Look At Us* was The Bee Gees' third Australian LP – effectively a compilation of tracks not previously released on an album. (*Festival Records*)

Left: West German picture sleeve for the non-album single 'Words'/'Sinking Ships' – January 1968. (*Polydor Records*)

Right: *Horizontal* UK album cover – February 1968. (*Polydor Records*)

Left: *Horizontal* Italian album cover – February 1968. (*Polydor Records*)

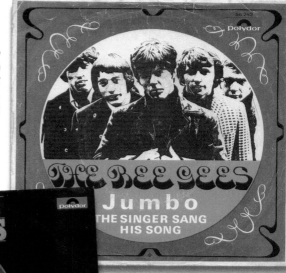

Right: Austrian picture sleeve for the non-album single 'Jumbo'/'The Singer Sang His Song' – April 1968. (*Polydor Records*)

Left: *Idea* UK album cover – September 1967. (*Polydor Records*)

Right: *Idea* US album cover with artwork by Klaus Voormann – September 1967. (*ATCO Records*)

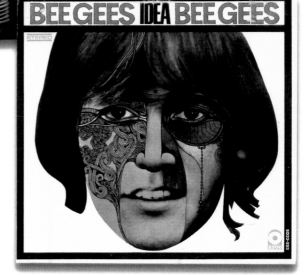

Left: The withdrawn German picture cover for the 'Lamplight'/'First Of May' single – February 1969. (*Polydor Records*)

Right: The revised German release with 'First Of May' as the A-side – February 1969. (*Polydor Records*)

Left: *Odessa* UK flocked album cover – March 1969. (*Polydor Records*)

Right: Robin Gibb's first solo single, 'Saved By The Bell'/'Mother And Jack' – Portuguese single, June 1969. (*Polydor Records*)

Left: 'Alexandria Good Time', the withdrawn original B-side to 'Saved By The Bell' – UK single, June 1969. (*Polydor Records*)

Right: 'Tomorrow Tomorrow'/'Sun In My Morning' – Norwegian single, May 1969. (*Polydor Records*)

Left: 'Don't Forget To Remember'/'The Lord' – French single, August 1969. (*Polydor Records*)

Right: A unique version of 'I Lay Down And Die' appeared as the B-side to 'Don't Forget To Remember' in Canada only – August 1969. (*ATCO Records*)

Left: Robin Gibb's second solo single 'One Million Years'/'Weekend' – Spanish single, November 1969. (*Polydor Records*)

I went to England, and somehow or other I connected with Long John Baldry, the English blues singer. He told me about The Easybeats, who were in town – I wasn't aware of that. I was living with my wife in a bedsitter at the time, and he knew where they were and had their contact. I then contacted them because they were old friends – we'd done tours and shows together. I used to call over and see them, they were living at Wembley Central. So, one day I was there, somebody who I don't know – perhaps somebody from their record company – mentioned that The Bee Gees were in town and they had a phone number. What an incredible coincidence – unbelievable! I contacted them, I phoned up and I spoke to Maurice and I said to him, 'How are things going? How was the boat trip? Blah, blah, blah …'. I said, 'We're a bit skint, you know, have you got any dough?'. He said, 'No, we're skint, as well! However, we've been signed up by this guy called Robert Stigwood and we're doing a recording next week. Why don't you come and play guitar? That would be great'. I said, 'That would be fantastic'. So, I got the details, and the only problem was that I didn't have a guitar, because I'd sold my guitar, my beautiful Epiphone Sheraton, to make money to come to England. But my friend Harry Vanda of The Easybeats was kind enough to lend me his Gibson 335, which I took real care of on the bus and the train into London and IBC. And that's where I met Colin Petersen for the first time.

In 2021, Vince recalled those earliest sessions with awe: 'I was completely awestruck by being in an English recording studio. It's like, you know, did I fall over and die and go to heaven or something? And so that night, it was great to see the guys – it was really good to see them after quite a bit of time since I sold my clothes to Maurice. And so, that night (21 March), I do believe we recorded 'New York Mining Disaster''.

Following his guitar contribution on 'New York Mining Disaster 1941', Melouney was soon invited to participate in more sessions:

In the beginning, I was there for about the first six weeks, I think, something like that – it may have only been a month, I don't really know, but I was a session player. Robert Stigwood said 'Go and buy any guitar you want, an amplifier, whatever you want' – which was fantastic – 'And buy some clothes'. So I did. I was actually on a wage for about a month to six weeks. And they said that they had a meeting, and they all agreed that I would become an official legal member of The Bee Gees. It would have happened before, but there were some contractual issues that were happening. So that was that!.

With Stigwood busily organising a packed concert schedule, the group was finally expanded to five, with Melouney formally coming on board as lead guitarist. Robin would later reflect: 'He was a tremendous, tremendous guitarist. He was on all the early sessions and just stayed on'. Barry was also excited with the five-man Bee Gees lineup, saying, 'Vince is a brilliant guitarist, Colin is a brilliant drummer. I don't think they'd ever leave the group, and I'd never think of replacing them with anyone else because I don't think anyone else is as capable as these two guys are'. After many years of being backed by anonymous musicians at shows with little rehearsal time, the brothers had long wished to be part of a real band where their performances could be more consistent and reliable. This was a great development for The Bee Gees.

More sessions followed over the next few weeks, producing 'House Of Lords', 'Mr. Waller's Wailing Wall', 'One Minute Woman', 'I Close My Eyes', 'All Around My Clock', 'I've Got To Learn', and 'Cucumber Castle'.

In the studio, Carlos Olms – a 37-year-old Polydor Records producer – was assigned to work with Ossie Byrne to produce what would become *Bee Gees' 1st*. Byrne – who the brothers had introduced to Stigwood – joined them, and relished the new opportunities to create in a properly established recording studio. It already seemed a long way from the back of a former butcher shop. Always enthusiastic musical experimenters, the Gibbs had long been frustrated by the lack of time and money Festival Records had invested in their preceding recordings. With Stigwood now giving them free rein in Polydor's studio, a great deal more time and better recording equipment, the brothers were delighted. 'We found out what we really wanted to hear was strings', Barry said, 'and we couldn't really get that in Australia. So, when we got to England, we knew we wanted to hear our music with an orchestra behind it. When we got a manager situation going with Robert Stigwood, he asked us what we wanted to do with our music, and we asked him for an orchestra. We always loved orchestras, and being in Australia, we were pretty starved of that. So, I think it was the starvation over those years that had us use orchestras with such enthusiasm when we finally had a manager and record company prepared to pay for them'.

The now five-man group's first British concert was on 17 March at the Palace Theatre, in their old hometown of Manchester – as an opening act for Gerry and The Pacemakers and Fats Domino. Just a few days later, on 1 April, the same show – promoted by Brian Epstein – began the first of a six-night run at the Saville Theatre. Despite their inclusion in a phenomenal lineup, Barry's recollection of the affair was not a happy one: 'All they wanted was Fats Domino – they were all teddy boys and they hated us'. Melouney told *Beat Instrumental*: 'We were cutting the LP and rehearsing, and were only together for two weeks before the show. We just about made it because we did rockers'. The Bee Gees' set included covers of rock classics like Larry Williams' 'Dizzy Miss Lizzy' and Gene Vincent and His Blue Caps' 'Be-Bop-a-Lula'.

On 14 April, The Bee Gees released their second international single, and the first from the forthcoming *Bee Gees' 1st*: 'New York Mining Disaster 1941'. *New Musical Express's* review was very positive, stating 'Fascinating harmonies, underlined by cello, and a lyric that keeps you glued to the speaker'.

Stigwood spared little expense in promoting the single, launching full-page advertisements in the 15 April editions of the UK music papers *Record Mirror*, *Melody Maker*, and *Disc & Music Echo* with the subheading 'The most significant new musical talent of 1967': a proclamation which understandably concerned the brothers – 'It was a big call to live up to', Barry recalled. As the official announcement that Vince Melouney had become a fully-fledged member did not occur until 29 April, publicity photos taken for the single release some weeks prior did not include him.

The unusually titled single was a simple pop-folk ballad that beautifully displayed their unique harmonies backed by an uncomplicated guitar arrangement. The song's protagonists – two men trapped in a coalmine – and the peculiar lyrics, raised questions in the press about the brothers' songwriting process, to which Barry responded: 'The old concept of writing about love and romance as the basis of every pop song, has changed. We still do write romance songs, but most of our writing is about contemporary things, situations, people. The Beatles have started to write about subjects not connected with love. We do too. 'New York Mining Disaster' is about some people trapped in a mine'.

The song title was also a deliberate attempt to attract public interest. 'As it was our first single (outside Australia)', Robin recalled, 'we wanted something to draw attention as well. So a title like that was not to be dismissed'. The gamble worked, as the single climbed to number 14 in the UK, and three back in Australia. In the US, where it was long-windedly labelled 'New York Mining Disaster 1941 (Have You Seen My Wife, Mr. Jones?)', it reached number 12. It was an excellent international debut. The Bee Gees were on their way.

The B-side – the beautiful, if grammatically incorrect 'I Can't See Nobody' – was another Barry and Robin co-write, the origins of which stemmed from the brothers' Brisbane days when they were at some point sharing a gig dressing room with a stripper, and their father told them to avert their eyes. Robin would later declare the song as 'one of my personal favourites, influenced by the soul music stable of Atlantic and Stax. Both lyrics and music were written in the basement of a seedy nightclub in Brisbane'. And true to Robin's often R-rated sense of humour, he added, 'That's why, even now, when I hear it today, it still manages to bring a lump'.

The single was credited as 'A Robert Stigwood Production', while Ossie Byrne received a 'co-producer' title. Another old Australian friend and producer assisting was Bill Shepherd, whose string arrangements on the B-side in particular, were masterful. Shepherd's reconnection with the group came courtesy of Colin Petersen, with whom Shepherd was sharing a flat until they both found work. Shepherd would remain with The Bee Gees until 1972, and his role in translating their musical ideas into complete songs should not be underestimated. Shepherd became The Bee Gees' valued musical adviser, and his orchestral arrangements became an essential part of their records and overall sound.

Meanwhile, work continued at a frenetic pace, with recording sessions to complete *Bee Gees' 1st* fitting in between live performances across the UK and Europe, and also several appearances on the BBC music TV programme *Top of the Pops*.

On 22 April, The Bee Gees made their first appearance on the BBC radio programme *Saturday Club*, performing specially recorded versions of four new songs: 'Cucumber Castle', 'In My Own Time', 'New York Mining Disaster 1941' and 'One Minute Woman'.

A group called The Gnomes of Zurich also appeared on the show, performing their new single 'High Hopes', which was released on the same day as 'New York Mining Disaster 1941'. Frank Sinatra originally recorded 'High Hopes' in 1959, with a children's chorus. The Gnomes' version included a number of guests on the chorus, including Radio London disc jockeys Keith Skues, Mike Lennox, and Ed Stewart; but for this exclusive BBC performance, lead singer Kevin Lear asked the show's presenter, Brian Matthew, if The Bee Gees could help out, which they ably did. In so doing, they provided us with probably the rarest of all Bee Gees guest appearances to be pressed on vinyl, if only on a BBC Transcription Services disc.

On 11 May, The Bee Gees made their first appearance on the very popular and influential *Top of the Pops*, performing 'New York Mining Disaster 1941'. Nine days later, they made their debut on the German music TV show *Beat-Club*, again performing their new single. The other guests on the show were Cream, The Equals, Small Faces; Dave Dee, Dozy, Beaky, Mick & Tich; The Who, The Kinks, Julie Felix and Whistling Jack Smith.

Two days later, The Bee Gees played the first of eight UK concerts, beginning in Northampton at the Maple Ballroom, followed by two shows the following day in Nottingham at the Britannia Rowing Club and The Beachcomber Club. After a show in Liverpool, they headed north for two gigs in Galashiels and Selkirk in Scotland, before finishing out the month with shows in Carlisle, and finally, Oldham at The Thing Club.

Also in May, little known Birmingham quartet The Monopoly released their take of 'House Of Lords'. Originally written and recorded in Australia in 1966, The Bee Gees revamped the song in 1967 for *Bee Gees' 1st*, but it didn't make the cut. The Monopoly's version on Polydor – which was their debut single – is quicker than The Bee Gees' version. Lead singer Raymond Froggat recalls not being too pleased with The Bee Gees reject-song, saying, 'We felt that we could write a better song than the one The Bee Gees wrote for us'. They also recorded 'Red Chair Fade Away' as a demo, but it was never released.

The Monopoly comprised Raymond Froggatt (vocals), Hartley Cain (guitar), Lou Clark (bass) and Len Ablethorpe (drums). Froggatt has remained active in music, becoming a fixture of the British country music scene, and Cain has remained in his band the entire time. Lou Clark became the string arranger for the Electric Light Orchestra and Renaissance before he became conductor of the Royal Philharmonic Orchestra.

During their 13 June spot on the ITV programme *As You Like It*, The Bee Gees performed 'To Love Somebody', which had been earmarked as their next single. They also featured it alongside 'Holiday', 'I Can't See Nobody' and 'In My Own Time' in the set comprising their second BBC session recordings for the Light Programme's *Saturday Club* on 26 June. 'To Love Somebody' received a shockingly tepid commercial response in the UK but fared much better in other parts of the world: in Canada, they would score their first top ten hit with it, and it would be their second-in-a-row in Australia. As a consolation, it would gain tremendous traction with other pop artists over the years and become one of the most covered songs in their catalogue.

The group were scheduled for four more shows in Britain later in the month, beginning on 19 June in Wishaw at The Belfry, and ending in Manchester at New Century Hall on 24 June. While they were focused on their own hectic schedule in the UK, they were likely unaware that their Australian songwriting catalogue was keeping a number of artists busy. 'Raining Teardrops'/'As Fast As I Can' by English-born singer Barrington Davis, had been recorded back in November 1966 with The Bee Gees assisting, just prior to their return to the UK. It was Davis' second single. Maurice Gibb and Nat Kipner wrote both songs. Exhibiting their flexibility as writers, the A-side is a decent fast rocker, whilst the B-side is a measured ballad. Although the single was not a hit, it did earn some solid airplay on Sydney radio.

In Melbourne, Dutch-born Australian singer Johnny Young released the Barry Gibb song 'Lady' as his final single before his departure to the UK on 6 June. The song had been written especially for him following Young's offer to pay Barry's return airfare to Sydney from Melbourne for a TV appearance. Barry returned the favour, presenting Johnny with the song. It was a top 30 hit in Australia. The single would also be released in the UK on the Decca label on 7 July. In December 1970, Canadian band Major Hoople's Boarding House also released 'Lady' as a single, but the songwriting credit was incorrectly attributed to both Barry and Robin on the label.

Also in Melbourne, 'Exit Stage Right'/'In The Morning' was Ronnie Burns' follow-up single to 'Coalman'; and like its predecessor, it was a big hit for Burns, who was one of Australia's biggest pop stars of the time. As with 'Coalman', Burns, to all intents and purposes, sang over The Bee Gees' demo of 'Exit Stage Right', it featuring the brothers' vocals, Barry's guitar, Maurice's piano and bass, and Colin Petersen on drums. The B-side 'In The Morning' would become the most covered Gibb song of their Australian years. Other people who recorded the song include Nina Simone, Mary Hopkin, Lulu and David Gray. Unlike the other Gibb songs that featured on Burns' ensuing debut album *Ronnie*, 'In The Morning' was re-recorded without any Bee Gees involvement and produced by now-legendary Melbourne bass guitarist Peter Robinson.

Festival Records also released Ronnie Burns' eponymous first album. The disc is now a collectable for Bee Gees enthusiasts, as it contains no less than eight Gibb brothers' songs. Seven of them were produced with Burns' vocal recorded over The Bee Gees' backing tracks laid down the previous year at St. Clair Studio. Only Barry's 'In The Morning' was a new recording. *Everybody's* magazine made *Ronnie* their 'Hot LP of the week' in the 9 August issue, and pop music columnist Maggie Makeig was very enthusiastic about the album: 'A winner from Ronnie Burns, who sings with control and sensitivity against splendid full production of the Bill Armstrong Studio Melbourne'. The *Brisbane Telegraph* was equally enthusiastic in their 16 August edition: 'For Australia's pop music industry, this is a boom time. There are artists who have made good on the teen scene, and move successfully on to become adult entertainers; others have made it at home and overseas. Ronnie Burns has put himself well and truly on the map with two hits – 'Exit Stage Right' and 'Coalman' – both Bee Gees compositions'.

However, amongst all the positive takes, there was at least one sour one, although The Bee Gees' songs were given some credit: 'Something less than ex but better than the average Australian pop LP. Bee Gee numbers are included; they reveal what a talented group has been lost to Australia. When Ronnie sings straight and unfettered, he sounds terribly dispirited. He depends more on an arrangement or a sound, than on his own voice'.

In June, UK pop group The Montanas released a cover of the Barry, Robin, and Maurice-penned song 'Top Hat', which was first heard on Ronnie Burns' debut earlier that month. The single was released in both the US and the UK. New Zealanders The Sounds also released the song as a single in February 1968 on the Philips label, exclusively in their homeland. Incorrectly credited to B. & M. Gibb on the label, this is one of the hardest cover records to locate and is on many collectors' want-lists.

On 14 July, the much-anticipated *Bee Gees' 1st* was released in most world markets but was delayed until August in North America.

Bee Gees' 1st (1967)

Personnel:
Barry Gibb: vocals, guitar
Robin Gibb: vocals, organ
Maurice Gibb: vocals, bass, organ, piano, guitar, Mellotron, harpsichord
Vince Melouney: guitar
Colin Petersen: drums
Additional personnel:

Orchestral arrangement: Phil Dennys: 'Red Chair Fade Away', 'One Minute Woman', 'New York Mining Disaster 1941' and 'I Close My Eyes'
Orchestral arrangement: Bill Shepherd: 'Turn Of The Century', 'Holiday', 'Cucumber Castle', 'To Love Somebody', 'I Can't See Nobody' and 'Close Another Door'
Recording engineers: John Pantry, Damon Lyon-Shaw and Philip Wade
Producer: Robert Stigwood
Co-producer: Ossie Byrne
Recorded between 7 March and 21 April 1967 at IBC Studios, London; Spot Studios (Ryemuse Sound Studios), London, and Central Sound, London
Release dates: UK: 14 July 1967, US: 9 August 1967
Chart positions: France: 2, West Germany: 4, Norway: 5, US: 7, UK: 8, Australia: 10

The now-classic *Bee Gees' 1st* was their international debut album, issued in both mono and stereo versions in many markets, as was the usual practice at the time. The mono version was important because it was heard on singles, radio and jukeboxes. Because future-proofing wasn't a consideration for many record buyers at that point, mono was still the bigger seller, even for LPs.

Whilst Robert Stigwood is credited as the album producer, he was more effectively acting as an executive producer. In reality, it was The Bee Gees' former producer Ossie Byrne – with recording engineers John Pantry, Damon Lyon-Shaw and Philip Wade – who really served as producer. No doubt, the Gibb brothers had their say in how the material developed, and as such, are uncredited producers.

What needs to be understood and appreciated from the outset, is that *Bee Gees' 1st* was released at the peak of the psychedelic era. Bear in mind that there was a mere seven weeks between the release of The Beatles' *Sgt. Pepper's Lonely Hearts Club Band* and *Bee Gees' 1st* – and 1967 was 'the summer of love'. Thus, the whimsically nonsensical lyrics of songs from this and the following two albums (songs such as 'Red Chair, Fade Away', 'Lemons Never Forget' and 'Kilburn Towers') were absolutely in tune with what was happening in pop music at the time. Songs such as Procol Harum's 'A Whiter Shade Of Pale' and The Beatles' 'I Am the Walrus' are notable examples of psychedelia that made the mainstream, and are probably the best-known nonsense songs of the period. But Procol Harum were looked upon as intellectuals; and The Beatles could do no wrong; but The Bee Gees were seen as their copyists and struggled with this tag for a number of years.

However, the younger generation of pop fans – having missed out on the initial craziness of Beatlemania – wanted their own groups to idolise, and this is where The Bee Gees fitted in. Of course, they had their detractors in the press, but they also had those who championed them.

The album was recorded mostly at IBC Studios in Portland Place, London, on four-track recording facilities: the standard in Britain at the time. This was undoubtedly an absolute luxury to the Gibbs and producer Ossie Byrne, who had all laboured with two-track facilities for their previous album – and in fact, almost their entire Australian recording career.

Barry remembers, 'Ossie was the first person who ever gave us the time to record. I mean, in the early Australian days, we were basically given three hours to make a record. In those days, you had to have had hits in order to get the studio time. That's how Festival Records in Australia used to operate in the mid-'60s. So, you did a three-hour session, and if you came up with something, great, and if you didn't, that was fine too. But they didn't extend any extra time to you if you didn't have a hit'.

Continuing, he reminisced that 'Ossie had his little home studio, and truly believed in us, and we'd basically work all night. He was a good engineer, and when we came to England, we all felt it was appropriate that he came with us. So that's what happened'.

With better studio facilities, a wider array of instruments available to experiment with, and great orchestra arrangers (primarily modelled by Bill Shepherd), The Bee Gees were in their element.

Robin was glowing in his praise of Shepherd, saying that he 'was a very, very, very important cog in the machinery. He had this vivid way with melodies in the arrangement. He came up with this great orchestral picture to complement the music. That was vital to us in that first stage'. He continued, saying, 'Bill Shepherd was a producer at Festival Records that came from England in '64, and produced a lot of big hits in Australia for other artists. We met Bill through this because he ended up producing some songs for us as house producer for Festival Records in Sydney. What we didn't realise at the time, was that he was a great musical arranger – a musician in his own right. And when he came over to England, he wasn't in his capacity as a producer – which he had been before we became connected – but more as a musical arranger. That was a whole new role for us to see Bill Shepherd in. He was brilliant and one of the best musical arrangers that ever lived'.

In addition, their new manager Robert Stigwood was very confident of his new protégés, and accordingly, quite benevolent in the allocation of studio time. The Bee Gees took full advantage of it, using that latitude to be industrious and innovative, thereby creating a classic album.

Combining all this with an already prodigious songwriting talent, a tight band and superb natural harmony vocals, the group was a force to be reckoned with. Add Stigwood's enthusiastic hype into the publicity mix, and there's little wonder that their international rise to fame was astronomical.

Bee Gees' 1st would produce three international hits. Some of the songs would remain in the group's concert setlist for their entire career, and, incredibly, there are cover versions of every single song on the album. It's an astonishingly strong international debut, made even more remarkable by the fact that the Gibbs had arrived in England essentially homeless and unemployed a month before they began recording it.

In what could only a few months earlier have seemed like the stuff of dreams, Klaus Voormann – a German-born musician, producer, artist, bassist for English rock band Manfred Mann, and designer of The Beatles' iconic *Revolver* album artwork – was commissioned to create the cover for *Bee Gees' 1st*. He captured the flavour of the psychedelic era perfectly, with a spectacular collage that encompassed every colour of the spectrum – complete with weird-out grass and flowers, a tree trunk with eyes, and a colour wheel. Central to the design was a round typographical motif emphasising the album title.

The illustration overlaps a casual but rather uninspiring group photograph – the only splash of primary colour being Barry's sweatshirt bearing the partially-covered slogan 'Made in USA'. Although the album title in a regular font style in the top left-hand corner was possibly surplus to requirements, it is pleasing to note that the new record company had employed somebody who understood how to use apostrophes!

On the down side, Voormann's involvement with The Beatles only served to reinforce some detractors' claims that The Bee Gees were merely inferior wannabes.

The back cover design varied greatly from country to country. In the UK, the large *Bee Gees' 1st* motif from the front cover, dominated, with a column of sleeve notes down the right-hand side. America opted for an elaborate antique illustration that included a variety of musical instruments to frame the sleeve notes, with the track listing above. Germany's issue featured several photographs of the group with sleeve notes below: strangely not translated into German.

Not unusually, Japan issued the album with a totally different sleeve design showing an enormous psychedelic flower upon which the group are seated.

'Turn Of The Century' (Barry Gibb, Robin Gibb)
Recorded at IBC Studios, London: 7, 8 and 15 March 1967

This was written during the passage from Australia to England on the *Fairsky*. Robin remembered that 'it was floating around for a while, and we never really completed it. We played it to Robert, and he wanted us to finish it and put it on the album. So, the inspiration was quite basic, you know, the sort of obsession with time and going back and how we'd incorporate that into a song'.

It's a perky little number about fantastical time travel back to the Victorian era. The harpsichord and oboe introduction perfectly set the scene for a wonderfully descriptive lyric.

This song epitomises the baroque-pop sounds popular at the time, and introduces alternating leads illustrating Barry and Robin's contrasting vocal styles: a tool that would see plenty of use throughout their career. Bill Shepherd provides a splendid arrangement that constantly builds as the song progresses, culminating with bold brass flourishes and full three-part vocal harmonies.

The final verse is a repeat of the first, which is not unusual in Gibb compositions. Whether this shows a lack of lyrical development is debatable, but as 'Turn Of The Century' is descriptive rather than a story, it merely reinforces the imagery of a bustling Victorian street scene.

The song was rarely performed live, with the notable exception of a 1973 episode of the American TV programme *Midnight Special*, where they sang live over the original backing track. A segment of the song was included in the medley section of their *BG2K Millennium Concert* on 31 December 1999.

'Red Rubber Ball' hitmakers The Cyrkle released 'Turn Of The Century' as a single in 1967, followed a year later by another song from *Bee Gees' 1st*: 'Red Chair, Fade Away'.

'Holiday' (Barry Gibb, Robin Gibb)
Recorded at IBC Studios, London: April 1967
Chart positions: Netherlands: 2, Spain: 8, US: 16, Canada: 18

The very simple-sounding but impenetrable lyric makes 'Holiday' one of The Bee Gees' most mysterious songs. It's a slow and meditative song with no chorus, just a verse sung by Barry once and then always by Robin.

The wordless refrain adds more intrigue to the inexplicable lyric, but the mood of the melody and arrangement is the main point of the song. Maurice supplies the Mellotron and Hammond organ, giving the first verse especially, an almost hymn-like timbre.

'Holiday' was released as a single in some countries, but notably not in Britain. 'Every Christian Lion Hearted Man Will Show You' was the B-side in the United States and Canada, while European releases opted for 'Red Chair, Fade Away'.

Later in the year, another of Robert Stigwood's charges – who assumed the stage name of Oscar – released 'Holiday' as a single on Stigwood's Reaction Records label, with backing vocals by The Bee Gees.

'Red Chair, Fade Away' (Barry Gibb, Robin Gibb)
Recorded at IBC Studios, London: 7, 8 and 13 March 1967

As with 'Holiday', 'Red Chair, Fade Away' has opaque lyrics. But while 'Holiday' can be looked upon as being somewhat philosophical, this one is The Bee Gees' first true foray into pop-psych. Lines like 'I can feel the speaking sky' and 'Rainbows all the time/We're all going higher', show the brothers confidently entering into the spirit of psychedelia – but it seems unlikely that the squeaky-clean boys that they were, ever dabbled in mind-altering substances like LSD, which, although undoubtedly responsible for sparking remarkable creativity in some, fried the brains of others. They have, however, copped to relying on medicinal speed at times to stoke their creativity.

Robin offered some insight into the song's origins: 'It was actually based on the chair of our grandfather. It was written about my dad's memories, rather than *our* memories of him because he died when we were quite young. He'd always dreamt of his father in this red chair. And we thought, you know, maybe he'd be a lot happier if he didn't see these things, so we wrote 'Red Chair, Fade Away''.

Phil Dennys wrote the orchestral arrangement, perfectly capturing the song's essence, throwing in slightly discordant accents, giving the track a somewhat chaotic feel – particularly the coda which is reminiscent of The Beatles' 'Rain'.

So influential was this song, that in the 1980s, a British band formed with the name Red Chair Fadeaway. They performed 1960s-style psych, and were active from 1988 until 1994. They released a few singles and two albums, but, curiously, didn't cover any Bee Gees songs. However, one track, titled 'Mr. Jones', did make some collectors more than a little curious.

'One Minute Woman' (Barry Gibb, Robin Gibb)
Recorded at IBC Studios, London: 9 and 15 March 1967

Early versions of 'One Minute Woman' featured Robin on lead vocal, but Barry's take won out for the final version included on the album. Barry's voice was in very good form on this record, and the beautiful tenor tone he used on this song and 'To Love Somebody' was never used in quite the same way again.

Two high-profile artists covered 'One Minute Woman': Jackie Lomax, as the B-side to his 1967 single 'Genuine Imitation Life'; and Billy Fury, as the B-side to his 1968 single 'Silly Boy Blue'. Both single labels incorrectly credited the songwriting to all three brothers.

'In My Own Time' (Barry Gibb, Robin Gibb)
Recorded at IBC Studios, London: 23 March 1967

No fancy orchestral arrangements for 'In My Own Time' – this is purely The Bee Gees as a complete pop/rock unit in full flight. Whether it was intentional or coincidence, we'll probably never know, but the guitar riff was always bound to draw comparisons with George Harrison's 'Taxman' from The Beatles' *Revolver* album.

The opening lyrics, 'I received an invitation/Come to the United Nations', proved prophetic, but more on that in the next volume ...

The Patterns were quick to cover 'In My Own Time' in late 1967, and though the vocal harmonies were good and the guitar solo even better, the rather feeble guitar sound and thin production left their version as somewhat lacking. However, the Dutch band Mega's 1968 take was more bass-driven, and their lyric interpretation occasionally bordered on the comical. In 1983, the Los Angeles alternative rock outfit The Three O'Clock introduced the song to a younger audience, with their great power pop version, which appeared on their *Sixteen Tambourines* album.

The Bee Gees opened the concerts on their 1974 Australian tour with this song, but it was never performed live again after that: a bit disappointing given its great, straightforward rock rhythm and powerfully brash harmonies.

The song title was used, albeit in modified form, as *In Our Own Time*: a 2010 Bee Gees documentary that was released on DVD.

'Every Christian Lion Hearted Man Will Show You' (Barry Gibb, Robin Gibb, Maurice Gibb)
Recorded at IBC Studios, London: 23 March 1967

This uncharacteristically dark and ominous song threw everything into the melting pot, with its droning Gregorian-like chant of 'O Solo Dominique' and a glorious, earthy Mellotron strings sound. The boldly-strummed guitar and double-tracked lead vocal with lots of echo, lead into a powerful chorus with booming bass, and probably Colin Petersen's best drumming on record. The harmonies are strong and get more interesting in the final coda, with channel separation of the voices. Robin later explained:

> We did the monks in the background. 'O Solo Dominique' is actually an expression we got from a church in Essex. I think it's 'Strength through fear of God and unity through church and family'. It was something to that effect, but it was in Latin, of course. And we repeated those words. We don't know, but it could be the hidden Da Vinci Code!

Barry told Bill Harry of *Record Mirror* in November 1967: 'When I was in Rome, I visited the Colosseum. I wrote a number about it on the last album, called 'Every Christian Lion Hearted Man Will Show You', which would be suitable for one of those Roman Empire films'.

Barry performed the song on his solo *Mythology* tour in 2013-2014, with his son Stephen singing the low-register chant.

Several cover versions exist, the earliest being by The Tangerine Peel in September 1967. That group included Mike Chapman who – when he later partnered with Nicky Chinn – created a string of hit singles for artists including The Sweet, Suzi Quatro, Smokie, Mud and Racey. Those recordings generated a sound that became identified as the 'Chinnichap' brand. He later produced breakthrough albums for Blondie and The Knack.

The Bee Gees' old Australian friend Johnny Young followed closely with his version in October 1967.

'Craise Finton Kirk Royal Academy Of Arts' (Barry Gibb, Robin Gibb)
Recorded at IBC Studios, London: 21 March 1967

A simple piano accompanies Robin's vocal, which sounds like it's sung through a megaphone – similar to the New Vaudeville Band's 'Winchester Cathedral': a huge global hit in 1966. But the style would be more correctly credited to Rudy Vallee, who popularised it in the late-1920s.

Barry explained: 'We just thought, well, why not just one instrument? Why does everything have to be a full band? We started to be more selective about what instruments are playing the songs. It became more of a fascination for us. Mo sat down at the piano, we started ad-libbing, Robin started ad-libbing, and once again, I think you can tell it's a very Beatlesque type of thing'.

Noteworthy as an early example of a Bee Gees' fantasy character song, it tells the tale of Craise Finton Kirk: an unusual name to be sure. What exactly the Royal Academy of Arts has to do with this is anybody's guess, although verse one's mention of 'a pencil in his hand' must surely imply he was an artist or an aspiring artist at the very least.

It's quaint in its own cheerfully chirpy way and an apt closer for side one. We should rejoice that the worst blow fate could throw at Mr. Kirk was that 'His wavy hair continued not to grow': as other song characters the brothers created would not be so lucky!

The Bee Gees reunited with Johnny Young – an old friend and presenter of the Australian television programme *The Go!! Show* – when he recorded the song, and they even provided backing vocals. Young's version was released as a single in the UK and Germany, where he performed it on the popular *Beat-Club* programme. Back home in Australia, however, it became a hit, peaking at number 14 on the national *Go-Set* chart. He later recorded and released 'Every Christian Lion Hearted Man Will Show You' as a single, but it didn't chart.

'New York Mining Disaster 1941' (Barry Gibb, Robin Gibb)

Recorded at IBC Studios, London: 21 March 1967
Chart positions: Netherlands: 3, New Zealand: 3, West Germany: 10, Australia: 11, UK: 12, US: 14, Canada: 34, France: 36

'New York Mining Disaster 1941' seemed to be a strange title for a pop song, and some may have considered it a little pretentious to not include the title in the lyric. The subject was also rather unusual – a tale of miners trapped below ground, hoping to be saved but fearing that the rescuers may have given up on them. But grim subject matter was to become something of a theme with many of their songs over the next few years.

The song was a pop-folk ballad that amply displayed the group's strongest asset: their harmony singing – which was backed with a very simple arrangement. The version decided upon for release was quite different to the two other more elaborate versions, the first of which was scored by Bill Shepherd and the other by Phil Dennys. Both later appeared on the expanded edition of *Bee Gees' 1st* released as part of *The*

Studio Albums 1967-1968 box set in 2006. All takes considered, Robert Stigwood was right to decide on the simpler version for release.

Robin recalled that the song 'was written at Polydor Records on a staircase. It was in the dark and it was echoey, and we had this strange inspiration to write this song about a mining disaster that occurred in New York in the year 1941. I suppose, you know, because it was the atmosphere'.

Barry elaborated further, saying 'The song itself was about the Aberfan mining disaster in Wales, killing over 200 children. Quite sad, really'. On 21 October 1966, a coal-waste tip slid down the mountainside into the village of Aberfan in South Wales. It engulfed the Pantglas Junior School and about twenty village houses before coming to a halt. Almost half of the schoolchildren and five of their teachers were killed. In all, the death toll was 144: 116 of them, children.

A colour promotional film was made at The Speakeasy club in London and featured Barry, Robin, Maurice and Colin Petersen – Vince had not yet officially joined the group. There were also TV appearances: in the UK on *Top of the Pops,* and in Germany on *Beat-Club*.

As the album's debut single, 'New York Mining Disaster 1941' performed very well, peaking at number 12 in the UK and at 14 on the *Billboard* Hot 100 in the US. New Zealand and The Netherlands gave The Bee Gees their first international top ten hit, with the single peaking at number 3 in both countries.

The song has since been covered over 100 times, with notable versions by the incredible psychedelic band Velvett Fogg on their eponymous 1967 debut album; and, interestingly, Ashton, Gardner and Dyke: the group that guitarist Vince Melouney joined after leaving The Bee Gees. Their version, however, was released in 1971 after he had departed the band. Also worthy of mention is the wonderfully sombre version by Chumbawamba, included on their 2000 album *WYSIWYG.*

Those doubtful of the Beatles influence, should listen to 'I Don't Want To Spoil the Party' from their *Beatles For Sale* album, for some melodic similarities.

'Cucumber Castle' (Barry Gibb, Robin Gibb)
Recorded at IBC Studios, London: 13 and 15 March 1967
A strange title for a song about an imaginary castle in an imaginary land. The enigmatic lyrics set it up to be a story song, but with just two verses, it's frustratingly short and doesn't develop as much as it

could have. It does, however, have a solid vocal from Barry, and Bill Shepherd embellishes the accompaniment with one of his best flowery arrangements. This pointed the way to a distinct Bee Gees sound that they continued over their next two albums.

A few years later, the song title became the inspiration for a television special and a supporting album.

'To Love Somebody' (Barry Gibb, Robin Gibb)
Recorded at IBC Studios, London: April 1967
Chart positions: Australia: 6, Belgium: 8, Canada: 9, South Africa: 10, US: 17, West Germany: 19, UK: 41, France: 65

This was conceived in New York during the Gibb brothers' first visit to the US, and written after Barry met legendary soul singer Otis Redding. Robert Stigwood suggested that Barry write a song for Redding. Robin would assist in writing this now-classic rock-blues ballad. Barry told *Mojo* magazine in 2001 that it was in fact written for Stigwood himself: 'I say that unabashedly. He asked me to write a song for him, personally. It was played to Otis but, personally, it was for Robert. He meant a great deal to me. (I had) tremendous admiration for this man's abilities and gifts. 'To Love Somebody' may have been all things to all men, but it was inspired by just one'.

Otis Redding never had the opportunity to record the song. He and most of his backing band The Bar-Kays, died on 10 December 1967 when his twin-engine Beechcraft plane crashed into Lake Monona near Madison, Wisconsin.

The Bee Gees' take, despite positive reviews and predictions, did reasonably well as a single in the biggest markets of the UK, US and West Germany. However, it reached the top ten in Australia, Belgium, Canada, the Netherlands and South Africa. The single's relative failure confused the Gibbs as Robin recalled: 'Everyone told us what a great record they thought it was. Other groups all raved about it, but for some reason, people in Britain just did not seem to like it'.

Barry suggested, 'The reason it didn't do well here was because it's a soul number. Americans loved it, but it just wasn't right for this country'.

However, greater recognition than mere chart positions lay ahead for the song. It became very important for The Bee Gees' standing as songwriters. When they were being dismissed as pop lightweights and Beatles mimics, critics had a far more difficult task in denying the power of their compositions, and 'To Love Somebody' was the best example.

When rock, blues and soul heavyweights like Eric Burdon & The Animals, Janis Joplin and Nina Simone recorded the song in the late-1960s, it was just the beginning. Since then, it's gone on to become one the most recorded and played songs of The Bee Gees' entire catalogue – and one of the most covered songs in pop music history. Some of the 300-plus versions are by artists like Ronan Keating, Roberta Flack, Billy Corgan, Rod Stewart, James Carr, Jimmy Barnes, Hank Williams Jr., The Revivalists, Blue Rodeo – and the list goes on. Michael Bolton's very dramatic version reached number 11 in the US in 1993, and number 2 in Canada, while former Bronski Beat and Communards vocalist Jimmy Somerville enjoyed a number 8 hit with it in the UK in 1990. New Zealander Keith Urban performed a scintillating version live on the 2017 CBS special *Stayin' Alive: A Grammy Salute to the Music of The Bee Gees*. Barry– the sole surviving brother by this point – was in the front row.

Of all the artists that covered the song, *Rolling Stone* magazine thought the US band The Flying Burrito Brothers' version was the best, saying that lead singer 'Gram Parsons makes this a hippie country-soul heartbreaker. Inspired by the Memphis Stax R&B sound, the Gibbs wrote it with Otis Redding in mind, but nobody ever sang it with more heart than Gram'.

The Bee Gees adopted a slower, blues-hued version of 'To Love Somebody' during their live sets in the mid-1970s. While they rarely performed their own songs with guest vocalists, Australian singer Helen Reddy joined them for a rendition of it on a 1975 episode of the US musical variety series, *The Midnight Special*. American singer Yvonne Elliman, who would cover a few of the Gibbs' compositions during her recording career, did the same during their appearance on the live concert series *Soundstage* for Chicago's WTTW television network shortly after they released the album *Main Course*. By the 1980s, they'd reverted to a more traditional interpretation when they performed it on stage.

Barry Gibb joined Jay Buchanan of California rock band Rival Sons for a duet on Barry's top-selling album *Greenfields*, released in early 2021.

The Gibb brothers even parodied their own classic on Howard Stern's 1993 *New Year's Rotten Eve Pageant* radio show, in a spoof fundraising effort for the *National Addadicktome Foundation* for people who found themselves in a similar unfortunate predicament to John Wayne Bobbitt, changing the words to 'To Lose Your Penis'.

In a 2017 interview, British journalist Piers Morgan asked Barry, 'If you thought to yourself, 'Right, of all the songs I've ever written, I'm going to sing one of them', which song would you choose?'. Barry chose 'To Love Somebody', as it has 'a clear emotional message'.

'I Close My Eyes' (Barry Gibb, Robin Gibb, Maurice Gibb)
Recorded at IBC Studios in London: 9 and 15 March 1967

A Phil Dennys arrangement, 'I Close My Eyes' has both Barry and Robin sharing lead vocals on the first verse, while Barry takes the second verse, solo.

Intriguingly, the brothers have said their song 'I Can't See Nobody' originated from their Australian years, when sharing a dressing room with a stripper, their father told them to avert their eyes. Whilst this song could be similar in concept, it's not believed to have been written during the same period.

Only two cover versions are known to exist – the first by the John Hamilton Band as the closing song on the 1971 medley album *28 Bee Gees Hits*, which was released in Australia, Italy and West Germany. In 1981, Singaporean cover band Radioactive recorded a portion of the song on their eponymous album, which contained a side-long medley of Bee Gees songs. This was released in their home country, Japan and Spain.

'I Can't See Nobody' (Barry Gibb, Robin Gibb)
Recorded at IBC Studios, London: 7, 8 and 13 March 1967

'I Can't See Nobody' was released as the B-side to 'New York Mining Disaster 1941' in April 1967. Half a century later, it's still the subject of much debate as to why it wasn't the A-side. It's an extremely strong song and should have been a hit in its own right. Robin said the song was 'influenced by the soul stable of Atlantic and Stax, and both lyrics and music were written in the basement of a seedy nightclub in Brisbane'.

Barry elaborated, saying, 'It was written with Robin and I sitting together in a dressing room with girls who weren't wearing anything, if that's how you want to visualise it. So, the comment 'I can't see nobody', it's pretty apt, actually. You just have to change the way it's written'. He continued: 'Being in the same dressing room with the dancing girls, when they changed, you are still sitting there. Nobody bothered to say anything. Well, you know, the fact that you are kids, it didn't cross their minds – but in our minds, we weren't kids!'.

Opening with cellos playing a melody over Barry's gentle electric guitar, the scene is well and truly set for Robin's soulful vocal performance. As the song builds with strings and wordless backing vocals, it's further lifted with a tympani flourish before going into a close three-part harmony chorus, while Maurice's beloved harpsichord makes an appearance at the beginning of verse two. The third verse ends with ad-libs, while the arrangement steps up a further gear before the chorus repeats twice to end the song over a choir of horns. It's a classic of the highest order.

Bee Gees' protégés The Marbles – who recorded a total of seven Gibb brothers' compositions, including the hits 'Only One Woman' and 'When The Walls Fell Down' – released 'I Can't See Nobody' in 1969 as their third single, though it failed to match the success of its predecessors.

Nina Simone chose 'To Love Somebody' as a single (from her album of the same name), which reached number 5 in the UK in 1967. 'I Can't See Nobody' was on the flip.

'Please Read Me' (Barry Gibb, Robin Gibb)
Recorded at IBC Studios, London: 23 March 1967
Another song arranged by the group themselves. On the face of it, it appears quite simple, but the wordless vocal break is probably the album's best showcase of the brothers' vocal talents. The melody and countermelodies work together wonderfully, but combined with the sibling harmonies, it becomes something special. There are fleeting moments reminiscent of The Beach Boys: particularly Maurice's high harmony part.

Nina Simone must have been quite The Bee Gees fan, as she also recorded 'Please Read Me', releasing both studio and live versions. Dutch beat group Nils Van Hill & The Gem released it as the B-side to their single 'Bulldog' in the Netherlands and Germany.

'Close Another Door' (Barry Gibb, Robin Gibb, Maurice Gibb)
Recorded at Spot Studios (Ryemuse Sound Studios), London: April 1967
The album's closing track was the only song on the original release to not be recorded at IBC Studios. Instead, it was recorded at Spot Studios, owned by Ryemuse Ltd., at 64 South Molton Street in London.

The song begins with Robin singing a cappella with a big echo effect. The lyrics and subject matter at this point are quite depressing. However, when the group joins in for the first chorus, it takes on a new life as a bouncy and upbeat number; but through tempo changes and repeats of the 'It's so sad, so sad' lyric, the listener is kept in check. The ending slows things down again before Robin takes off on an ad-lib *tour de force* in his full chest voice: which sadly fades out far too soon.

American singer Jennifer (better known to most as Jennifer Warnes, who began using her full name in the 1970s) included 'Close Another Door' as the opening track on her 1968 debut album *I Can Remember Everything*. She also recorded a cover of 'In The Morning' in 1972 for her eponymous third album.

Bee Gees' 1st – 2006 edition bonus songs

'Gilbert Green' (Barry Gibb, Robin Gibb)
Recorded at Central Sound, London: sometime in 1967

'Gilbert Green' was originally included in the recordings and demos that Hugh Gibb sent to Brian Epstein's company NEMS in November 1966. They re-recorded it for possible inclusion on *Bee Gees' 1st*. Whilst the song didn't make the album's final cut, it was part of their concert setlist for their 1967/1968 tours.

It's a song epitomising Bee Gees story songs – a tale of a wannabe songwriter who meets a tragic end while an undiscovered song lies in the basement.

The song gives a better appreciation of Maurice's bass-playing, as it melodically lifts the song, particularly in the instrumental outro, which sadly fades out early on the studio version, but was extended for concert performances.

Unfortunately, the studio version is just the group performing on their own, which is a great pity, as we know from concert performances that Bill Shepherd actually created an orchestral arrangement for it.

The best-known cover of 'Gilbert Green' is by Gerry Marsden of Gerry and The Pacemakers fame. Dutch group Soft Pillow released the song in 1969, also opting for the baroque sound which remained rather faithful to Marsden's version.

The Robert Stigwood Orchestra also recorded the song, with the intention of including it on *The Bee Gees Hits* album. This was something that Robert Stigwood allowed Bill Shepherd to make as a vanity project, and a very worthwhile one it was. 'The End Of Gilbert Green', as it was known for that album, was in fact just the outro melody, though it was vastly extended and began quietly with the melody played solely on piano before building to a spectacular climax. Unfortunately, it didn't make the cut and remains unreleased.

'House Of Lords' (Barry Gibb, Robin Gibb)

Recorded at IBC Studios, London: 5 April 1967

Written and originally recorded in Australia, 'House Of Lords' was re-recorded twice during the sessions for *Bee Gees' 1st*. It's another story song, and it comes as no surprise that Sir Frederick didn't survive to the end of the song. It should have been a contender for inclusion, but with so much other strong material to compete with, it didn't quite make the grade in Robert Stigwood's book.

Ronnie Burns recorded it in 1966 using the original Bee Gees backing track in Australia during sessions for his first album *Ronnie*, but ultimately it was not included.

'I've Got To Learn' (Barry Gibb, Robin Gibb, Maurice Gibb)

Recorded at IBC Studios, London: 13 March 1967

This is a rocking little track with a Gene Pitney-esque vocal by Robin, and some characteristically-1960s lead guitar from Vince. It's a very underdeveloped recording though, and it never progressed beyond this demo stage.

'All Around My Clock' (Barry Gibb, Robin Gibb, Maurice Gibb)

Recorded at IBC Studios: 9 and 15 March 1967

In the first verse of this very short song, Barry takes the lead vocal to a minimal accompaniment of Maurice's bass before the chorus – sung by Robin – takes you by surprise when the full band joins in. The constant pounding beat of snare drum, bass and guitar then continues for the remainder of the song, except for a brief dreamlike sequence in the middle. It's not a particularly strong song, and still sounds quite incomplete, even though it was worked on across two sessions.

'Mr. Wallor's Wailing Wall' (Barry Gibb, Robin Gibb)

Recorded at IBC Studios, London: 4 April 1967

A fun song, but surely never a serious contender for release. That being said, it's quite incredible the amount of work that went into its creation and that two different versions exist. Best described as vaudevillian in style, it has a rather intricate arrangement of barroom piano, banjo, muted trumpets, trombone slides and farting sounds; not to mention a variety of strange vocals by Robin.

Whilst *Bee Gees' 1st* was both a strong critical and international commercial success, in retrospect, the album may have suffered slightly from being released just a month after The Beatles' groundbreaking album *Sgt Pepper's Lonely Hearts Club Band*. The Gibbs later lamented their inability to return to the studio to tweak their debut after being awestruck upon hearing the fab four's instant masterpiece. But *Bee Gees' 1st* would also perhaps be devoid of its pure unceremonious creation had they had the opportunity. Prior to their album's release, Barry tipped his hat to Ossie Byrne and his production team for their patience: 'We drove the producer and technicians mad. We have nothing worked out. We sit about and think up a subject, then write a song on the spot. We did the whole of the album like this. It's really the only way we can work – spontaneously, off the cuff'.

Sharing The Beatles' management team NEMS had some distinct advantages in terms of the time, energy and resources that backed The Bee Gees' now escalating careers, but the two bands' paths were kept distinctly separate. Although The Bee Gees were not aware of it at the time, The Beatles had expressed interest in their new NEMS stablemates: 'They wanted to come in on one of the boys' earlier sessions', Robert Stigwood recalled, 'but I asked them not to, because I didn't think it would be particularly good'.

Successful British band Unit 4 + 2 released a cover of 'Butterfly' on 23 June 1967. One of the best B., R. & M. Gibb songs from their Australian years, it was yet another song that had made its public debut on Ronnie Burns' debut album *Ronnie*. Italian pop group, I Favolosi also recorded 'Butterfly' (as 'Come La Rondini') in 1967, and Scottish hitmakers Marmalade would do so in 1969.

Immediately after *Bee Gees' 1st* was released, the group were back in the studio recording new material. At Central Sound Studios from 17 July through to 1 August, they wrote and committed to tape, ten songs, four of which would make the tracklist of their forthcoming second album – they were 'And The Sun Will Shine', 'Day Time Girl', 'Birdie Told Me' and 'Harry Braff'. The band took a break for a live date at The Palladium in Stockholm on 21 July. They also appeared on Dick Clark's popular and iconic *American Bandstand* TV show on 22 July, performing 'New York Mining Disaster 1941', though this was a filmed performance and not actually live in the studio.

In August, Stigwood told *New Musical Express*, 'Everyone is clamouring for Bee Gees songs. At least fourteen artists are considering songs by the group'. He wasn't exaggerating – several covers of brothers Gibb songs were released as singles that month. English pop singer Dave Berry – a Stigwood-contracted singer – released 'Forever' on 11 August. Written in 1966, it was originally offered to Ronnie Burns, who declined to record it. The Bee Gees' original demo of the song was unheard and unreleased until 1970s *Inception/Nostalgia* set.

Regarded by some as one of the finest songs that Gerry Marsden recorded, 'Gilbert Green' is a lost diamond in the Gibb brothers' song catalogue. Marsden's version was released on 25 August 1967, and was just his second solo single following his split from The Pacemakers the year before. It's a wonderful piece of baroque pop, despite Marsden's pronounced posh Scouse accent and enunciation. It included Shepherd's fabulous all-bells-and-whistles arrangement with its ridiculously overblown yet glorious outro.

Speaking of Marsden's cover of the song, Barry recalled: 'The mixture of our song and Gerry's voice, didn't work. The trouble was that we knew how the song should be done, and the whole character of it was completely changed at Gerry's session. We realised that it would be better if we actually went along to the session and explained exactly how the song should be done. Unfortunately, that's easier said than done. Really, the composer doesn't even expect to be allowed to dictate how one of his songs should be done'. The song was released on CBS/Columbia and arranged by Bill Shepherd. It's one of a few Gibb songs with a real narrative – almost a Gilbert and Sullivan mini-epic.

Meanwhile, in Australia, an unknown duo called The Kids released their first and only single 'Big Chance'/'How Many Birds', both sides being Barry Gibb songs from the *Spicks And Specks* album. The Kids were Sydney university students Michael Griffiths, aged nineteen, and his friend Tony Borg, aged twenty, who sang over The Bee Gees' original backing tapes recorded at St. Clair Studio. At the time, The Kids had been together about six months, originally formed from the remnants of a band called George Waters and The Kids that had broken up earlier in the year. When their debut single failed, the duo disappeared from the music scene. As Nat Kipner had curtailed his own production work during 1967, it's probable that Festival house producer Pat Aulton helmed The Kids' record at Festival Studios.

Also in August, Australian singer Johnny Young was in the UK trying to launch his international career– only, quoting Young himself, 'to die on my feet'. Whilst there, he lived for some of the time with Barry. Young's second UK single release was covers of 'Craise Finton Kirk Royal Academy Of Arts'/'I Am The World', backed by The Bee Gees and produced by Barry. The single was released on the Polydor label in Britain, and Clarion in Australia. The B-side was the first cover of a solo Robin composition. The single made the Australian National Top 30, peaking at 14 on the local Melbourne charts, and at 29 in Sydney.

The Bee Gees played another round of shows that month, starting on 4 August at the Tiles Club in London, while their final appearance was The Festival of the Flower Children, held 26-28 August at Woburn Abbey. Apart from The Bee Gees, the bill included Jimi Hendrix, Small Faces, Eric Burdon, The Jeff Beck Group, Dantalian's Chariot, Family, Al Stewart, The Alan Price Set, Marmalade, Tomorrow, Blossom Toes, The Syn, Zoot Money's Big Roll Band, Breakthru and Tintern Abbey.

Due to the overwhelming popularity of 'Holiday' on US radio, it was released there as a single in September. It peaked at number 16 – their third consecutive American top twenty hit, and a perennial fan favourite. Following its success overseas, NEMS artist Oscar – real name Paul Oscar Beuselinck – recorded 'Holiday' for UK audiences. Despite Robin Gibb providing backing vocals, Oscar's single failed to break into the British charts, where The Bee Gees' original had not been released as a single. He relaunched his career in the 1970s as Paul Nicholas, appearing in many films including *Tommy*, *The Jazz Singer* and The Bee Gees-headlined *Sgt Pepper's Lonely Hearts Club Band*. He recalled:

I'd heard the record because Robin sang it on their album. It was recorded in a studio in Portland Place I remember, and he came down and did the backing on it. I'm not sure if Barry was there, but Robin was certainly there, and I think Maurice was. Robert Stigwood was credited as producer on the single, and Bee Gees arranger Bill Shepherd was attributed for musical direction.

8 September saw the release of popular Israeli duo Esther & Abi Ofarim's cover of Barry's 'Morning Of My Life'. The single was very successful, climbing to number 2 in Germany, staying in the top 40 for over 25 weeks. The B-side – the melodic 'Garden Of My Home' – was written by all three Gibb brothers and is the only known recording of that song. Esther & Abi Ofarim's album *2 In 3* – which included 'Morning Of My Life' – became their third number one album in Germany, and it reached six on the UK chart. Both songs were obviously favourites of the husband-and-wife duo,

as they re-appeared on their *Live 1969* album. The duo are possibly best-known for their hit 'Cinderella Rockefella', released the following year.

On 13 September, The Bee Gees' new single 'Massachusetts' – one of the songs written the previous month for their upcoming sophomore set – was released to rave reviews. On the same day, the group recorded the song along with 'To Love Somebody' for the BBC radio Light Programme's *Easy Beat*. The show was aired on 24 September.

Three days earlier, they'd performed 'To Love Somebody' on the German *Beat-Club* TV show, but strangely, not the new single. Normally 30 minutes in length, this episode of the iconic show was 45 minutes long, to celebrate the introduction of colour TV in Germany, where it was also broadcast a few days later. Other artists on the special – filmed in black and white from Bremen – were Small Faces, Manfred Mann, Alan David, Twice As Much and Anita Harris. The Bee Gees were among the artists filmed in colour from the Berlin 'Funkausstellung' broadcast, which also included Cat Stevens, P. P. Arnold, Keith West, Eddie Floyd and Truly Smith.

On 22 September, British teen idol Adam Faith released the psychedelic-flavoured and oddly-titled Barry, Robin, and Maurice composition 'Cowman Milk Your Cow'. Recorded in August 1967, The Bee Gees provided backup vocals – unfortunately, that didn't help the song break into the charts and relaunch Faith's career, which was stumbling at the time. In a seven-year period up to late 1966, Faith had achieved 24 chart hits on the Parlophone label, including two number ones. Of 'Cowman Milk Your Cow', he recalled: 'The Roulettes – my backing group at the time – had heard it and thought it would make a great record. It was pure chance that it happened. I think we did hear a demo. I loved the song – it was one of those mad moments where you hear somebody, a writer, sing their own song so brilliantly, it fools you into thinking that you can achieve the same effect'.

Back in Australia, Noeleen Batley released the fourth and final song Barry wrote for her. 'The Wishing Song' was the second of the series to be issued as a single A-side. A pleasant enough ballad, it perhaps was aimed at a more adult market. Noelene, though still young at 23, was at this time something of a veteran of the pop music industry and was perhaps seeking an older audience.

Before September was over, certainly one of the oddest ever Gibb songs was released by their NEMS stablemates The Sands. With their ode to the large kitchen appliance in song – 'Mrs. Gillespie's Refrigerator'

– the Gibb brothers were some 20 years ahead of Dire Straits' mention of white goods' in their classic hit 'Money For Nothing'. While the Gibb's song is certainly not in that league, it is one of the trio's most curious compositions. Maurice recalled it in 1994, saying, 'It came from our experimental days in Australia'. Written by all three brothers, the song was re-recorded in London soon after Colin Petersen and Vince Melouney joined the group, and they also performed it live on a BBC radio program. With Robert Stigwood becoming the manager of The Sands following the death of Brian Epstein that summer, it's no great surprise that The Sands heard the song, or that the ensuing single – 'Mrs. Gillespie's Refrigerator'/'Listen To The Sky' – was released on Stigwood's own Reaction Records.

The song got another chance for fame when San-Francisco indie pop outfit The Sneetches covered it on the Bee Gees tribute collection *Melody Fair* in 1994. This was a tribute album with a difference, as most of the artists were little-known independent and alternative bands from California. Speaking of the album at the time, Maurice said, 'I was quite surprised with some of the older songs. I thought most of these songs may not have been heard in America. I mean, those songs were jam sessions. To see these songs like 'Mrs. Gillespie's Refrigerator' – Good grief!'.

On 28 September, The Bee Gees performed 'Massachusetts' on the German programme *Der Goldene Schub*, whilst in the UK, their performance of the same song was broadcast on *Top of the Pops* on the same day. It would repeat three more times in October as the single continued to build momentum.

On 30 September, the dynamics of BBC radio radically changed when Radio 1 was established. It was the successor to the BBC Light Programme, which had broadcast popular music and other entertainment since 1945. The new station Radio 1 was conceived as a direct response to the popularity of offshore pirate radio stations, which had been outlawed by an Act of parliament.

Radio 1 launched at 7:00 a.m. on Saturday, 30 September 1967, with DJ Tony Blackburn presenting. Blackburn had previously been a DJ for pirate stations Radio Caroline and Radio London. The first record played on Radio 1 was 'Flowers In The Rain' by The Move. The second was 'Massachusetts' by The Bee Gees.

On 13 October – the same day The Bee Gees guested on the popular children's television show *Crackerjack* – another unusual cover version was released. 'Like Nobody Else' was a little-known Gibb song that was covered some years before the release of their original recording. Spanish group Los Bravos recorded the song as one of the follow-ups to their big 1966 hit 'Black Is Black'. They recorded versions in English, and in Spanish as 'Como Nadie Mas'. Their recording is a more psychedelic rock cover and is somewhat better than The Bee Gees' demo.

On 15 October, The Bee Gees also appeared on the BBC radio programme *Top Gear*, performing specially recorded versions of 'Cucumber Castle', 'I Close My Eyes' and 'Mrs. Gillespie's Refrigerator'.

On 17 October – just as they prepared to release their next single 'World' – they received news that 'Massachusetts' had topped the UK singles charts: their first number 1 there. It remained in the pole position for four weeks through to 7 November. It also reached number 1 in Germany and Australia. In the US – where it was released under the extended title '(The Lights Went Out In) Massachusetts' – it was also a great success, peaking at number 11 – their biggest hit to date and their fourth consecutive top twenty single in that market.

Johnny Young released another Bee Gees track – 'Every Christian Lion Hearted Man Will Show You' – in early November before returning to Australia. Also produced by Barry and backed by The Bee Gees, the single failed to chart. However, Young's short stay in London was not wasted. House-sharing with Barry and his new girlfriend Linda Gray, Young was encouraged by Barry to compose his own songs. Over the next few years, Young would become a very successful songwriter in Australia, achieving three number 1 singles amongst other successes. All four Gibb songs that Young recorded would later appear on the compilation album *Johnny Young – The Festival Years*.

Another Bee Gees cover that would surface that month was 'The Storm': the first single by UK band Family Dogg. Their members included Albert Hammond and Steve Rowland, who would achieve great success as songwriters over the next twenty years. Hammond would also have an enduring solo career. The song is titled 'Waiting In The Storm' on some printed sheet music issues.

The following month, The Bee Gees made two more *Top of the Pops* appearances – the first on 2 November reprising 'Massachusetts', and the second on 30 November, when they performed their new single 'World'.

The Bee Gees' fifth UK single, 'World', was released on 17 November. It would become their second top ten success in Britain, reaching number 9. In Germany, it became their second number 1 single, and it also took them to the top of the charts for the first time in Holland and Switzerland.

On 19 November, The Bee Gees made a triumphant return to the Savile Theatre, where just seven months ago, as unknowns, they'd faced off a very unappreciative audience as a support act. This time, they were the headliners, supported by The Bonzo Dog Doo Dah Band and The Flower Pot Men.

On 25 November, the band again appeared on the German TV show *Beat-Club*, performing 'Massachusetts'. Other artists featured on that date were Sam and Dave, Scott McKenzie, Felice Taylor, Family Dogg, Barry Mason, The Flower Pot Men, Sharon Tandy, and Johnny Young, who sang his cover of 'Craise Finton Kirk Royal Academy Of Arts'.

As a repeat performance of 'World' was broadcast on *Top of the Pops* on 14 December, The Bee Gees were recording a Christmas Special at Liverpool's Anglican Cathedral. The special – *How On Earth* – was broadcast on ITV on Christmas Eve.

Two more Bee Gees *Top of the Pops* appearances were broadcast during December. The show's Christmas edition on 26 December featured a new rendition of 'Massachusetts', and on the regular weekly show two days later, their previous performance of 'World' was reprised. In Germany, the 30 December edition of *Beat-Club* included a repeat showing of their 'Massachusetts' clip, plus a new performance of their current hit 'World'.

Without any consultation with The Bee Gees or their management, Festival Records issued a new compilation of the group's Australian songs: *Turn Around, Look At Us*. Though not a big seller at the time, the album has since become rare, expensive and very collectable. The Gibbs weren't happy about the new release, as Barry told *New Musical Express*: 'Someone sneaked a copy of our Australian album over to the States, and they were playing things like 'Claustrophobia' over the air there. But these old discs bear so little relation to what we are doing now; it would be ridiculous for anyone to issue them'.

Turn Around, Look At Us (1967)

Australia release date: 1967

Side One: 1. 'Turn Around, Look At Me' 2. 'The Battle Of The Blue And The Grey' 3. 'The Three Kisses Of Love' 4. 'Theme From Jamie McPheeters' 5. 'Every Day I Have To Cry' 6. 'I Want Home'

Side Two: 1. 'Cherry Red' 2. 'All Of My Life' 3. 'I Am The World' 4. 'I Was A Lover, A Leader Of Men' 5. 'Wine And Women' 6. 'Peace Of Mind'

Festival Records in Australia were quick to exploit The Bee Gees' newfound international success by compiling an album of recordings that they owned the rights to. Released in late 1967, *Turn Around, Look At Us* was a worthwhile exercise in gathering up all the songs which had previously been released as singles but had not yet appeared on an album.

The tracklist was comprised of both sides of the first single: 'The Battle Of The Blue And The Grey' and 'The Three Kisses Of Love'; the three non-Gibb compositions from 1964/1965 – 'Turn Around, Look At Me', 'Theme From Jamie McPheeters' (listed on the label as 'Theme From The McPheeters') and 'Every Day I Have To Cry'; both sides of the 'I Want Home'/'Cherry Red' single, and the two Spin B-sides from 1966: 'All Of My Life' and 'I Am The World'. To bring the album up to twelve tracks and a more respectable playing time, three A-sides from the Leedon singles were added – 'Peace Of Mind', 'Wine And Women' and 'I Was A Lover, A Leader Of Men'.

While 1965's *The Bee Gees Sing And Play 14 Barry Gibb Songs* was similar in concept, it did at least include three new songs. More by luck than good judgement, it spanned the period from July 1963 to November 1965, whereas *Turn Around, Look At Us* encompasses that era and extends it at both ends from March 1963 to November 1966. With most groups, one would expect growth and progression in sound and style over a four-year period. But there are limits to what should be expected. When we speak of growth in terms of a musical act, we seldom do so in reference to their hormones. 'The Battle Of The Blue And The Grey' and 'The Three Kisses Of Love' – recorded when the twins had just turned thirteen and still had pre-pubescent high-pitched voices – sit uncomfortably next to the 1966 recordings where their voices had dropped an octave or two.

Although the album didn't trouble the chart compilers, it is significant in terms of The Bee Gees' catalogue, as their first complete compilation album – and Festival can't be blamed for trying to take advantage of the group's rising star. In fact, The Bee Gees' international labels also tried to capitalise on these recordings with the release of the three volumes of *Rare, Precious And Beautiful* in 1968-69, with much the same result in terms of commercial success.

The album artwork title styling was appropriate for the era, but the cover would have benefitted enormously from a splash of colour rather than the drab monochrome. The photograph used was from a shoot of the now-five-piece group posing around an Austin Mini, one shot of which was used on the cover of the December 1967 edition of British music magazine *Beat Instrumental*, although Colin Petersen and Vince Melouney were cropped out.

The album's front cover image was presented in its negative form, but in black and white, it severely lacks impact, bearing in mind what it was competing with in the record store racks at the time from a design perspective.

With the financial rewards of their growing success now rolling in, Barry, Robin and Robert Stigwood returned to Australia for a quick visit with their families over the Christmas holidays.

The music industry was also beginning to recognise The Bee Gees. In Holland, they received a Best Pop Stars award, while in the UK, the *New Musical Express* gave them their Best New Group award, and the Carl Alan Awards anointed them Top Musical Group. Radio Luxembourg gave them the Golden Lion Best Record award for 'Massachusetts', and in the US, *16* magazine awarded them Most Promising Group.

For these young men – still teenagers in the case of Robin and Maurice – these were exhilarating times indeed. But according to Barry, amidst all the excitement, Robert Stigwood was trying to help them maintain a level of composure: 'Robert was very good with us, he was almost like a parent. He wouldn't let us get bigheaded about it, and he would always bring us down to earth and say, 'One hit does not a career make'. He was always there to tell us that 'Two hits does not a career make', and even on our third hit, he would say 'Stay calm''.

Sadly, despite Stigwood's best efforts, their long and disciplined Australian apprenticeship, and a strong and supportive family, some tough and tragic times lay ahead for the brothers. But even greater success was ahead also – perhaps even beyond their wildest dreams.

1968

Near the close of the decade, popular music on both sides of the Atlantic was maturing and becoming more complex, and artists were diversifying their sounds and seeking new ways to express themselves as their work reflected the wildly changing world surrounding them. 1968 in particular, was a year mired in global social unrest. International political conflicts – especially the Vietnam War and the Cold War – spurred agitation in cities around the planet, where some took to the streets to protest racism, sexism, authoritarianism and capitalism, amongst other issues.

Pop music had had a broadly uniform sound for at least the first half of the 1960s, but that was no longer. The Beatles – who had built their empire on the simple beat music of songs like 'I Want To Hold Your Hand' and 'She Loves You' – moved on to more intricate tracks like the ones that comprised the *Sgt. Pepper's Lonely Hearts Club Band* and *Abbey Road* albums.

1968 would be a year of tremendous change on many fronts for The Bee Gees, too, when they'd achieve new career heights and a few startling setbacks.

Considering the band were virtual unknowns until 'New York Mining Disaster 1941' broke through in April 1967, their trajectory over that year and into late 1968 was quite incredible. *Bee Gees' 1st* firmly established them as consistent hitmakers in the US and the UK with top ten appearances in both country's album charts, and they'd scored their first number one single on British soil with 'Massachusetts' – a remarkable achievement for a band who'd started off the year nearly penniless and without any prospect of a recording contract.

Wasting little time capitalising on the momentum, The Bee Gees wrote and recorded furiously, ultimately resulting in the release of two original full-length albums in 1968: *Horizontal* in February and *Idea* in September.

The recording of *Horizontal* began in July 1967, a mere three days after *Bee Gees' 1st* landed in UK retail stores. The sessions would extend over five months – from 17 July to 29 November – a relative eternity compared to the short seven weeks they spent making their debut.

In January, they released the classic ballad 'Words' as a stand-alone single. It peaked at 15 in the US and became their fifth consecutive top twenty hit there. It earned them their first Canadian number one hit, and reached the pole position in Germany, the Netherlands and Switzerland. 'Words' was also their third top ten UK single in a row, reaching number 8.

Whilst covering Bee Gees/Gibb brothers' songs would successfully launch and/or compliment many artists' careers, in the case of Decca band The Majority, it was their final grasp for success. The Majority – who had been performing since 1965 – covered a new Gibb brothers song, 'All Our Christmases', and also performed it in the 1967 film *The Mini-Affair*. The film's director Robert Amram recalled that Robert Stigwood asked him to include The Majority in the film as part of the deal that got Amram another Bee Gees song, 'Words', which was performed by Georgie Fame, the star of the film. Released on 12 January, this was The Majority's final single, and they split up shortly after it failed to break into the charts. The Bee Gees own recording of 'All Our Christmases' from 1967 was finally released in 2006 on *The Studio Albums 1967-1968* box set.

They were finally able to see their receptive American fans in person with their first-ever gig on US soil, at the Anaheim Convention Center in Orange County, California, on 27 January. During their Stateside visit, they also taped performances on three high-profile television shows, which would be broadcast over the next few months.

Early February saw the arrival of *Horizontal*: The Bee Gees' second international album. Like its predecessor, the set was anchored by a strong batch of eclectic compositions – many of which – like 'Massachusetts', 'World' and 'And The Sun Will Shine' – would become stalwarts of the Gibbs' catalogue and remain permanently fixed in their live sets. The album landed at numbers 12 and 16 on the US and UK charts, respectively. In Germany, it became their first chart-topping entry. 'Bee Gee-mania' was quickly usurping the stronghold of Beatlemania in that market, with the brothers claiming the country's 1968 *Bravo* magazine Golden Otto award – which recognises achievements in film, television and music. The fab four settled for silver, while The Monkees received the bronze prize.

Horizontal (1968)

Personnel:
Barry Gibb: vocals, guitar
Robin Gibb: vocals, organ
Maurice Gibb: vocals, bass, Mellotron, piano
Vince Melouney: guitar
Colin Petersen: drums
Additional personnel:
Orchestral arrangements: Bill Shepherd

Engineers: John Pantry, Mike Claydon and Damon Lyon-Shaw
Producers: Robert Stigwoodand The Bee Gees
Recorded between 17 July and 29 November 1967 at Central Sound, Chappell, and IBC Studios, London
Release dates: UK and US: February 1968
Chart positions: West Germany: 1, France: 2, Norway: 7, Australia: 8, US: 12, UK: 16

Confident and excited after achieving widespread success with *Bee Gees' 1st*, the Gibbs were soon back in the studio working on its follow-up. Prodigious writers that they had always been, Barry, Robin, and Maurice were actively writing for their next project before *1st* had even been released. 'Harry Braff', at least, appears to have been written around the same time as 'To Love Somebody', 'Holiday' and 'Every Christian Lion Hearted Man Will Show You', but there may have been others in the works.

Horizontal is a strong album that seems to have withstood the rigours of time better than many Bee Gees albums. It saw their sound develop from what was sometimes quite simple and raw on *Bee Gees' 1st* into a more mature, refined, but somewhat darker style. With its rich mix of definitive Bee Gees ballads and heavy guitar-oriented rock, *Horizontal* makes for an interesting listen.

Much like *1st*, *Horizontal* must be revisited with the clear understanding that it was created in an era when artists were navigating a quickly-shifting and fiercely competitive musical landscape; chasing psychedelic hipness while still being careful not to abandon their already well-established pop sensibilities and instincts. Fortunately, The Bee Gees didn't abandon their penchant for melody and harmony, but *Horizontal* – like its late-1960s counterparts – took the Gibbs down some strange paths: many of them wonderfully weird.

Horizontal's two hits – 'Massachusetts' and 'World' – didn't really showcase the group at their best or define the album. Certainly, they were good commercial pop, and it was probably sensible from a marketing perspective to stick with a formula that sold records. However, there were less obvious single choices on the album that were better songs. The songs frequently singled out for having odd lyrics – 'Lemons Never Forget', 'Birdie Told Me', 'The Earnest Of Being George' and 'Horizontal' – may have made perfect sense to someone dabbling in sundry illicit substances of the day (including the songwriters themselves). But since the Gibb's musical abilities continued to improve, the tunes are better remembered than the verbiage anyway.

On release, *Horizontal* got a mixed response from the band's growing number of followers, but the critics loved it; though it would be the last Bee Gees album for some time that wouldn't be criticised for being *lightweight*. Although not as big a hit as their previous album, *Horizontal* was still a global success, cementing The Bee Gees' reputation as chart movers with tremendously broad appeal.

It's evident that Vince Melouney influenced the album's underlying blues-rock sound, but seemingly with the support of the other guitarists: Maurice and Barry. Melouney recalled, 'We started to experiment, on *Horizontal*, away from everything they'd previously done. Not that there was anything wrong with what they'd previously done: it was terrific. They just started to experiment more with sounds and arrangements'.

Certainly, Barry's versatile tenor voice lent itself well to singing a good rock lead vocal. But heavy rock and blues was never Robin's preference. So did this cause some dissension among the group? Robin had only two lead vocals on this album, while Barry had five, but the two did share lead vocals on five other songs, including the two hit singles. While it wasn't uncommon for The Bee Gees to feature a rockier number or two on future albums, they would never again return to the darker mood that at least half of this album offers.

The production team retained John Pantry and Damon Lyon-Shaw as engineers, adding Mike Claydon for good measure. Ossie Byrne and Phillip Wade – who helped guide the *Bee Gees' 1st* sessions – were not involved in *Horizontal*. Bill Shepherd, exclusively, took care of all the orchestral accompaniments, which became as much a trademark of the early Bee Gees sound as their harmonies. Robert Stigwood acted as executive producer, meaning that he was responsible for business decisions and organising studio time, as opposed to actually producing the music.

The band themselves – including Vince and Colin – were highly involved in the production. Vince recalled: 'It was a band effort. We all felt that we were a part of one thing; we'd just try different things. It wasn't like it was the Gibb brothers, Colin and me. We were all in The Bee Gees together'. Barry confirmed, '*Horizontal* is more of us doing what we wanted to do. The first album was like trying to make a band out of us. The second album was more of us wanting our own way, wanting to experiment'.

In 2006, Reprise Records reissued *Horizontal* as part of the *Studio Albums 1967-1968* release. The box set included both the album mono and stereo mixes on one disc, and previously unreleased songs, non-album tracks and alternate takes on the second.

The album cover was a far more staid affair than the colourfully surreal art developed for *Bee Gees' 1st*. Paragon Publicity – a London company that'd already worked for The Who, Cream, and Julie Driscoll, Brian Auger and The Trinity were tasked with the design.

The group photograph – taken at Robert Stigwood's house at 16 Adams Row in Mayfair, London – is set within an oval frame on a background of what can best be described as the colour of French mustard. The typeface used on the UK edition is a bold and curvaceous display-font style. The back cover uses the graphic from the rear of the US edition of *Bee Gees' 1st,* with song titles in another whimsical typeface with swirly embellishments.

The US edition front cover features a slightly different photograph from the same photo session, but this time as a genuine reflection in a gilt-framed mirror on a wood-panelled wall. The back cover is a poorly lit group photo taken on a railway freight wagon with cranes in the background. The entire group wear the same outfits for both photographs, so it's assumed they were taken on the same day.

South Africa issued the album with the UK design but replaced the murky brown cover with plain white, with the group name and album title in black. Japan released the album in May 1968 as *Massachusetts*, featuring a photograph from a TV show performance, while Italy offered an awesomely wild psychedelic alternate sleeve – mimicking the style of *Bee Gees' 1st* – with the band suitably attired.

'World' (Barry Gibb, Robin Gibb, Maurice Gibb)

Recorded at IBC Studios, London: 3 October 1967
Chart positions: West Germany: 1, Netherlands: 1, Singapore: 1, New Zealand: 2, Switzerland: 2, Belgium: 3, Sweden: 3, Denmark: 4, Austria: 5, Australia: 6, Norway: 6, UK: 9, Italy: 10, Spain: 10, France: 20, Japan: 24

Taking off from where Hamlet wondered whether 'To be, or not to be', this song's lyric is patently existential. Though that's where the Shakespeare comparison ends, as here the Gibb brothers conclude that 'Now I found that the world is round/And of course it rains every day'.

Barry explained the lyric's simplicity: 'What we are saying is that you can't live in your own little world, because somewhere there's trouble, rain, and you must face up to it. It may be sun, flowers and beauty in England today, but it's rain and misery somewhere else. It's always raining somewhere in the world for somebody'.

The song features Maurice's bold compressed piano introduction, Robin playing a spacey organ, and wailing guitar licks verging on the edge of distortion from Vince, who commented, 'I had this idea to play the melody right up in the top register of the guitar behind the chorus'. It also showcases some unusually powerful drumming from Colin, and heartfelt vocals by Barry and Robin. It's a classic late-1960s Bee Gees song.

Maurice had 'vivid memories of Robin's great performance on the organ, and me playing a very compressed piano, which we also used on 'Words'. A big thank you to Mike Claydon, our engineer, for helping us in the making of this little epic'.

'World' was written in the studio, and was originally planned as a band-only arrangement with no orchestra, but it was deemed worthy of some embellishment. This late decision caused a few studio issues, as the group had recorded the song using all four tracks available to them. To save the day, these four tracks were then mixed down to one track, and the orchestra was added to the mix.

The song remained in the group's concert setlist throughout their career, albeit as part of a medley of older material, from 1975 onwards.

The promotional film for 'World' began dramatically with the launch of NASA's unmanned Apollo 4 space flight on 9 November 1967 – which occurred just a week before the single release on 16 November. Further space footage shows Buzz Aldrin's space walk from Gemini 12 on 13 November 1966, with Earth in the distance. The group footage features the five Bee Gees standing in a circle with the camera in the middle, spinning from one to the next.

'And The Sun Will Shine' (Barry Gibb, Robin Gibb, Maurice Gibb)

Recorded at Central Sound Recording Studio, London: 17 July 1967; Chappell Recording Studio, London: 30 July and 1 August 1967
Chart position: France: 66

With a beautiful melody, lush orchestration by Bill Shepherd and a great lead vocal from Robin, this is a fine example of what The Bee Gees were about at that time. Robin remembers the song as being 'written, sung and recorded in a seedy, little-known, broken-down old studio off Denmark Street in London. This track, believe it or not, was put down and sung purely ad-lib – one of the many cases where the demo actually became the finished recording. The raw intensity of the original pilot vocal proved to be more moving than anything we could achieve on the finished product. Not only that, it was cheaper!'.

The studio Robin referred to was Central Sound Recording Studio – a small demo studio suite located on the first floor above the shops at 9 Denmark Street in London's West End – which was used for the first session. Two further sessions took place at the Chappell Studio, located within the Chappell music store at 50 New Bond Street, London.

'And The Sun Will Shine' was always a fan favourite, and was regularly performed in concert until 1974. It returned to the set for the *One Night Only* concerts in the late-1990s. 'That's one of my favourites too', Robin said: 'It was a very emotional song, but a lot of the words just came ad-libbed. The song actually wasn't planned. We just played the record down and sang it as we felt it. We kept the original demo the way it was and just added the orchestra. It's got a great feeling to it, a great atmosphere – sometimes you know you can't recapture that feeling if you keep recording something'.

Former Manfred Mann frontman Paul Jones released his version of the song as the B-side of his 1968 single 'The Dog Presides'. It's highly collectable due to a stellar cast of backing musicians, including Jeff Beck on guitar, Paul Samwell-Smith of The Yardbirds on bass, noted session musician Nicky Hopkins on keyboards, and none other than Paul McCartney playing the drums. The track was produced by Peter Asher, formerly of the pop duo Peter and Gordon, and brother of McCartney's then-girlfriend, actress Jane Asher.

Puerto Rican singer Jose Feliciano also released the song as a single, achieving moderate success, peaking at number 25 in the UK in August 1969. Other versions include those by P. J. Proby, and actor Joe Pesci in a previous incarnation when he was known as Little Joe.

The Bee Gees' recording was also released as a single, but only in France. Despite its popularity, its peak position there was a disappointing 66.

'Lemons Never Forget' (Barry Gibb, Robin Gibb, Maurice Gibb)
Recorded at IBC Studios, London: 4 September 1967

Barry recalls that the odd title was a bit of a send-up of Apple Records. 'It was all over the industry that Apple was in disarray and that The Beatles were breaking up. So, it was a bit of a play-off on that situation'.

A very different Bee Gees song to anything they'd crafted to date, Robin thought it one of his elder brother's 'supreme rock songs. When Barry gets into that rock mode, he's unique and very original. He's got a great sound'.

'Lemons Never Forget' – the album's first true psychedelic outing – is one of the band's most atmospheric and unsettling recordings. It is but one of four heavier rock tracks on *Horizontal*. Coming across as almost a live recording, it showcases Vince Melouney's lead guitar and Maurice Gibb's robust compressed piano. Barry's lead vocals are markedly harder and edgier than previously heard.

'Really And Sincerely' (Barry Gibb, Robin Gibb, Maurice Gibb)

Recorded at IBC Studios, London: 29 November 1967

On Sunday, 5 November 1967, the busy 19:43 Hastings to Charing Cross train service derailed between Hither Green and Grove Park railway stations. Of the twelve coaches – many full of standing passengers – eleven were derailed, and four of those turned onto their sides, resulting in 49 fatalities and 78 injuries. Robin Gibb and his girlfriend, Molly Hullis, were among the passengers: 'What I didn't realise was the engine had just become uncoupled. Then the carriage rolled over, and big stretches of railway line came crashing in straight past my face' he told reporter Camilla Beach the following day. 'Suddenly, it felt as if we were going over great boulders. Rocks were hitting the side of the compartment. Molly and I held on to each other as the train turned over and over, still going forward along the line. It almost seemed as if the train was going to pieces around us. One minute we were in the luggage rack, the next, we were on the floor. The train finally came to a halt on its side, 1,400 yards from where it had come off the rails'.

'Really And Sincerely' was Robin's response to his involvement in the crash, explaining that 'It was written on a piano accordion that I bought in Paris'. He later told Nick Logan of the *New Musical Express*, 'I was told to spend three days in bed, but that is the worst thing you can do. You should get straight back into reality. I wrote the song on the first day and recorded it on the second. It doesn't mention the train crash, but it does reflect the mood I was in'.

The first recording was actually made on 28 November, with piano as the main instrument. This can be heard as a bonus track on the second *Horizontal* disc included in the 2006 *The Studio Albums 1967-1968* box set. The second and final version was recorded the next day, substituting piano for the original piano accordion, which gives the song a far more melancholy feel.

It's another classic Robin Gibb vocal performance – poignant and emotional, showcasing his unique voice. Robin said the song was about his relationship with Molly at the time, 'So it had a personal tone to it. We nearly got killed …'.

'Birdie Told Me' (Barry Gibb, Robin Gibb, Maurice Gibb)
Recorded at Chappell Recording Studio, London: 30 July 1967

There are two theories regarding 'Birdie Told Me'. The first is that it relates to the old-fashioned expression 'a little bird told me' or 'a little birdie told me' – the origins of which emanate from the biblical verse Ecclesiastes 10:20: 'Do not revile the king even in your thoughts, or curse the rich in your bedroom, because a bird in the sky may carry your words, and a bird on the wing may report what you say'. The second is that 'Birdie' was a woman, although, at the time the song was written, it was not a very common name. It was at the height of its popularity around the turn of the 20th century but was used less and less until around 1950, when it essentially disappeared.

It may simply be an employment of the then-in-vogue colloquial slang term 'bird' – describing a woman – but that's speculation. Barry has never revealed who or what 'Birdie' is.

Robin remembers, 'The original idea that Barry had for 'Birdie Told Me' came at Chappell Recording Studio, which is the original Chappell Music (Publishers' office), but they had a studio upstairs. We used to alternate between there and the IBC Studios in Portland Place, which was just opposite the BBC'.

Barry recalled the song simply as 'something I think I brought in, really about love on the rebound. Obviously, the person has lost the one he loves, and she's telling him it's going to be alright'. Barry, who sang the lead vocal, remembers it rather unpretentiously, as 'a pretty song'.

With a pleasant but subtle lead guitar break on the first-verse repeat, and fine orchestration by Bill Shepherd, Robin thought it had a 'flavour of the late-Sixties in it – that's the kind of song you would hear from a film of the time. I really love the chorus; it's a very poignant song'.

It's the shortest song on *Horizontal* but one of the more melodious tracks on an otherwise heavy-sounding album.

'With The Sun In My Eyes' (Barry Gibb, Robin Gibb, Maurice Gibb)
Recorded at IBC Studios, London: 3 October 1967

Sparse but beautifully arranged, Barry again takes the lead vocal on this pretty, but melancholic, track which closes side one. With songs like this containing a solo vocal without contributions from the others, it's difficult not to class them as Barry songs or Robin songs, which tends to obscure their input on each other's tunes, and also Maurice's instrumental contributions generally. In much the same way as Beatles songs were always credited to Lennon/McCartney no matter who wrote them, all the *Horizontal* songwriting credits – plus those for the two following albums *Idea* and *Odessa* – are assigned to all three Gibb Brothers.

Barry once said that this was a love song to his wife Linda, and cited it as one of his favourites, surprising and delighting the hardcore element of the audiences on his solo *Mythology* tour in 2013/2014. He also included an outstanding new version as a bonus track on his 2021 album *Greenfields*, with the arrangement taking it to heights never before imagined. It is truly the record's *goosebumps* moment.

'Massachusetts' (Barry Gibb, Robin Gibb, Maurice Gibb)
Recorded at IBC Studios: 9 August 1967
Chart positions: Austria: 1, Belgium: 1, West Germany: 1, Japan: 1, Netherlands: 1, New Zealand: 1, Norway: 1, South Africa: 1, Sweden: 1, United Kingdom: 1, Australia: 2, Canada: 2, Denmark: 2, Ireland: 2, Switzerland: 2; France: 4, Italy: 5, US: 11

One of the most iconic Bee Gees songs of all, and a staple of their live performances throughout their career, 'Massachusetts' was also their first number 1 hit in important territories including the UK and Germany, and their highest charting single in the US up to that point, peaking at number 11.

The song was written at the St. Regis Hotel in New York City during The Bee Gees' first promotional visit to America. Barry explained, 'It's basically anti-flower-power – 'Don't go to San Francisco, come home'. We wanted to write the opposite of what it's like to lose somebody who went to San Francisco. The lights all went out in Massachusetts because everybody went to San Francisco because they left'.

Robin remembered, 'We worked out the basic melody in about five minutes when we were in New York'. Maurice added, 'Robin and I began, then Barry started throwing in ideas. I'm not quite sure why we thought of Massachusetts in the first place because we weren't even sure how to spell it!'. Indeed, when they wrote the song, The Bee Gees had never actually been to the state of Massachusetts some 200 miles northwest of New York – they just liked the sound of the name.

Maurice never forgot the thrill of being told they'd just reached number one on the British charts for the first time:

The Bee Gees were standing on a revolving stage, waiting to perform. The Merseybeats were performing, and Dick Ashby, who was our road manager at that time, came rushing up just as the stage was about to turn around, and said "Massachusetts' just went to number one!'. We were so high from that news because that was the first number 1 we had in England. All that time we were in Australia, dreaming of that; it was such a kick for us that I couldn't stop crying. We did the lousiest show you ever saw; we were so excited. That moment of being told – that stands out like it was this morning.

Some earlier pressings of the single incorporated a subtitle, which, depending on the country of release, either read '(The Lights Went Out In) Massachusetts' or 'Massachusetts (The Lights Went Out In)'. Presumably, this was to help make the single more easily identifiable for DJs and record buyers; but how could one mistake a title like 'Massachusetts' for anything else? The extraneous text was dropped for later pressings.

According to legend, the song was originally offered to the Australian group The Seekers, who rejected it because of the somewhat typical abstract Gibb lyrics. 36 years later, in 2003, The Seekers finally recorded the song as a tribute to Maurice following his death earlier that year.

'Harry Braff' (Barry Gibb, Robin Gibb, Maurice Gibb)
Recorded at Chappell Recording Studio, London: 30 July 1967

There was possibly some fraternal tongue-in-cheek humour here, as 'braff' is – or was – according to the brothers, allegedly an Australian slang expression for 'fart'.

'Harry Braff' – or 'Chequered Flag' as it was originally known – was first recorded as far back as 21 April 1967. That early version appears on the *Bee Gees 1st* bonus disc included in the *Studio Albums 1967-68* box set. It was written – according to the brothers' memories – during a very drunken night at the house of Roland Rennie: then president of Polydor Records in England. Barry said the group 'spent the whole day and night at this guy's house, and he was legless. And we were all legless by the end of the night. 'Harry Braff' came from that. In the middle of the night, coming back from this guy's house, we went and woke Robert (Stigwood) up in London at his flat, and got him out of bed at 3 a.m. In The Morning so we could sing him this song! It's amazing how young and enthusiastic you can be!'.

Easily the album's most vociferous song, 'Harry Braff', has a storyline about a racing driver that's evocative of The Beatles or The Kinks. The track is stereotypical of 1960s Britain. Whether there was talk on that drunken evening about the Gibbs' early days singing between races at Australia's Redcliffe Speedway will never be known, but the line 'The mayor of Gordon cheers him on' could also be a reference to the suburb of Gordon on Sydney's Upper North Shore.

All three brothers sang the song in unison, though Robin takes the verses – but this is brief respite from a full-on band performance that changes pace several times, each movement building to a crescendo. The finale sees a sole trumpet introduced into the mix, forcefully blowing fanfares at Harry's victory.

'Day Time Girl' (Barry Gibb, Robin Gibb, Maurice Gibb)
Recorded at Central Sound Recording Studio, London: 17 July 1967; Chappell Recording Studio, London: 30 July 1967

A very underrated ballad, 'Day Time Girl', sees Barry and Robin sharing the lead vocal – both solo and in unison, so intricately that at times, one starts s line and the other finishes. With voices so radically different to each other, this technique would seem to be impossible to carry off, but somehow their sibling timbres meld seamlessly to make this effective.

Once again, whilst *Horizontal* adopted a somewhat heavier sound, this light and melodic track offered a reprieve. Maurice contributes a conservatory-like piano, bass, and to some ears, possibly a lead vocal at times. The string arrangement makes this a prime piece of baroque pop.

'The Earnest Of Being George' (Barry Gibb, Robin Gibb, Maurice Gibb)
Recorded at IBC Studios, London: 7 September 1967

Featuring a strong Barry lead vocal with tricky dead-stops and carefully-timed silences, 'The Earnest Of Being George' had the bizarre original working title of 'Granny's Mr. Dog'. With its blues/rock feel, one senses that lead guitarist Vince Melouney was in his element.

The title – which doesn't appear in the lyric – could be a tip of the hat to *The Importance of Being Earnest* by Irish poet and playwright Oscar Wilde, whose name Robin would summon on more than one occasion during interviews. While sometimes criticised for inscrutable lyrics, Barry was the first to admit the song was 'in the realm of just being as abstract as possible; going for the musical adventure rather than having a meaning to the song, because I don't think there is one'. Robin, however, disagreed on this point, explaining, 'It's about a guy that's being used – 'You bought my love and I paid' – the usual story where he's been trampled on'.

Noel Gallagher of the band Oasis has long cited *Horizontal* as one of his all-time favourite and influential albums. In 2005, he wrote a song called 'The Importance Of Being Idle', which topped the UK charts that summer. Although Gallagher says that it sounds like songs from two British bands – The Kinks and The La's – the title must surely be a veiled homage to The Bee Gees.

'The Change Is Made' (Barry Gibb, Robin Gibb, Maurice Gibb)
Recorded at IBC Studios, London: 29 November 1967
Another strong blues/rock track, 'The Change Is Made' gives Barry a chance to experiment, with a pleading, impassioned vocal. It's one of his finest performances of the time. Vince Melouney gets a rare opportunity to showcase how he could make an electric guitar wail. Though the song fades out at the end, one senses that the original recording could have descended into an elongated blues jam.

It was probably the album's weightiest track and a reminder to those critics who would pigeonhole the Gibb brothers as ballad singers, that they could also cut it as a legitimately hard-edged rock band when they wanted to.

'Horizontal' (Barry Gibb, Robin Gibb, Maurice Gibb)
Recorded at IBC Studios, London: 4 September 1967
The title track and closing song sums up the album's moody soundscape. Maurice leads the track with pounding piano chords, while Barry takes the lead vocal in the main parts of the verse. Robin laments, 'This is the start of the end' in the latter portions. Maurice adds some glorious Mellotron to the mix before an almost cacophonous melange of wordless psychedelic vocals envelops the listener in the middle section. Eventually, the song cuts out, leaving a solitary Mellotron note before resuming the verses before the fade. It's a truly satisfying conclusion to the album.

In 2006, Robin remembered it as 'an interesting track, because it's mysterious and can't really be classified as any kind of style except probably psychedelic. He concluded by saying, 'It does have a strong message somewhere in there. I just love the atmosphere of the whole song'.

Horizontal – 2006 edition bonus songs

'Out Of Line' (Barry Gibb, Robin Gibb, Maurice Gibb)
Recorded at IBC Studios, London: November 1967

Beginning with a bit of slick guitar-noodling from Vince, 'Out Of Line' is quite a powerful song melodically speaking, and the verses feature an unusual amount of harmony singing. The outro, however, is weaker, with half a minute of the Gibbs merely repeating the phrase 'we say yes' over and over to a fade.

While the track does have a couple of neat little hooks, it would not have sat comfortably within the context of the album as it developed. It's easy to see how it was passed over in favour of other, stronger songs, which also because of their mood, were better-suited.

'Ring My Bell' (Barry Gibb, Robin Gibb, Maurice Gibb)
Recorded at Chappell Recording Studio, London: 30 July 1967, 1 August 1967 and probably other dates.

Opening with a gentle piano introduction, 'Ring My Bell' sees Barry taking the lead vocal on the verses, all three brothers in harmony on the choruses, and Robin solo on the bridge.

As with 'Out Of Line', its shortcoming is once again in the repetition – this time in the chorus. The fact that the song was worked on over at least two days implies that its lyrical form was complete, but a better effort than 'Ring my bell if you want me to' repeated four times as a chorus was required. Even in the days of abstract lyrics, contextually, these make less sense than most.

The outro becomes even more tedious, with two choruses – thankfully separated by a drum break – one after the other, and more again, still audible as it fades out.

New life was breathed into 'Ring My Bell' when San Francisco duo Strangers In A Strange Land collaborated with former Bee Gee Vince Melouney. Released on digital platforms on 29 January 2021 via the UK label Ace Records, it features a stellar cast of Strangers members Paul Kopf on vocals and Alec Palao on bass, piano and organ, with Vince contributing his distinctive lead guitar. Joining them are Blondie's Clem Burke on drums and Jonathan Lea of The Jigsaw Seen, adding guitar and

Mellotron. Adding his production skills, giving the song a wonderfully fresh but still retro feel, is legendary producer Shel Talmy, who revealed, 'After the session, all of us reconvened at a local North Hollywood restaurant, and so I got the opportunity to tell Vince that back in 1967, I had tried hard to sign The Bee Gees for my Planet label when they arrived in the UK from Australia. I lost out to Robert Stigwood, who was another Australian with a gift of gab!'.

'Barker Of The U.F.O.' (Barry Gibb)
Recorded at Chappell Recording Studio, London: 30 July 1967, 1 August 1967 and other dates.

This was originally released as the B-side of the 'Massachusetts' single, except in the US, where 'Sir Geoffrey Saved The World' was used instead. It's a very short and quirky song, revealing Barry's lifelong fascination with U.F.O.s. 'I'm sort of a U.F.O. freak', he admitted. 'It's easy to write because I loved the subject so much. It started when I was really young and just continued. I guess that's where that came from. That's one of my favourites'.

The accompaniment is an unusual combination of instruments: tuba, xylophone, cello and drums – but it was Barry's idea to record the cymbals but play them backwards, which became the song's trademark. As Robin recalled, 'That was the first time we did backward tapes. Again, it was a great idea that Barry had about reversing the tapes. He came up with the whole idea of 'Barker Of The U.F.O.', and I thought it was really cool'.

Maurice was in agreement, saying they always had 'experimentation in mind; this was a fun time. The memories of this session will always be remembered. I loved the tuba and reverse cymbal effect'.

'Words' (Barry Gibb, Robin Gibb, Maurice Gibb)
Recorded at IBC Studios, London: 3 October 1967
Chart positions: Canada: 1, Netherlands: 1, Switzerland: 1, West Germany: 1, Belgium: 3. Austria: 4, South Africa: 5, Norway: 7, UK: 8, New Zealand: 9, Italy: 11, Australia: 13, Ireland: 14, Spain: 15, US: 15, Chile: 19, Japan: 19

Barry affectionately recalls that 'Words' 'came about at the Adams Row, London home of Robert Stigwood. Robert had the gift of bringing out the very best in any artist and I feel that this particular song justified his faith in us'.

Robin said that 'Words' 'was written after an argument: 'Barry had been arguing with someone, I had been arguing with someone, and happened to be in the same mood. (The arguments were) about absolutely nothing.

They were just words – that is what the song is all about; words can make you happy, or words can make you sad'.

Barry remembers the first recording session clearly: 'Robin and I were in the studios at nine o'clock in the morning and Robin kept on falling asleep over the piano. I wanted him to write the piano part of the song and play it because I'm not much of a pianist, but he just couldn't keep his eyes open, so I ended up doing it myself'.

The song was used to launch a new piano sound, as Maurice explained:

We accidentally discovered the sound on 'Words'. When we were recording, after everyone had gone to lunch, I was sitting at the piano mucking about and I wrote a riff. I went upstairs and switched on the mic for the piano, and then I started playing about with the knobs in front of me. When I played the tape back, I had all these incredible compressed piano noises. Mike Claydon at IBC Studios, who engineered all our records, then said 'What the hell was that?' when he heard the piano sound. 'Come up here and listen to that sound'. It was just compression, but he didn't know what to call it then. I think he called it 'limited'. It made the piano sound like it was about 40 pianos playing at the same time and very, very thick. In 'Words', it was very beautiful, but that sound on it made it sound like the L.A. Symphony on it. If you listen to all our records, the piano sound is on it.

Issued as a single in January 1968, neither 'Words' nor its very fine B-side 'Sinking Ships' were on the *Horizontal* album, which was released in February. Years later, Barry said, 'I didn't know it wasn't on an album – that's strange how it used to work in those days. We used to bang singles out one after another'. The song's first appearance on a Bee Gees album was on 1969's *Best Of Bee Gees*.

The label on some US and UK single pressings bore the notation 'from the film *The Mini-Mob*', which intrigued fans at the time and for many years later. It was a movie directed by Robert Amran, starring British pop star Georgie Fame, but which had its title changed to *The Mini-Affair*, which would have initially made it difficult to find based on the single label note alone. Ultimately, the film never saw a general release. The Bee Gees' version of 'Words' was never actually used in the movie – included instead was a cover performed by Georgie Fame in a scene where he was walking through a garden. An instrumental take was also incorporated. Both of those iterations were arranged by long-time Bee Gees musical director Bill Shepherd. Georgie Fame's version was issued as an extremely rare, limited promo single on the Lyntone label.

Now considered a classic Bee Gees song, 'Words' topped the charts in several countries, and made the top ten in the UK and many other territories. In the US – where it peaked at 15 – it was their fifth consecutive top twenty hit.

In a vast catalogue of Bee Gees songs, 'Words' is one of the most popular, with well over 300 cover versions in existence. The calibre artists who have covered it is quite extraordinary – including, amongst many others: Lynn Anderson, Acker Bilk, Cilla Black, Glen Campbell, Donna Fargo, Engelbert Humperdinck, Brenda Lee, The Lettermen, Barbara Mandrell, Al Martino, Roy Orbison, Patti Page, Sandie Shaw, LabiSiffre and Terry Wogan.

Cliff Richard also recorded the song, claiming Barry told him years later that 'Words' was written with him in mind. Elvis Presley performed the song in his late-1960s concerts, and included it on his live 1969 album *Elvis In Person At The International Hotel*. American singer Rita Coolidge had a UK top 30 hit with it in 1978.

In 1993, The Bee Gees made a guest appearance on Brazilian duo Chitãozinho & Xororó's Portuguese version of 'Words' – titled 'Palavras' – on their album *Tudo Por Amor*. The two brothers who made up the duo – José De Lima Sobrinho and Durval De Lima – went under the stage name José & Durval in other Spanish-speaking South American countries. The song's Spanish version – again with The Bee Gees on backing vocals – was titled 'Palabras'.

Irish boy band Boyzone enjoyed their first number 1 with the song in 1996. On 29 August 1998, their lead singer Ronan Keating joined The Bee Gees on stage as a special guest to perform the song with them at their *One Night Only* concert at Dublin's RDS Arena. Two weeks later, Boyzone appeared with them on the acclaimed *An Audience With The Bee Gees* television special. Keating recorded the song solo for his 2004 compilation album *10 Years Of Hits*. In an interview on *BBC Breakfast* on 12 December 2020, Barry remarked that Boyzone's cover was his favourite.

Dolly Parton chose 'Words' when she was asked to join Barry for a duet on his best-selling album *Greenfields*. While the pairing is pleasant to listen to, it certainly wasn't the country or bluegrass version that was expected.

On a December 2011 UK TV special titled *The Nation's Favourite Bee Gees Song*, the public voted 'Words' as the fourth most popular.

'Sir Geoffrey Saved The World' (Barry Gibb, Robin Gibb, Maurice Gibb)

Recorded at IBC Studios, London: 9 August 1967

This began life as a demo titled 'You Know How You Gave Yourself Away', the entire backing track being retained for the finished version. Only the lyric hook line was changed to make it a song about the British government's Clean Air Act.

It's a buoyant little number, similar in a way to The Beatles' 'Penny Lane' – Maurice acknowledged it as such when he divulged that it was 'one of my favourite bass lines and obvious Beatles influence here; but what the hell, they were great songwriters and we loved what they did'.

The song appeared as the B-side of 'World' in most countries, though in the US and Canada, it was the B-side of 'Massachusetts'. The French picture sleeve for the 'World' single gave prominence to a man in a suit of armour holding a large sword with the B-side song title on his shield, somewhat deceptively implying that it was the A-side when it wasn't. However, The Bee Gees did perform the song on television during a promotional trip to France.

The song has been covered a few times by the likes of The Big Deals and The Typhoons, but most notably in French as 'Sir Geoffrey La Saveur' by F. R. David.

Though not a cover version, the East German band Puhdys recorded a song called 'Wenn Ein Mensch Lebt' in 1973. Whilst immediate comparisons would be to 'Spicks And Specks', the verse melody is highly reminiscent of 'Sir Geoffrey Saved The World'.

'Sinking Ships' (Barry Gibb, Robin Gibb, Maurice Gibb)

Recorded at IBC Studios, London: 7 November 1967 and other dates
Released as a single B-side to 'Words', January 1968

Reported in the press at the time as a likely single release, 'Sinking Ships' was ultimately used as the B-side of 'Words'. The title implies another song of doom and gloom, but only verse one refers to sinking ships and crashing planes. The first lines use the literary technique of alliteration, where the initial consonant sounds repeat in multiple words: 'Sinking ships, watching them sail and the sun as it sinks in the sea'.

An instrumental version turned up on the Robert Stigwood Orchestra's *Bee Gees Hits* album, and as Maurice recalled, 'Bill Shepherd – our arranger and master of the orchestra in the late-Sixties and early-Seventies – once said to me, 'Let's build it beautifully', and he did'.

The melody of The Nocturnes' single 'Look at Me' – released in July 1968 on the Columbia label – is uncannily similar to 'Sinking Ships'.

'Mrs. Gillespie's Refrigerator' (Barry Gibb, Robin Gibb)
Recorded in late-1966 or early-1967: location unknown

Recording details are sketchy for this track, and could even date as far back as a late-1966 Australian session. It's believed to be one of the songs sent on acetate to Brian Epstein at NEMS, prior to The Bee Gees' return to England.

It's another humorous track The Bee Gees would mix into their more serious material – this one about a woman advertising refrigerators on a television commercial.

This is one of many songs The Bee Gees recorded for the BBC at special sessions used exclusively for radio play. This case is particularly noteworthy as the arrangement was significantly different. It's also interesting to note that when the song was covered, this was used as the model.

The Sands' version on Robert Stigwood's Reaction label is a harder-edged guitar-driven pop-psych classic, and is a legendary collectable that attracts attention from both Bee Gees and psych collectors – although the latter are more interested in the single's B-side 'Listen To The Sky'.

Australian band Five Sided Circle had their version consigned to oblivion for half a century, only to be rediscovered in 2018 when it saw its first release on *Big Beat Cellar Scene Vol. 3: Even More Lost Sounds of Adelaide, 1964-69*. It's a very rough take with some incoherent lyrics, as the group struggled to accurately transcribe the words from the recording they made of The Bee Gees version from a syndicated BBC *Top of the Pops* radio show in 1967.

'Deeply, Deeply Me' (Barry Gibb, Robin Gibb, Maurice Gibb)
Recorded in late-1966 or early-1967: location unknown

A difficult recording to date, but known to have been recorded in Australia initially – with 'Gilbert Green' and 'Mrs. Gillespie's Refrigerator' – around November 1966. On 25 November 1966, an acetate of these was sent to Brian Epstein's NEMS, along with the *Spicks And Specks* LP and a covering letter from Hugh Gibb.

The three songs were recorded again in England, and Vince remembers that 'Deeply, Deeply Me' was a very weird tune! A very Indian thing'. Indian musical influences were subtly surfacing in western pop recordings at this time. With The Rolling Stones' 'Paint It Black', George Harrison's 'Love You To' from The Beatles' *Revolver* album, and The Cyrkle's 'Turn Down Day' all released in 1966, could these have offered the Gibbs some inspiration?

Barry has vague memories of the song being committed to tape on the same day as 'Day Time Girl', which would place them at Central Sound in London on 17 July 1967. Vince also remembers playing the rather good lead guitar part on it.

However, it was all a rather scattered effort in trying to keep up with trends, and it really didn't work, as Barry admitted: 'It was just us screwing around. That's why 'Deeply, Deeply Me' never made it, because we never thought it was much of a song'.

'All My Christmases Came At Once' (Barry Gibb, Robin Gibb, Maurice Gibb)
Recorded at IBC Studios, London: 31 August 1967

Throughout their long career, The Bee Gees avoided releasing a Christmas album or even Christmas songs in general. Although their hit song 'First Of May' did have a memorable reference to Christmas trees, it was released as a single in February, and is about longing and regret rather than festive cheer. In an interview with *BBC Breakfast* on 12 December 2020, Barry said, 'We've always avoided it. I think it was appropriate maybe 50 years ago. These days I think it's too much of a marketing trick'. That being said, in 2006, Robin had released a solo album of traditional Christmas songs – *My Favourite Carols* – but perhaps Barry was speaking exclusively of The-Bee-Gees-proper catalogue.

Despite its title, 'All My Christmases Came At Once' is not an actual Christmas song. It was initially written for *The Mini-Mob* – the film referred to earlier – but The Bee Gees' version did not appear. English group The Majority – who had a bit-part in the film – performed it instead.

In the *Horizontal* reissue booklet notes in *The Studio Albums 1967-68* box set, Barry said, 'I think it's Robin singing lead, but it may be all of us in lots of places. I haven't heard it since those days'.

Speaking of *The Mini-Mob* movie, Barry said, 'It was a Sixties spy thing, there were a whole bunch of those things out at that time I never saw. We were going to do *Wonderwall*, which George Harrison ended up doing. We actually visited the set. I remember that very well'.

'Thank You For Christmas' (Barry Gibb, Robin Gibb, Maurice Gibb)
Recorded at IBC Studios, London: 1 December 1967

This was written especially for a Christmas Eve television special called *How on Earth?*, filmed at Liverpool's Anglican Cathedral on 14 December

1967. Reverend Edward H. Patey – dean of the cathedral – presented the programme.

Other performers on the show were folk group The Settlers – best-known for their hit single 'The Lightning Tree': theme to the popular television programme *Follyfoot* – and Radio 1 disc jockey Kenny Everett, who read the gospel in Scouse. In the late-1970s, Everett was to famously parody The Bee Gees on *The Kenny Everett Video Show* with his 'Do-It-Yourself Bee Gees Kit' sketch.

This is a very short song, clocking in at less than two minutes, comprising a single verse between two choruses. Robin sings lead throughout, and the accompaniment is quite simple, with just the group playing organ, guitars, bass and drums. The introduction's simple mandatory Christmas bell-like sound embellishment is probably played on a glockenspiel or possibly a celeste.

Medley: 'Mary's Boy Child' (Jester Hairston)/'Silent Night' (Joseph Mohr, Franz Xaver Gruber, John Freeman Young)/'The First Noël' (William Sandys, Davies Gilbert, John Stainer)/'Mary's Boy Child' (Jester Hairston)
Recorded at IBC Studios, London: 1 December 1967

A medley of Christmas songs arranged by The Bee Gees for the *How on Earth?* TV special, opens and closes with an excerpt from 'Mary's Boy Child'. The track listing on the 2006 expanded edition of *Horizontal* in the *The Studio Albums 1967-68* box set incorrectly states that song's title as 'Hark! The Herald Angels Sing' – an error which may have been carried over from the recording engineer's notes on the tape reel box. What appears to have caused the title confusion revolves around the opening lines of each portion of the song as performed here, both of which are actually incorrect. The lyrics should be 'Hark, now hear the angels sing', but the Gibbs actually sing 'Hark, the herald angels sing'. We can, therefore, assume that the brothers were attempting to sing the songs from memory.

'Mary's Boy Child' was not a traditional carol, but a popular hit recorded by Harry Belafonte. The brothers would have been familiar with the song from their childhood days in Manchester, when it spent seven weeks topping the UK chart – in November and December 1957.

'Silent Night' dates back to 1818 as the German-language original titled 'Stille Nacht, Heilige Nacht', with music written by Franz Xaver Gruber and lyrics by Joseph Mohr. It wasn't until 1859 that John Freeman Young

– a priest at Trinity Church in New York City – wrote and published the English translation.

In 1979, The Bee Gees sang an impromptu a cappella version on *The Official Bee Gees Fan Club* single, and in 1981 on *The Michael Parkinson Show*. In 1983, their families sang the carol on *Cilla Black's Christmas Eve* TV programme, beamed in by satellite from Miami. Robin also recorded 'Silent Night' for his 2006 solo album *My Favourite Carols*.

'The First Noël' is a traditional English carol of Cornish origin, most likely from the 16th or 17th century, but possibly dating from as early as the 13th century. Therefore it's frequently noted as being 'traditional' rather than having specific composer credits. But in its current form, it was first published in *Carols Ancient and Modern* (1823) and *Gilbert and Sandys' Carols* (1833), both of which were edited by William Sandys, and arranged and edited with extra lyrics by Davies Gilbert. Robin also included this song on *My Favourite Carols*, but rewrote the chorus to reflect an anti-war message.

On 11 February, The Bee Gees achieved an important milestone, making their first American television appearance on *The Smothers Brothers Comedy Hour*, during which they reprised 'Words' in addition to 'And The Sun Will Shine'.

They embarked on a short six-concert Scandinavian tour on 9 February, visiting Stockholm, Gothenburg, Oslo and Copenhagen. On 27 February, they began an 18-date stint in Germany, launching their road trip at Hamburg's Musikhalle, concluding at the Stadthalle in Braunschweig on 8 March. The 17-piece Massachusetts String Orchestra accompanied the group, and the support band were Essex rockers and Polydor labelmates Procol Harum. The setlist consisted of 'New York Mining Disaster 1941', 'Every Christian Lion Hearted Man Will Show You', 'Words', 'Gilbert Green', 'Turn Of The Century', 'To Love Somebody' and 'Holiday'. Then came a medley comprising: 'In My Own Time'/'C'mon Marianne' (Four Seasons cover)/'I Can't See Nobody'/'Strange Brew' (Cream cover)/'In My Own Time', followed by 'In The Morning', 'Massachusetts', 'Spicks And Specks' and 'World'.

On 17 March, The Bee Gees made their second American TV appearance, performing 'To Love Somebody' and 'Words' on the iconic *Ed Sullivan Show*. The latter song was a striking rendition with a live lead vocal from Barry and a large standing string section flanking the band in a long parallel line. Since Maurice was needed to play bass, Robin instead is seated in his usual place at the piano, rather obviously miming over the recorded backing track. Two weeks later – on 1 April – they appeared on *Rowan and Martin's Laugh-In*.

After inking their first major-label recording contract with Polydor in the UK in 1967, their new label issued their own collection of the Gibbs' Australian recordings. In April 1968, *Rare, Precious And Beautiful* – or the album formerly known as *Spicks And Specks* in updated packaging – arrived in the UK and Europe. The US release was delayed until November.

Rare, Precious And Beautiful (1968)

Release dates: UK: April 1968, US: November 1968
Chart positions: West Germany: 15, US: 53
Side 1: 1. 'Where Are You' 2. 'Spicks And Specks' 3. 'Play Down' 4. 'Big Chance' 5. 'Glass House' 6. 'How Many Birds'
Side 2: 1. 'Second Hand People' 2. 'I Don't Know Why I Bother With Myself' 3. 'Monday's Rain' 4. 'Tint Of Blue' 5. 'Jingle Jangle' 6. 'Born A Man'.

Such was The Bee Gees' rapidly expanding popularity in the United States in 1968, *Rare, Precious And Beautiful* eventually made it to number 53 on the *Cashbox* album chart. Considering their lack of success in Australia up to late 1966, ironically, this chart-placing made it the most successful Australian-produced album to date. Though the album didn't break into the UK or Australian charts, it *was* successful in Germany – peaking at number 15 – a market that by 1968 was huge for The Bee Gees' music.

The songs were released as part of an agreement between Polydor UK and Festival Australia. Other territories followed suit, with releases on ATCO in the US and Canada, and on Polydor's budget imprints Karussell in Scandinavia and Triumph in France.

Robert Stigwood was vocal in his objection to releasing these older songs, quite rightly concerned that the material was outdated and not representative of what the group was currently producing, and fearful it could be damaging to their reputation. However, this deal was out of Stigwood's control, as his arrangement with Polydor was purely to provide new recordings. In telling this to the head of Polydor Roland Rennie, Stigwood insisted the boys deserved better and that their talent was 'rare, precious and beautiful'. Inadvertently, he'd provided the title for a project to which he was staunchly opposed.

Stigwood eventually penned the album's liner notes – undoubtedly with reticence. But in the writing, he proved himself to be a great spin doctor:

This album comprises tracks recorded by the Gibb Brothers, and some of them with Colin Petersen, four to two years ago in Australia. It was hearing these tracks for the first time that first drew my attention to The Bee Gees. They are described as rare, precious and beautiful because they have now indeed become a collector's item. They show the blossoming of a gigantic songwriting and performing talent that has now burst forth and is appreciated from all corners of the globe. They are not being released as current examples of the group's work, but to please their millions of fans who are genuinely interested to hear what the group sounded like a few years ago. I regard these recordings with great affection, as they represent a landmark in the extraordinary career of this incredibly talented group.

Rare, Precious And Beautiful eventually became a three-album franchise, encompassing 35 of the group's Australian-era tracks, 'electronically reprocessed for stereo from the original monophonic recordings'.

The first of the three compilations was more coherently compiled than the second and third, as it included all the songs from the original 1966 Australian album *Spicks And Specks*: albeit in a different order.

Polydor in the UK took the lead with the artwork, farming the design out to Paragon Publicity, who created very uninspiring covers featuring a Malaysian butterfly. For each volume, only the background colour was changed. ATCO in the US and Canada emulated the artwork, as did Festival in Australia. Other territories were a little more adventurous, with Germany and France using a fanned-out paper Christmas decoration on the first volume. In Japan – where the first volume was released using the prototypical title *Spicks And Specks* – it had a more elaborate gatefold sleeve, but the cover was no more inspiring with an open book and scattered miscellanea, including a blue butterfly.

In March, two tracks that weren't included on *Horizontal* – 'Jumbo' and 'The Singer Sang His Song' – were issued as a single. The decision was strange on a couple of fronts: the first being that there were clearly stronger album cuts to choose from relative to both of these outtakes; the second was favouring the bizarre lyrics and quirky blues-esque cadence of 'Jumbo' for the single's A-side, over the more accessible ballad that was relegated to the B-side. The Bee Gees' soulful melancholy had served them well so far, and the break in the formula yielded uninspiring results. The single broke the band's consecutive run of top twenty US hits, peaking at number 57. In the UK, it interrupted their string of three top ten hits in a row, reaching 25. However, their affectionate German fan base propelled 'Jumbo' to number 5.

Returning to the UK from their short New York jaunt, The Bee Gees resumed live shows promoting *Horizontal*. Their 27-stop outing began on 27 March at The Royal Albert Hall in London, with Dave Dee, Dozy, Beaky, Mick & Tich, and Grapefruit supporting. The show was nothing short of spectacular, with the accompaniment of a 67-piece orchestra, the Royal Air Force Apprentice Marching Band (backing 'I've Decided To Join The Air Force': a new song that was not on *Horizontal* but *would* make the final cut for *Idea*) and 40 members of the renowned London choral group Ambrosian Singers (on 'Birdie Told Me'). The tour's final date was at the Ritz in Belfast, Northern Ireland, on 3 May.

For a pre-recorded guest appearance on the German television series *Beat-Club* broadcast of 18 April, The Bee Gees performed 'World'; and appearing again on 27 April, performed 'Harry Braff'.

On 11 May, The Bee Gees appeared on the weekly Southern Television show *Time For Blackburn* which honoured the group with a 'Bee Gees Special' and a guest appearance by former Manfred Mann front man Paul Jones. During the show, it was mooted that The Bee Gees were writing a song for the presenter, Tony Blackburn, to record.

Little-known American band Sounds Of Modification released their only album on 1 June 1968. It included the little-known Barry Gibb song 'You'. Drummer Butch Cavouto remembers that Barry 'taught it to us at Jubilee Studios at 1790 Broadway, Manhattan, New York. Great times!'. The song – beautifully produced and arranged by Bob Gallo – was released on Jubilee Records in the US, and on Stateside (an EMI subsidiary) in the UK.

In August, The Marbles released the Barry, Robin, and Maurice song 'Only One Woman'. The duo featured the Gibbs' Australian mate and collaborator Trevor Gordon. Gordon – a native of Skegness, England – had also returned to England from Australia, joining his cousin Graham Bonnet's rock outfit The Graham Bonnet Set. The two established The Marbles and worked together in 1968 and 1969.

'Only One Woman' – a pop-soul ballad – reached number 5 in the UK, becoming The Marbles' sole hit single. It was backed with another Gibb song: 'The Walls Fell Down'. Bonnet – who was gifted with a powerful voice custom-built for hard rock and heavy metal – continued to cultivate a successful recording career as a solo artist and as a member of rock bands like Alcatrazz, Rainbow, The Michael Schenker Group, Stratovarius and Impellitteri. He released new material as recently as 2020. Gordon released a solo album in 1970 but left the industry to become a high school music teacher. He later published a music theory volume: *Caged for Jazz Guitar – A Chord-Shaped Approach To Jazz Mastery.* He died of unspecified causes in London on 10 January 2013.

In between the steady stream of live shows and small-screen gigs, The Bee Gees had been writing and recording tracks for their third studio album *Idea*. 'Swan Song' – the first of the batch to be recorded in mid-December 1967 – was originally a candidate to be a non-album single that would launch the group into 1968. Ultimately, they decided to release 'Words' instead, which seemed to be a good choice in hindsight. Recording for the album was complete by the end of June, with the now-iconic 'I Started A Joke' bringing up the rear as the last addition.

Idea (1968)

Personnel:
Barry Gibb: vocals, guitar
Robin Gibb: vocals
Maurice Gibb: vocals, bass, organ, piano, Mellotron
Vince Melouney: guitar, vocals
Colin Petersen: drums
Additional personnel:
Orchestral arrangements: Bill Shepherd
Recording engineers: John Pantry, Mike Claydon and Damon Lyon-Shaw
Producers: Robert Stigwood and The Bee Gees
Recorded 13 December 1967-25 June 1968 at IBC Studios
Release dates: UK and US: September 1968
Chart positions: West Germany: 3, France: 4, UK: 4, Australia: 8, Canada: 10, US: 17

Idea was The Bee Gees' third album release in just fifteen months. It was an important album from a creative and statistical perspective, showcasing a further evolution in their singing and songwriting, and adding to their already impressive commercial successes.

Both *Bee Gees 1st* and *Horizontal* were strong records that sold well and were critically acclaimed. With shifting industry trends – to which

The Bee Gees had thus far adapted well – music critics and fans were curious to see how they would proceed. The previous two albums yielded superb ballads, classic pop melodies and whimsical forays into psychedelia, but they also contained definitive soul and R&B vehicles like 'To Love Somebody', which had quickly become a genre-transcending standard, embraced by audiences and fellow musicians alike. *Horizonal* strengthened the cohesion of the five-piece as a band. So, where would they go next?

They answered with a consistently good pop album. 'I've Gotta Get A Message To You' and 'I Started A Joke' are among their all-time great tracks and have remained evergreen.

On the UK edition of *Idea* – which was released in advance of other markets – 'I've Gotta Get A Message To You' was not included. There were five ballads, and the only rock tracks were the title song and guitarist Vince Melouney's 'Such A Shame'. Following the success of the 'I've Gotta Get A Message To You' single, the song was included on the US and South African releases of the album, but at the expense of 'Such A Shame'. With a lead vocal by Vince, it would be the only non-Gibb Bee Gees song included on any of their post-Australia studio albums. When *Idea* was issued on CD in 1989, both songs were included, and the track list was stronger for it.

Vocally, *Idea* is a superb set, with no less than five combinations of vocal leads. Barry has lead vocals in three songs, Robin four, and Barry and Robin share in three (four if you count the later addition of 'Message'). Maurice has no solo leads but does share a harmony vocal with Barry on 'Kitty Can', and with Vince on 'Such A Shame'.

Following the success of the singles 'I Started A Joke' and 'Message' on the US singles charts (numbers 6 and 8 respectively), the album reached number 17 in *Billboard*. Strangely, 'I Started A Joke' was not issued as a single in the UK, but the album – even without the UK-chart-topping 'Message' – peaked at number 4. It was their highest-charting LP in the UK to date. In Germany, it was their third successive top four album.

In 2006, Reprise Records reissued *Idea* (using the European cover) as part of the excellent *Studio Albums 1967-1968* box set, with both mono and stereo album mixes on one disc, plus a second disc of unreleased songs, non-album tracks and alternate mixes.

The European album artwork features a twin helical filament light bulb with a small group photograph on the screw shank, set against a deep purple background. The group logo is in pink capital letters, matching the glowing bulb filament, while the album title above is in white with outward-pointing red arrows on either side. The back cover is a vignette of a slightly different photograph to that on the front. No design credits are shown on the album cover, but the group photographs were by famed German photographer Wolfgang 'Bubi' Heilemann.

The United States, Japan and Australia opted for a different design: a montage comprising elements of the five Bee Gees' faces. This was made up of Maurice's hair and eyes, Robin's nose, Barry's upper lip and teeth, Vince's chin and Colin's left cheek. Despite there being less of Barry in the picture than the others, his teeth are enough to give the overall impression that it's a picture of him. The photographic facial elements are combined with swirly patterns and a monocle. It wasn't of quite the same calibre as The Beatles *Revolver* artwork, but there was something familiar about it – it came as no real surprise when the designer was revealed to be Klaus Voorman (designer of the *Revolver* cover). For a group who bristled when they were labelled as Beatles clones, making this album cover such an easy target for comparison was probably not Robert Stigwood's best management decision.

The back cover of these album editions was a group photo taken at Robert Stigwood's house in London, along with a black and white line drawing of the front cover's face composite with a numbered legend clueing the listener in to which parts belonged to each band member. Curiously, the Canadian issue used this photograph and drawing on both the front and back of the sleeve – but without the context of Voorman's original face composite, the line drawing and legend make absolutely no sense.

The outfits they're wearing in this image look a little familiar, as the photo is from the same session that gave us the *Horizontal* cover photos.

The album credits quite helpfully note who sings each song, the only Bee Gees album to do so on the cover itself.

'Let There Be Love' (Barry Gibb, Robin Gibb, Maurice Gibb)

Recorded at IBC Studios, London: 12 and 21 June 1968
Chart position: Netherlands: 16

The lush ballad 'Let There Be Love' opens the album, and Barry recalls that it 'was written next to St. Paul's Cathedral in a penthouse apartment that we rented when we first arrived in England. That song was written in that penthouse 'round about midnight. Me and my then-girlfriend, who is my wife now, we'd just fallen in love, and it was that type of mood I was in that night'.

In March 1970, it was belatedly released as a single, but only in Belgium and the Netherlands: where it peaked at 16.

The song was included in The Bee Gees' concert setlist for their 1974 United States tour, and was performed with a full orchestra as heard on a *King Biscuit Flower Hour* broadcast.

'Kitty Can' (Barry Gibb, Robin Gibb, Maurice Gibb)
Recorded at IBC Studios, London: 12 June 1968

This catchy, fast track sees Barry and Maurice doubling on lead vocals, giving it a unique sound not heard on a Bee Gees record up to this point. Barry recalls that 'Kitty Can' 'was written by Maurice and I during a night with Maurice and Lulu at their place in London – the early apartment they shared before they moved to Hampstead'.

It features some interesting percussive vocal sounds, which would today probably be referred to as beatboxing. Examples contemporary to *Idea* include Pink Floyd's 'Pow R. Toc H.' from their 1967 album *The Piper at the Gates of Dawn*, and Paul McCartney's 'That Would Be Something' from his 1970 debut solo album *McCartney*.

'In The Summer Of His Years' (Barry Gibb, Robin Gibb, Maurice Gibb)
Recorded at IBC Studios, London: 14 and 21 February 1968

On Friday 25 August 1967, Robin was visiting secretary Molly Hullis – later to become his wife – at the NEMS offices when Brian Epstein arrived in tears and entered Robert Stigwood's office. Robin tells how 'He closed the door and there was a lot of shouting. When he came out, he was still crying. I said, 'What's the matter?'. He said, 'I can't talk', and he went straight out'. Moments later, Stigwood told Robin that The Bee Gees would be leaving on a trip to Monte Carlo that night. 'Brian had pleaded with Robert to go to Sussex with him that weekend because he didn't want to be alone. The Beatles were in Bangor (North Wales) with the Maharishi. And Robert had said no'.

On Sunday in Monte Carlo, Stigwood and The Bee Gees received the news that Brian Epstein had died from an accidental drug overdose. 'It was awful', remembered Robin. 'We had this terrible midnight cruise to Nice, so Robert could catch a plane back. He had nothing to do with Brian's death, but he felt tremendously guilty, because if he'd stayed, that might not have happened'.

'In The Summer Of His Years' is Robin's touching tribute to Brian Epstein. With its delicate arrangement of piano, flute, harp and glockenspiel backing Robin's plaintive vocal in the first verse, it intensifies, adding guitar, drums and backing vocals in the second, while the orchestra enters in full flow on the third wordless refrain.

'Indian Gin And Whisky Dry' (Barry Gibb, Robin Gibb, Maurice Gibb)
Recorded at IBC Studios, London: 17 June 1968

A fun song – originally demoed by Robin solo on 13 June 1968 – which appears on the superb *Saved by the Bell – The Collected Works Of Robin Gibb 1968-1970* triple CD-set released in 2015. On the tape reel, the title appears as 'Indian Gin And *Whiskey* Dry', contrary to the completed track that appears on the album.

Robin explained that he 'came up with the idea in New Delhi. I actually saw the title on a menu in a restaurant in India, and sort of took the title from that and then finished it up together with Barry and everyone in London when I got back. I think we got the idea to finish up the song from that demo'.

Vince's Duane Eddy style guitar in the introduction implies drunkenness and slurred speech. Vince explained: 'We detuned a guitar on that and tried to get Indian – not exactly like a sitar, but leaning in that direction, experimenting a bit'. Maurice's Rickenbacker 4001 bass guitar heavily processed through a wah-wah pedal and sliding from note to note, further emphasises the effect.

'Down To Earth' (Barry Gibb, Robin Gibb, Maurice Gibb)
Recorded at IBC Studios, London: 8 and 9 January 1968

'Down To Earth' gives an insight into Robin's strange writing ability. The song is splendidly atmospheric, but as with many pop songs of the era, the lyrics are actually best described as just words which fit the meter. As profound as a single line may sound, combined with everything that surrounds it, it makes absolutely no sense.

The song opens dramatically with an introduction of heavily compressed piano chords and lightly-strummed acoustic guitar before Robin chimes in with a bell-clear vocal swathed in oodles of reverb. The first verse builds steadily, tasteful alto sax accents providing breaks between lines before the powerful chorus. There, Robin's voice is double-tracked before his brothers join in for the climax, then returning to the initial sparse verse arrangement. It begins building again, through to an extended chorus and Robin's quavering wordless outro.

'Such A Shame' (Vince Melouney)
Recorded at IBC Studios, London: 14 June 1968

Vince Melouney's song 'Such a Shame' is unique as the only Bee Gees recording written by a Bee Gee that wasn't a Gibb brother. It was included on international editions of *Idea* but was not included on the US or Canadian issues.

The song had a great country feel and lent itself perfectly to a dual lead local by Vince and Maurice. However, Vince now appears to regret the decision to sing it himself, saying, 'Barry loved it, wanted to sing it, and I said 'No, I want to sing it!'. I wish I had let Barry sing it now. Not that I don't think I didn't sing it really spectacularly or anything, but Barry would have sung it much better'.

Referring to the tensions bubbling up between the brothers at the time, Vince said, 'It's all about that it was such a shame that everything was falling apart. There were just too many problems' – Vince even admitting that 'It mentions Stigwood in the lyrics to the song'. Evidently, a sufficiently-veiled reference to pass muster!

It was good to see that the lead guitarist didn't use the song as a showcase for himself – the only guitar solo is in the outro. Instead, there's some rather accomplished chromatic-harmonica-playing, although who the player is, is unknown. Vince only remembers that it was a friend of the recording engineer.

The song also made it onto 7" formats, as a track on two Australian EPs: *I've Gotta Get A Message To You* and *I Started A Joke*.

'I've Gotta Get A Message To You' (Barry Gibb, Robin Gibb, Maurice Gibb)
Recorded at IBC Studios, London: 12 July 1968
Chart positions: Italy: 1, Ireland: 1, South Africa: 1, UK: 1, Netherlands: 2, New Zealand: 2, Australia: 3, Canada: 3, West Germany: 3, Denmark: 5, Norway: 6, Switzerland: 6, US: 8, Belgium: 9, Austria: 12, France: 21

This classic track was not recorded during the *Idea* album sessions, which had concluded the previous month. The song originated with Robin, who wrote most of the lyrics: 'This is about a prisoner on death row who only has a few hours to live. He wants the prison chaplain to pass on a final message to his wife'. Barry recalled the night of recording as 'memorable':

We wrote it together, all three of us. I think that night, I know for a fact; we didn't sing the choruses in harmony. Robert called us back to the studio at eleven o'clock at night and said, 'I want the choruses in harmony, I don't want them in just melody. I want three-part harmony choruses'. So, we went in and attempted that 'round about midnight. Everyone drove back to the studio, and that's what we did.

Barry was also very complimentary of Maurice's bass-playing: 'He had a lot of intensity in his bass – Mo was a real McCartney bass freak, as a lot of us were. He would pick up on all the things that McCartney would do. Maurice was very good on different instruments, you know – good lead guitarist, good bass player, good keyboard player. He was versatile. He loved playing bass more than anything else, I think, at that time'.

Featuring Robin and Barry's characteristic, alternating lead vocals, all three brothers combined to sing the powerful chorus with their distinctive sibling harmony. Close scrutiny reveals a superb underlying vocal countermelody that could stand alone as the basis for a song in its own right.

'I've Gotta Get A Message To You' was an immediate hit across the globe, and it became The Bee Gees' second UK chart-topper. Also, it peaked at 8 in the US, earning them their first *Billboard* top ten entry and their highest-charting single there to date.

Whilst it was too late to include the song on the UK and European editions of *Idea*, its success *did* force its inclusion on the US and Canadian releases, at the expense of 'Such A Shame'. Both songs, however, appeared on all *Idea* CD editions.

Apart from the single's mono mix, 'I've Gotta Get A Message to You' has since appeared in several slightly different versions, including the stereo mix on the US and Canadian issues of *Idea* and *Best Of Bee Gees*, and the 1990 *Tales From The Brothers Gibb* and 2006 *The Studio Albums 1967-1968* box sets. Some vary somewhat in pitch and speed. For some reason, the single omits two things: the album mix's distinctive vocal-and-orchestra hit on the fifth note of each bar of the introduction, and Robin throatily singing the line 'I've just gotta get a message to her/Hold on' immediately following the key-change after the third chorus. On close listen, the album version also reveals two rather comical ad-libs, one of which sounds like someone answering Robin's aforementioned 'Hold on' with 'How?'; and as Barry belts out the last line of the refrain near the song's end, someone (maybe Robin) almost interrupts him by uttering 'Save your voice!'.

Over four decades later, The Soldiers – a singing trio consisting of enlisted British Army servicemen – recorded 'I've Gotta Get A Message

To You' with Robin as guest vocalist. The single was released on 23
October 2011 as the Royal British Legion's charity single for the annual
poppy appeal. Robin sings the first and third verses, just as he did on the
original. The single reached 75 in the UK.

On 11 June 1988, before an audience of 72,000, this was one of two
songs The Bee Gees performed at the *Nelson Mandela 70th Birthday
Tribute* concert at Wembley Stadium. The concert – which included Stevie
Wonder, Sting, George Michael, The Eurythmics, Al Green, Meat Loaf, Peter
Gabriel and Harry Belafonte – was broadcast to more than 60 countries.

When Barry performed the song on his *Mythology* concert tour in
2013/2014, his son Stephen sang the verses that Robin had sung.

In 2021, Barry re-recorded 'Message' with country star Keith Urban for his
2021 duets album *Greenfields*. It was one of the best songs on a fine album.

Notable performers of well over 150 cover versions of the song, include
José Feliciano, Tim Rose, American soul singer Percy Sledge, and Welsh
singer Mal Ryder, who had a hit with his Italian version in 1969. More
recently, in 2017, American singer-songwriter Bobby Osbourne released a
brilliant bluegrass revamp.

'Idea' (Barry Gibb, Robin Gibb, Maurice Gibb)
Recorded at IBC Studios, London: 20 and 25 June 1968

The fast rocking title song leads off side two of the original LP. On an
album so jam-packed with ballads, this is a welcome addition and lifts its
rhythm substantially.

Barry recalls 'wanting to do something with more aggression, with more
energy. That's my greatest memory of it – looking for something that was a
little more angry, and that just came out in the studio'.

The track would be Vince Melouney's last guitar solo before leaving the
band later that year. Barry recalls that Melouney was a 'rocker at heart,
(and he) would influence us'. Maurice played an important part, too, with
his pounding piano introduction being immediately recognisable!

Barry would later say the song 'was Jagger-influenced. In those days of
course, everything was either The Stones or The Beatles, and everybody
wanted to be in that sort of zone. So, I think that it was certainly
influenced by that'.

'We always loved one word titles', Robin said of the track. 'Just the angle
of coming up with a title like 'Idea', and then coming up with the formula
to match the title, like 'Holiday', 'Idea' is one of my favourite songs. Barry
was really powerful vocally'.

As with *Bee Gees 1st* and *Horizontal*, *Idea* was released in both mono and stereo. While the differences between the two versions usually boiled down to the way they were mixed, the title track's mono and stereo takes are actually completely different recordings.

In the introduction, as the opening guitar and crashing piano notes decay, the mono version has whistling and clapping, which are not on the stereo version. Most noticeably, after Vince's guitar break, the mono take switches to a different guitar and vocal track, with Barry singing in a much looser manner. An alternate mono mix – released for the first time on the *Idea* bonus disc of *The Studio Albums 1967-1968* box set – also uses that different vocal take for the entirety of the track.

'When The Swallows Fly' (Barry Gibb, Robin Gibb, Maurice Gibb)
Recorded at IBC Studios, London: 18 June 1968
Chart position: Netherlands: 20

This song's opening lines are a tip of the hat to William Wordsworth's best-known poem, which opens with the titular line 'I wandered lonely as a cloud', with the third line being 'When all at once I saw a crowd'.

Barry's recall of how and where the song was written is rather vague: 'That's something I brought in, but I don't remember how the song came about. It was probably written in Eaton Square or at the penthouse. A lot of the ballads in those days were written that way, like 'Words''. Despite this, Robin asserts, 'It was one of my favourites. I think Barry's vocal on that is fantastic'.

This was another song belatedly released as a single, this time only in the Netherlands, with 'Give Your Best' from the 1969 album *Odessa*, as the B-side. It peaked at number 20 on the Dutch chart in 1971.

'I've Decided To Join The Air Force' (Barry Gibb, Robin Gibb, Maurice Gibb)
Recorded at IBC Studios, London: 15 and 21 February 1968

This was first performed several months before *Idea* was released, at the Royal Albert Hall on 27 March 1968: the opening night of The Bee Gees' 26-date UK tour with British pop/rock outfit Dave Dee, Dozy, Beaky, Mick & Tich.

Robin joked that the show 'had everything on there except The Bee Gees. It was like a Roman spectacular, a bit overdone. But it was exciting!'.

Band manager Robert Stigwood explained: 'It was a particular stage of their career, and I wanted to create a big event. These boys are brilliantly talented and their music shows so. Big things are happening for them, and therefore there is no reason why their affairs shouldn't be treated with a certain amount of flamboyance'.

After Robin introduced the new song to the audience, the group played the song through; Stigwood boasted, 'I had the doors of the hall open in all different directions, and this Air Force band marched through the audience playing a reprise of the song'.

'I Started A Joke' (Barry Gibb, Robin Gibb, Maurice Gibb)
Recorded at IBC Studios, London: 20 June 1968
Chart positions: Australia: 1, Brazil: 1, Canada: 1, Denmark: 1, New Zealand: 1, South Africa: 2, France: 3, Netherlands: 3, Norway: 3, Switzerland: 5. US: 6, Belgium: 8, Spain: 14, Austria: 16, Italy: 19

'I Started A Joke' has always been recognised as Robin Gibb's signature song, and he is primarily credited with its creation: 'The melody to this one was heard aboard a British Airways Vickers Viscount about a hundred miles from Essen', he recalled. 'It was one of those old four-engine *prop* jobs that seemed to drone the passenger into a sort of hypnotic trance, only with this it was different. The droning, after a while, appeared to take the form of a tune, which mysteriously sounded like a church choir'.

Everybody has a theory about this song – probably the most controversial being that it's about Adolf Hitler. That theory could very well be correct, but then again, it could be well wide of the mark. Only one thing is certain: Robin took the secret of the song's meaning to his grave.

The closest we ever got to an explanation was when Robin offered that it 'was a very spiritual song, about faith and survival in life. It wasn't a love song; it was one of the first songs we wrote about struggling to survive emotionally alone in the world'.

In all likelihood, the song wasn't written about anybody or anything specific; it was just words set to a melody, and thanks to their ambiguity, listeners over-thought it and came up with their own ideas as to what it was all about. The Bee Gees added to the mix, saying it was up to the listener to decide what it was about, and that is what many did. Barry even commented to this effect, saying, 'There was a lot of that in those days. There was a lot of psychedelia and the idea that if you wrote something, even if it sounded ridiculous, somebody would find the meaning for it, and that was the truth'.

Likewise, Maurice added there 'were people coming up to us saying 'I really know what you're saying in that song', and we'd be like, 'That's great, because we don't!''.

No matter what it's about, it's a classic, and was always a concert favourite with Robin taking the spotlight for what was effectively a solo spot – nobody else mattered when Robin sang 'I Started A Joke'. His unique voice was perfect to deliver the song, and he hit the soaring high notes with ease every time.

Because of its omnipresence throughout The Bee Gees' career, most are surprised to learn that the song wasn't released as a single in the UK, and therefore, was not a hit there. But it reached number 6 on the *Billboard* Hot 100 in the US, beating 'I've Gotta Get A Message To You' as their highest-charting single there to that point. It also reached number 1 in Canada, Australia, Brazil, Denmark and New Zealand.

Notable covers include that by alt-metal rockers Faith No More, who turned in an acclaimed version for their 1998 album *Who Cares a Lot?*. The Wallflowers – fronted by Jakob Dylan (Bob Dylan's third-born son) – recorded a version featured in the 2001 comedy film *Zoolander*. British singer-songwriter Robbie Williams and electronic music duo The Orb also turned in a take, included on the 1999 *Bee Gees Tribute Album/Gotta Get A Message to You* – a charity project benefitting *LIVE Challenge '99*, which sought relief for homeless people in Northern England.

By way of a tribute to his late brother, Barry performed 'I Started A Joke' on his *Mythology* tour in 2013/2014, though he only sang the first verse himself. The rest of the song used a live performance video from the 1998 *One Night Only* tour, projected onto a big screen on stage, and Robin's inimitable voice again filled concert halls across the globe, every time to rapturous applause. After the audience shed emotional tears and the song concluded, an appreciative standing ovation was always guaranteed.

'Kilburn Towers' (Barry Gibb, Robin Gibb, Maurice Gibb)
Recorded at IBC Studios, London: 14 June 1968

The epitome of whimsy, 'Kilburn Towers' is a wonderfully light and breezy song. As convincing as they may sound, the flutes are actually Maurice playing a Mellotron – and Colin abandons his drum kit in favour of bongos.

Barry says he wrote 'Kilburn Towers' in his apartment near St. Paul's Cathedral in London: 'I would just sit and strum on my own. I think it was just something that I sort of came up with and that was it'.

He must have had something on his mind by way of influence, and the obvious thoughts are of some old towers in the north west London district of Kilburn. However, the more likely inspiration goes back a few years to Barry's days living in Australia. Kilburn Towers is a striking pair of circular apartment buildings which were built in 1960 on Smedley's Point in Manly on Sydney's North Harbour. Their shape earned them the nickname the 'toilet rolls building'.

Barry is obviously fond of the song, as he performed it on the Australian leg of his Mythology tour in 2014 when he introduced it as being 'about people who sit in a field and get drunk – and I remember that'.

'Swan Song' (Barry Gibb, Robin Gibb, Maurice Gibb)
Recorded at IBC Studios, London: 13 December 1967

A very powerful ballad, 'Swan Song' dates back as far as December 1967, and as such, is the earliest Bee Gees song included on *Idea*. It was once touted as a possible single but was eventually overlooked in favour of 'Words'.

As with some other songs, it subliminally infers a desire for a break from their current situation. Written by all three brothers, was this a veiled message to each other? With lots of media talk of Barry leaving The Bee Gees to go solo and into movies at the time, was this more a statement from him? Whatever the message, it's a good lead vocal from the eldest brother, and a fitting closing track to a very strong set.

Idea – 2006 edition bonus songs

'Chocolate Symphony' (Barry Gibb, Robin Gibb, Maurice Gibb)
Recorded at IBC Studios, London: 8 and 9 January 1968

Robin explained that 'Chocolate Symphony' 'was written for a movie called *Pippi Longstocking*. It was being made in Stockholm at the time in '68. It didn't have music in it in the end. We actually wrote it in Stockholm and then went back to London to record it. Then the song didn't get used'.

At the time Robin was referring to, *Pippi Longstocking* – or *Pippi Långstrump* in the native Swedish – was a television series in the making, based on children's books by Astrid Lindgren. The show ran for thirteen episodes: the first broadcast on 8 February 1969 on Sveriges Television. A movie released the same year consisted of re-edited footage from the TV series, and was dubbed for the release in Germany. In 1973, it was again dubbed, this time for English-speaking markets including the UK and US.

The Bee Gees wrote at least four songs for *Pippi Longstocking*: 'Chocolate Symphony', 'We Can Lift A Mountain', 'Treacle Brown' and 'Four Faces West'. 'We Can Lift A Mountain' exists as an early work-in-progress demo and a superb completed version. The lyrics changed significantly during the development of the song, which, sadly, remains unreleased. 'Treacle Brown' and 'Four Faces West' were released in November by Lori Balmer.

'Jumbo' (Barry Gibb, Robin Gibb, Maurice Gibb)

Recorded at IBC Studios, London: 10 January 1968

Chart positions: Netherlands: 2, Switzerland: 4, West Germany: 5, Austria: 9, Denmark: 10, Canada: 16, Belgium: 18, Australia: 20, France: 25, UK: 25, US: 57

'Jumbo' was recorded amongst the *Idea* tracks, but The Bee Gees and Robert Stigwood's ambivalence towards it likely kept it out of the track list. It was released as a stand-alone single in March 1968.

Compared to the international accolades 'Words' had received just a couple of months earlier, 'Jumbo' may have been a bit of a let-down. Whilst most groups would consider a top ten single in several European countries to be a major success, relatively low chart placings of 25 in the UK and 57 in the US caused the song to be seen as something of a failure. Maurice later said that fellow group members Colin Petersen and Vince Melouney were so excited by 'Jumbo', that they convinced Robert Stigwood to release it as a single, against his better judgement:

> Robert was executive producer on everything we did; he was the overriding decider. He would say, 'That's the single that's coming out'. We would say, 'Oh no, we want that one'. I think we really pushed him for 'Jumbo' to be the single, and he put 'The Singer Sang His Song' on the other side. Of course, nobody really played 'Jumbo', and he reversed the A-side practically immediately. Then we had a hit again, not a number one, but after that, we didn't complain any more – 'Okay, you can select them', you know.

The choice of 'Jumbo', with a Barry lead vocal, over 'The Singer Sang His Song' with a Robin lead vocal, was evidence to Robin that their manager was favouring Barry's voice over his. Barry years later agreed that Stigwood had made a mistake by making 'Jumbo' the A-side: 'Personally,

I think 'The Singer Sang His Song' – the flip side – was a much stronger A-side'.

Stigwood quickly recognised his error and tried to turn 'The Singer Sang His Song' into the A-side, but it was too late for the US market in particular. These days – despite its strong showing in many countries – it remains a little-known Bee Gees song.

Of the song's origins, Barry said it's 'Mo playing The Beatles mellotron, a very experimental period. I think it's about a child's fantasy elephant, but when I listen again, there are some very phallic overtones'.

The first appearance of 'Jumbo' on an album was on *Kitty Can* – an 1973 RSO compilation initially issued only in Argentina. It was released in Uruguay a couple of years later.

In 1974, the mono recording was reprocessed to simulate stereo for its inclusion on the *Gotta Get A Message To You* compilation album on Polydor's budget label Contour.

In 1990, the first genuine stereo mix of 'Jumbo' was included in the *Tales From The Brothers Gibb* box set. That was also the song's first appearance on CD.

'The Singer Sang His Song' (Barry Gibb, Robin Gibb, Maurice Gibb)

Recorded at IBC Studios, London: 8 and 9 January 1968

A classic Bee Gees production, 'The Singer Sang His Song' is the sure-fire hit that wasn't. Badly misjudged and selected as the B-side to 'Jumbo', it faded outside the knowledge of all but serious Bee Gees fans, following the single's relative failure in major international markets. Some territories ignored Stigwood's decision and hastily nominated 'The Singer Sang His Song' as the A-side, but it was generally overlooked. Stigwood acknowledged his error almost immediately, saying, 'It was a mistake to release 'Jumbo' as an A-side in Britain, because the public still want big, emotional ballads from the boys'.

It's quite tragic that such a fine song with an excellent lead vocal from Robin should be consigned to semi-obscurity.

The first album, 'The Singer Sang His Song' appeared on was *World Star Festival*: a UNICEF charity LP released in 1969. Polydor's budget label Contour brought the song and other B-sides to a wider audience on the 1973 *Massachusetts* compilation. It sold well enough to be reissued in 1978, and riding on the coattails of *Saturday Night Fever* and *Spirits Having Flown*, the album achieved BRIT Certified Gold Award status. It also saw release on the South American compilation album *Kitty Can*.

The song's first appearance on CD was in 1990's *Tales From The Brothers Gibb* box set, for which it was mixed in stereo for the first time. The stereo mix extended the song by twelve seconds to 3:19 – this was also included on the 2006 box set *The Studio Albums 1967-1968*.

'Bridges Crossing Rivers' (Barry Gibb, Robin Gibb, Maurice Gibb)

Recorded at IBC Studios, London: 10 January 1968

This appears to be a quite early work-in-progress, with a basic accompaniment of strummed acoustic guitars, drums and bass, with Barry and Robin sharing the lead vocal. The lyrics consist of a single verse and chorus repeated twice, implying that they were placeholders for possible later lyrical development. However, that didn't happen, and we're left with a desperately short and quite unremarkable track.

'Completely Unoriginal' (Barry Gibb, Robin Gibb, Maurice Gibb)

Recorded at IBC Studios, London: June 1968

A bit of a spoof song, more befitting The Bonzo Dog Doo-Dah Band than The Bee Gees. The verses and chorus are quite cleverly written, but Viv Stanshall, Neil Innes and company would have probably made a little more of it.

The accompaniment appears to be played entirely by Maurice, with only an organ and bass guitar, implying that this was just a bit of studio fun and was never intended to go any further. Indeed, Robin confirmed, 'That was just a joke track that we did. We called it a therapy break, so we'd just make up stupid songs and put them down anyway. We never really seriously meant for them to have been used for anything. We just wrote them to have some fun, just to keep ourselves fresh so we wouldn't get bogged down too much in writing. We'd just go off at a tangent'.

The protagonist claims that Rodgers and Hammerstein, and Gilbert and Sullivan, plagiarised his songs and that their material was 'completely unoriginal'. Robin's lead vocal, though well within his range, seems unusually strained at the top end.

The middle section degenerates into what was probably quite amusing at the time, but now fails to strike the funny bone in quite the right place and is rather cringeworthy. Barry introduces an alleged example of one of the stolen songs, while Robin wails in the background before performing the said work in an over-exaggerated way, actually becoming a parody of himself.

The first verse is reprised with added handclaps, and a final run-through of the chorus concludes the song.

If the middle section had been jettisoned, this would have been a quite passable fun song.

'Come Some Christmas Eve Or Hallowe'en' (Barry Gibb, Robin Gibb, Maurice Gibb)
Recorded at IBC Studios, London: 20 and 25 June 1968

A strange yet mesmerising song that Robin recalled as 'one of the ideas I had in India when I came up with 'Indian Gin And Whisky Dry'. That was a working tape. I'm positive it's Maurice playing the guitar and me doing the singing. It's very morose, but it's not even a demo really. It's sort of like writing in progress, just singing what comes into your mind'.

Sure enough, the lyrics were obtuse, but melodically it was very sound. With a little more work to streamline the lyrics and create a smoother transition from verse to chorus, the song could have had great potential.

The tenuous Christmas reference gave rise to the song's inclusion on the German edition of Robin's 2006 solo album *My Favourite Carols*.

'Gena's Theme' (Barry Gibb, Robin Gibb, Maurice Gibb)
Recorded at IBC Studios, London: 10 January and 25 June 1968

A special album titled *Eine Runde Polydor* was released for a Polydor Records anniversary in 1968. The album contained 28 short tracks by Polydor artists, including The Bee Gees. Their contribution was 'Gena's Theme' – an instrumental track with a Greek influence, although the strummed instrument played here is a mandolin, not a bouzouki.

The version released on the original LP was just 1:30 in length. This was reissued on the *Rarities* album, which was part of the Germany-only seventeen-LP *Bee Gees* box released in 1983. The full-length version on the 2006 *Idea* bonus disc is 3:18, and close analysis shows that the version on *Eine Runde Polydor* is merely an edit of this, but an absolutely flawless one.

The album credits are quite evidently incorrect: noting the track as being arranged and produced by James Last. It's quite obvious that with the recording having been done at IBC Studios in London, trusty Bill Shepherd was in charge of musical direction.

In the booklet notes accompanying the 2006 album reissue, Robin said, 'It was actually written for a film, but I've forgotten what that film was going to be. There was another along with that, that Sounds Incorporated did – 'The Square Cup' – It was in the same period that was written. I remember writing it with Barry and Maurice'. Robin's memory failed him when he said this, as it was in fact, Max Greger that covered 'The Square Cup'.

'Another Cold And Windy Day' (Coke Spot #1) (Barry Gibb, Robin Gibb)
Recorded in 1968: location unknown

In the 1960s – the golden age of ad jingles – Coca-Cola's advertising executives had a bold idea – work with the world's most talented musicians to create ads so good they felt like hit records. The Bee Gees were an obvious choice, and their performances for Coke were among the plethora of Coca-Cola commercials that set a new bar for quality.

The Bee Gees wrote two jingles, penned especially for the campaign, with instructions to include Coca-Cola's strap-lines: 'Things go better with Coca-Cola, Things go better with Coke'.

The first ad is slow and begins in a minor key with Robin singing over an accompaniment of harpsichord and strings: prime-time baroque pop. A key change to major for the strap-lines adds a clever twist, leaving the listener convinced that drinking Coke will make things good!

Two different versions of 'Another Cold And Windy Day' were used in commercials of differing lengths. The version on the *Idea* bonus disc is the shorter of the two at just 0:55, while the longer 1:27 version is a completely different recording and remains unreleased. That version includes two extra lines in the verse and repeats the chorus fully twice before the voice-over.

'Sitting In The Meadow' (Coke Spot #2) (Barry Gibb, Robin Gibb)
Recorded in 1968: location unknown

A much faster upbeat song, 'Sitting In The Meadow', is the second of the Bee Gees Coca-Cola ads. Little is known of the recording history of these, but it's likely they were recorded in the United States, as the campaigns were for the American market. Whoever produced and arranged the tracks did an amazing job in emulating The Bee Gees' trademark sound. Bill Shepherd may well have been involved, but there's no evidence to support this.

Robin takes the lead vocal, and the beloved harpsichord appears again. But the lead instrument here is more difficult to identify, but a best guess would be a double-reed instrument – most likely a cor anglais (English horn) or bassoon.

There are three different recorded versions of 'Sitting In The Meadow', the longest of which is 1:28 in length – it repeats the first verse and a full chorus to make up the additional time. The version on *Idea* is one minute long and includes a brief instrumental introduction not heard on the long version. The third and shortest version is just 33 seconds long and is simply a verse and chorus.

In a rather strange quirk, this was not The Bee Gees' first association with Coca-Cola. In 1964, as part of a promotional campaign in Australia, photos of pop stars were printed on the inside of Coke bottle tops. Barry, Robin, and Maurice were included individually, though Robin and Maurice's names got mixed up.

While The Bee Gees were riding high on the crest of their first wave of fame, the breakneck pace of their schedule and the mounting pressure to maintain their explosive success began to take a toll on everyone involved. The band members' relationships began to fragment significantly, as Barry recalled: 'We weren't getting on, and that was it. I think it was a mixture of the group not getting along very well and egos. Ego, I think, is the keyword for this group. It's not unlike any other group in that everybody wants to be the one that gets the attention. Unfortunately, I think that happens a lot. Certainly, it happened to us'.

The magnificently dramatic 'I've Gotta Get A Message To You' was recorded on 12 July – just days after the completion of *Idea* – and was quickly released within weeks as their third non-album single of 1968. 'Message' became their second number one hit in the UK. It reached number 8 in the US – the first in what would become a long list of top ten singles there. In Germany, the single extended The Bee Gees' run of top ten hits to five with a number 3 peak. On 25 July, they appeared on *Top of the Pops* performing the song.

The group's internal unrest – particularly that between Barry and Robin as the band's most influential members – began to reach the ears of the media, with persistent whispering that the Bee Gees were on the outs. From multiple perspectives, it seemed Robert Stigwood frequently championed Barry as the leader of the group and the charismatic object of their fans' affection. Certainly, this didn't sit well with Robin, who was also a defining force in The Bee Gees' sound and direction. It was a widening rift that would only grow in the coming months.

The Bee Gees were scheduled to begin a US tour in early August at the prestigious Hollywood Bowl in Los Angeles, but despite their consistent success in the American market, ticket sales for some of the dates were reportedly lacklustre. A few days before they were to make the trip west, Robin collapsed at home. The incident was spun in the press as him 'suffering from a mystery illness' (more than likely exhaustion given the band's circumstances), accompanied by a series of photos taken of the other Bee Gees visiting him while in bed recovering at the Regent's Park Nursing Home. However, this did little to quell rampant speculation that perhaps the entire affair was staged to purposely avoid tout shows that were projected to be poorly attended. Regardless, the outing was delayed by eight days, and they instead started at Forest Hills Stadium in New York on 10 August. The audience was apparently intrepid as they sat through a half-hour-long downpour during the show. The Bee Gees also received a long ovation and thirteen curtain calls at the show's conclusion. The remainder of the tour took them mostly to major centres in the Midwest and on the east coast for single-date appearances, save for two shows on 26 and 27 August at Fairgrounds Coliseum (now Taft Coliseum) during the Ohio State Fair in Columbus. The tour concluded on 1 September at the Merriweather Post Pavilion in Columbia, Maryland – a suburb of Baltimore.

On 20 August – the inaugural broadcast day for the UK's Thames Television network – The Bee Gees shared a headlining spot on their first made-for-television special *Frankie Howerd Meets The Bee Gees*. The band performed a number of comedy sketches and songs. Howerd was a well-known English comedian and comic actor whose career had begun on stage and on radio in 1946. By 1968, he'd been associated with four different television series' bearing his name, in addition to a 1966 radio serial. While Howerd was widely recognised in Britain, he was likely only remembered elsewhere for his turn as Mr. Mustard in Robert Stigwood's disastrous 1978 cinematic indulgence *Sgt. Pepper's Lonely Hearts Club Band*, during which he would be reunited with The Bee Gees – probably rather regrettably for all involved.

On 12 September, the group travelled to Brussels to begin two weeks of filming an *Idea* television special with Jean-Christophe Averty: a Parisian producer and film director renowned in France for his experimental approach to video art – particularly in the use of graphics and special effects – before it had become a mainstream concept in other parts of the world. Averty had won an Emmy Award in the US for his 1965 French TV variety show *Les raisins vertes*, in addition to directing the video short for The Beatles' 'A Hard Day's Night'.

The programme featured guest appearances from Julie Driscoll, Brian Auger and The Trinity, and Swedish singer Lil Lindfors, who performed 'Words' in her native language.

The show was first broadcast on 11 December 1968 in Germany. The Bee Gees performed a number of songs from both *Horizontal* and *Idea*: namely 'Massachusetts', 'Idea', 'I Started A Joke', 'Such A Shame', 'When The Swallows Fly', 'Indian Gin And Whisky Dry', 'I've Gotta Get A Message To You', 'Harry Braff', 'Swan Song' and 'I've Decided To Join The Air Force'. French viewers were treated to three additional songs – 'Kitty Can', 'Let There Be Love' and 'Down To Earth' – when the show aired on the night of 31 December 1968.

The programme has been aired twice since its first broadcast – the first instance in France in 1978 on the France 2 channel, and the second on Germany's ZDF Theaterkanal in 2010.

The following month, The Bee Gees began a 26-date tour of Germany, Austria and Switzerland, with the inaugural show scheduled at The Stadthalle in Bremen on 31 October. However, they completed only fourteen of the stops, cancelling the remaining dates after appearing at the Deutsches Museum in Munich on 18 November. The set list was, 'New York Mining Disaster 1941', 'To Love Somebody', 'Jumbo', 'The Singer Sang His Song', 'I've Decided To Join The Air Force', 'I Started A Joke', 'Words', 'In The Morning', 'Really And Sincerely', 'Massachusetts', 'I've Gotta Get A Message To You' and 'Spicks And Specks'.

On 1 November 1968, Lori Balmer released her first single on the Polydor label – two new Gibb brothers songs: 'Treacle Brown' and 'Four Faces West'. Both were written for a new *Pippi Longstocking* film. All backing and production for the single were provided by The Bee Gees, with Bill Shepherd doing the arrangements. Even at the age of eleven, Balmer was something of a showbiz veteran. Like the Gibb family, the Balmers had migrated from the UK to Australia in the late-1950s, and like the Gibbs, they'd returned to the UK. On their return in 1968, her family contacted Barry Gibb with a request for any assistance in establishing Lori in the UK entertainment scene. The Gibb and Balmer families were good friends back in Australia, and Lori had recorded and released two Barry Gibb songs in Australia in 1966. In the UK, Lori had worked regularly on children's TV and radio shows, including *The BBC 1 Club*. She had also appeared on a few shows with The Bee Gees.

Another record release at this time with an Australian connection was little-known Melbourne quartet The Brigade's cover of Maurice's 1966 composition 'All By Myself', as the B-side of their debut single 'Joan'. The Bee Gees' original demo of 'All By Myself' didn't see a commercial release until the *Inception/Nostalgia* album in 1970. The Brigade released just one more single before disbanding, but not before supporting The Rolling Stones on their first Australian tour down under. Legendary Australian music producer, engineer, label owner and record industry executive Ron Tudor co-produced the single.

On 16 November, The Bee Gees reappeared on *Beat-Club* in Germany performing 'I've Gotta Get A Message To You', further bolstering their most recent release in a market that continued to laud them generously. Other guests on the programme were The Who, The Easybeats, Spooky Tooth, Blue Cheer; Dave Dee, Dozy, Beaky, Mick & Tich; The Hollies, Barry Ryan and The Family Dogg. A week later, on 23 November, The Bee Gees performed 'I've Gotta Get A Message To You' and 'Massachusetts' on the American variety series *The Hollywood Palace* on the ABC network.

Meanwhile, Polydor – satisfied with the success of the first volume of their *Rare, Precious and Beautiful* compilation of the group's Australian-era output – decided to issue a second volume.

Rare, Precious and Beautiful – Volume 2 (1968)

Release date: UK: November 1968, US: February 1970
Side 1: 1. 'I Was A Lover, A Leader Of Men' 2. 'Follow The Wind' 3. 'Claustrophobia' 4. 'Theme From Jamie McPheeters' 5. 'Every Day I Have To Cry' 6. 'Take Hold Of That Star'
Side 2: 1. 'Could It Be' 2. 'To Be Or Not To Be' 3. 'The Three Kisses Of Love' 4. 'Cherry Red' 5. 'All Of My Life' 6. 'Don't Say Goodbye'

While this compilation's first volume had at least some coherence in terms of its track listing, there was no rhyme or reason behind what was presented on the following two – suffice to say, the choice of material was limited to the remaining 23 songs that needed to be split between two LP records.

The logical way would have been to place them in chronological order to create a sensible career retrospective showcasing the group's development. But the compiler threw all caution to the wind and presented a totally mixed-up catalogue. The material is good, but in this context – and with The Bee Gees riding high on their now three-albums-deep international career – any attempt to cash in was, as Robert Stigwood had said, an ill-advised move, as it merely served to confuse the listener. Needless to say, the album didn't sell particularly well.

The artwork used the same Malaysian butterfly design as the first volume, only this time on a purple background, at least in the UK. Germany and France used a photograph of a wine glass filled with colourful marbles, while the Japanese pressing featured a collection of bottles and a dried-flower arrangement. In later years as the sleeve variations became more widely known, they became interesting items for collectors to search out.

Australian country singer Johnny Ashcroft's November 1968 cover of the obscure 1966 Barry song 'Don't Forget Me Ida' has become something of a collectable single among fans and completists. It was the B-side of his 'Think Pink' single, released on the Columbia label.

The Bee Gees recorded the song themselves in September 1970 during sessions for the *2 Years On* album. It's a beautiful and emotional song featuring the famous Bee Gees harmonies in full flight. Ashcroft's cover version, in comparison, feels dull and emotionless. The Bee Gees' original has never been officially released.

The final month of 1968 was a veritable rollercoaster for The Bee Gees. 'I Started A Joke' – which became Robin's definitive signature song over the ensuing decades – was released as a single in the US, becoming their highest-charting single there, peaking at number 6. It reached the top spot in Canada (their second following 'Words') and New Zealand (their third following 'Spicks And Specks' and 'Massachusetts').

On 8 December, as Christmas approached, The Bee Gees appeared on a Southern Television special called *A Carol For Christmas*. The programme commissioned popular songwriters to write new Christmas carols. Contributions included 'Warm Your Heart' by the husband-and-wife songwriting team of Tony Hatch and Jackie Trent, and 'The Christmas Message' by The Bee Gees.

On 9 December, Robin wed his fiancée Molly Hullis, who he'd met the previous year during her tenure on the administrative staff at NEMS headquarters. The ceremony took place in London at Westminster's historic Caxton Hall, which since its construction in 1883 had been used as a political, social and artistic centre – and as a registry office for civil marriages for a long list of high-society figures and celebrities.

On 28 December, Maurice appeared on the first episode of BBC1's prime-time Saturday evening show *Happening For Lulu*. Maurice and Lulu (soon to be married), duetted on a performance of 'What A Beautiful Creature You Are', a song written by Donovan. The song had been recorded earlier in the year as a duet with Lulu and the Scottish balladeer during the sessions for his album, *The Hurdy Gurdy Man*, but was not released at the time. It eventually appeared as a bonus track on the 2005 CD reissue of the album.

While The Bee Gees' list of achievements and accolades was still growing exponentially, the cracks in the band's foundation were only too evident by the end of 1968. Adding fuel to the already hot flames of their clashing egos and priorities was their increasing dependence on drugs and alcohol to numb the immense stress of their jet-setting existence. It was a recipe for disaster that would continue to have an impact on the band for decades.

The most devastating blow came when guitarist Vince Melouney announced he was leaving to concentrate on record production. He'd auditioned for ex-Zombies keyboard player Rod Argent's new group Argent, but ultimately, Vince formed the group Ashton, Gardner and Dyke as his first project after The Bee Gees. Their first single, 'Maiden Voyage' with Vince's song 'See The Sun In My Eyes' on the B-side, was released on 24 January 1969. Ashton Gardner and Dyke would cover 'New York Mining Disaster 1941' in 1971, but Melouney would have no involvement, as by that time he was in a group called Fanny Adams – a progressive rock group formed in the UK by Australians and New Zealanders in mid-1970. They relocated to Australia in December 1970 and disbanded in early-1971.

The Bee Gees had already begun to prepare *Idea*'s follow-up – *Odessa* – during the summer of 1968. After completing eight tracks with his bandmates, Vince exited without finishing the sessions. His departure was bittersweet. 'We had an amazing time', he told the authors in May 2021:

That period of time was incredible. We were always off to do a television show somewhere or other. There are times in America which were literally mind-blowing, staying in hotels that I couldn't even imagine, travelling first-class and all that, and it was like another world. We were always in the office and doing interviews and photo sessions, so, after a time, it really was getting pretty stressful and the tension was gaining. There were a few fingers in the pie that shouldn't have been there, and

Barry and Robin were having a bit of a difficulty because Robin wanted to
sing more songs and there was a bit of a problem there as brothers seem
to have, which does happen. I mean, it doesn't happen all the time, of
course, but it does sometimes. And so, it really just got too crazy – the
tension was really high. When we started at IBC on 'New York Mining
Disaster' right in the beginning, we were innocent young lads from
Australia, and then all the fame and the fortune came and it was all too
much. The whole thing imploded and it was really sad. If all that hadn't
happened, I would have really loved to have stayed on and been able
to give more of myself, and also learn an enormous amount, and it was
really sad. That's what my song 'Such A Shame' was about. It was such a
shame that this whole fantastic thing was coming to an end.

The 'end' to which Vince refers was still a few months away. If 1968 was
The Bee Gees' unravelling, 1969 would be the final tug of the thread that
was holding their entire career together.

1969

The Bee Gees entered 1969 with *Idea*'s second single – 'I Started A Joke' – rising high in the global charts. It hadn't yet peaked in many markets when the first – and ultimately only – single from their forthcoming and fourth studio album *Odessa* was released on 14 February.

'First Of May', despite its beautiful arrangement and wistful lyrics, now lives in infamy as the hit that brought The Bee Gees to a screeching halt. Arguments about whether the A-side should be 'Lamplight' (sung by Robin) or 'First Of May' (sung by Barry) caused tremendous friction within the group. Robert Stigwood chose the latter, which cemented Robin's perception that he was the victim of favouritism benefitting his older brother. Despite Stigwood stating publicly that the new album's title song 'Odessa' – which was ostensibly Robin's composition – was one of his favourite Bee Gees recordings, Robin was convinced that his own songs couldn't get the required attention within the restraints of the group structure. 'First Of May' only managed to reach a disappointing number 37 in the US, but maintained steady top ten performances in Britain and Germany: peaking at 6 and 3 respectively.

In February 1969, David Garrick was a 23-year-old *veteran* English pop singer best known for his 1966 hit 'Mrs Applebee', which was a top 5 hit in parts of Scandinavia and reached number 22 in the UK. He was a personal friend of Barry, who gave him the song 'Maypole Mews' to record. The single was released on the Pye label on Valentine's Day, but failed on the charts. The song – along with his cover of 'Spicks And Specks' – was included on the 1998 CD *David Garrick: The Pye Anthology*, where all three brothers were credited as the writers. Garrick's recording of 'Maypole Mews' was included on the 2004 Bee Gees tribute album *Maybe Someone is Digging Underground*. Garrick also covered The Bee Gees' 1968 hit 'Words' on his 1968 live album *Blowup*.

A little-known and unreleased Bee Gees song called 'In The Middle Of The Grass' dating back to April 1968 was picked up by an obscure Essex group called 1984. They were signed by Transatlantic Records in early 1969 and released two singles on their Big T label in January and March that year. They recorded the song at Regent Sound in London's famous Denmark Street, although it's noted as 'There Is Music All Around Me' on the acetate label. The recording has gained cult status among psych collectors, and it's still not widely known that it's a Gibb brothers composition, despite its release on a couple of excellent CD compilations specialising in obscure psych: *In King Solomon's Minds* and *Talking About The Good Times, Volume 1*.

To close out February, Polydor released the third volume of their *Rare, Precious And Beautiful* compilations.

Rare, Precious And Beautiful – Volume 3 (1969)

Release date: UK: February 1969

Side 2: 1. 'Wine And Women' 2. 'I Don't Think it's Funny' 3. 'Turn Around, Look At Me' 4. 'I Am The World' 5. 'The Battle Of The Blue And The Grey' 6. 'How Love Was True'

Side 2: 1. 'And The Children Laughing' 2. 'You Wouldn't Know' 3. 'I Want Home' 4. 'Timber!' 5. 'I Was A Lover, A Leader Of Men' 6. 'Peace Of Mind'

The release of the final instalment of the *Rare, Precious And Beautiful* album series, arrived at a rather inopportune time, with The Bee Gees scheduled to debut *Odessa* – a double album of new material – the following month.

With 24 of the 35 Australian-era tracks already released on the first two albums in the series, there were only eleven songs remaining to make up the album, the compiler facing the dilemma of having six songs on one side and five on the other, leaving a significant durational difference between them. To remedy this, 'I Was A Lover, A Leader Of Men' – which had also appeared on the previous volume – was placed as side two's penultimate track, but in a bizarre twist, it did not appear in the sleeve's track listing.

The album was released in many countries, but not the United States – ATCO had opted out: probably indicative of poor sales of Volume 2. The German release was issued on Karussell, while Festival handled the Australian and New Zealand versions.

The artwork maintained the Malaysian butterfly design but on a turquoise background in the UK. Germany and France used a photograph of a different exotic butterfly on a white background, and the Japanese pressing showed a collection of chemical laboratory equipment.

On 18 February, Maurice married Scottish pop star Lulu at St. James' Church in Gerrards Cross, Buckinghamshire. The two had met backstage at *Top of the Pops* a year earlier and began dating. The event caused a media stir after nearly a thousand onlookers crowded the church grounds hoping for a glimpse of the newlyweds. Although tensions between the brothers at the time were noticeably high, Barry and Robin were in attendance.

Following the success of The Marbles' debut single 'Only One Woman' six months prior, their follow-up 'The Walls Fell Down' – released on 28 February – was also a Gibb brothers composition, as was the B-Side 'Love You'. Barry, Maurice and Colin Petersen provided the backing, while Barry, Robin, and Maurice are credited with production. Whilst 'Only One Woman' was a massive worldwide hit, 'The Walls Fell Down' did not repeat that success, although it reached numbers 3 and 10 in the Netherlands and New Zealand, respectively. Like its predecessor, the A-side has a very powerful chorus led by the commanding vocals of Graham Bonnet, but is somewhat let down by some very pedestrian lyrics.

American songstress Rosetta Hightower – who also sang with Joe Cocker – released a wonderful version of 'The Walls Fell Down' on the Philips label in 1973.

By mid-March, the personal and creative rifts between the Brothers Gibb had become too wide to repair, at least for Robin. On 19 March – just eleven days before *Odessa* was to land on record shop shelves – he formally announced he was leaving The Bee Gees. Rumours of the group's split had been swirling around the British press for at least six months while their management categorically denied them.

Years later, all three brothers would concede that immaturity, ego, exhaustion and some substance abuse had all contributed to their breakup. 'We were all very selfish at that point', Barry admitted in the 2020 documentary *The Bee Gees: How Can You Mend A Broken Heart*:

The testosterone kicked in, and the competition of life began. (Robin and I) both wanted to be individual performers. We all wanted individual recognition. And therein lies the issue. The three of us stopped looking inwards to each other and all started looking outwards to what we could be individually. 'To hell with what my brothers think' – and each one of us was thinking that ... Robin was first to say, 'Well, I'm quitting the group'. I stopped really knowing Robin and his personal life once we became famous. And the same with Mo. Our three lives were three different lives. We were no longer living the same life.

Barry and Robin ceased to communicate directly with one another for about eighteen months. However, this didn't stop them trading barbs through the UK music media. Barry said, 'We had this fascination with calling the newspapers up. You called *NME*, or you called *Disc* or *Music Echo*, and you'd say, 'Robin said this about me, and I just want to be able to correct the record', and all that stuff'.

Robin affirmed: 'It was a whole strange episode of our lives, but a lot of things had gone down at that time, and we needed time apart to think about them'.

Maurice began serving as his elder brothers' go-between – a role he would essentially play in perpetuity. He recounted in 2001:

Story of my life, really (laughs). Barry would call me up and say, 'Well, can you call Robin and tell him if he wants to do this?'. And Robin would go, 'Well, give Barry a call and let him know that I'm gonna be over'. I said, 'Robin, you call Barry. Barry, you call Robin'. And they both said, 'No, we won't!'. And for 18 months, they never did!.

In response to Robin's announcement of his departure, Barry and Maurice declared they would continue to record and tour together with drummer Colin Petersen as The Bee Gees.

Carrying the rather heavy weight of The Bee Gees' undoing, *Odessa* was released on 30 March.

Odessa (1969)
Personnel:
Barry Gibb: vocals, guitar
Robin Gibb: vocals, keyboard
Maurice Gibb: vocals, bass, piano, guitar
Colin Petersen: drums
Vince Melouney: guitar (Atlantic Studio sessions only)
Bill Keith: banjo on 'Marley Purt Drive' and 'Give Your Best'
Benjamin Franklin 'Tex' Logan Jr.: fiddle on 'Give Your Best'
Paul Buckmaster: cello on 'Odessa'
Additional personnel:
Orchestral arrangements: Bill Shepherd
Recording engineers: Philip Wade, Edward 'Ted' Sharp, Andy Knight (IBC); Adrian Barber (Atlantic Studio)
Producer: Robert Stigwood
Recorded between 12 July 1968 and December 1968 at IBC Studios; Trident Studios, London; Atlantic Studios, New York
Release date: UK: March 1969, US: February 1969

Chart positions: Spain: 3, West Germany: 4, France: 7, Canada: 7, UK: 10, Australia: 13, US: 20

More than half a century after its release, *Odessa* remains one of the most pivotal Bee Gees albums of their long recording career. Its ambition should have made it the best-known album from their first round of international success in the late-1960's. But despite it comprising so many well-written-and-arranged tracks, it became a commercial casualty of the now-dismantled group.

It's the only studio album The Bee Gees released as a double-LP set. Barry recalled years later, 'It wasn't supposed to be that, but everybody was doing that, like The Beatles'. The fab four released their *White Album* at the end of 1968.

Interestingly, *Odessa* was initially touted to be a concept album, and to this day, many still refer to it as such. While the definition of a concept album is somewhat murky and there's no consensus among music critics as to the specific criteria, it's generally defined as an album where the songs have greater meaning collectively than they do individually – typically achieved through a single central narrative or theme which can be instrumental or lyrical. There is no central unifying theme linking the songs on *Odessa*, so this definition does not apply. However, the term is sometimes applied to albums considered to be uniformly excellent rather than having a specific theme. If this interpretation is applied, *Odessa* is most certainly a concept album – however, this status would be bestowed by critics, not the creators.

Prior to The Bee Gees entering the recording studio in July 1968, a number of key groups – many of whom were particularly influential to the Gibb brothers – had released critically and commercially successful concept albums, including The Beach Boys' *Pet Sounds* (May 1966), The Beatles' *Sgt. Pepper's Lonely Hearts Club Band* (May 1967), Nirvana's *The Story of Simon Simopath* (October 1967), The Moody Blues' *Days of Future Passed* (November 1967), Simon and Garfunkel's *Bookends* (April 1968) and The Pretty Things' *S.F. Sorrow* (December 1968). The Who's *Tommy* would be released two months after *Odessa*.

Odessa's recording would be split between London and New York: the first time the group would record in the United States. The Bee Gees were scheduled to begin a 15-city American tour in August 1968. Days before they were to depart the UK, Robin collapsed due to nervous exhaustion. The remaining four Bee Gees – likely not wanting to forfeit their plane tickets – took the opportunity to spend a week laying down demos and instrumental tracks for the album at Atlantic Studios in Manhattan while Robin recovered at home. After a few weeks' break, sessions resumed back in London at IBC in October, but some tracks were recorded at Trident Studios – a short jaunt away in Marylebone.

Unfortunately for all concerned, *Odessa* – possibly the most important Bee Gees album to date – came at a time when the group was imploding. It's important to remember that at the time recording began, Maurice and Robin were still only nineteen years old. Big brother Barry himself would only turn 22 midway through the sessions. After two years of fame, fortune and a strenuous timetable of recording and touring, The Bee Gees were emotionally and physically exhausted.

Going through a phase the brothers themselves later referred to as 'first fame syndrome', they were at each other's throats – particularly Barry and Robin – fighting and bickering about songs, their lyrics, and importantly, who would sing the lead vocals. After years in Australia, striving for success, their recent accomplishments had inflated their egos. By their own admission, other influential factors – immaturity, drugs and alcohol – played a part and were having an impact. Vince Melouney left the group in September 1968, only contributing to a few *Odessa* songs. Ironically, he'd written the song 'Such A Shame' for their previous album *Idea*, about his feelings on the group tensions. By now, they were running rampant.

Odessa was originally intended to be titled *An American Opera*, before it was changed to *Masterpeace*. Both titles were puns commenting on America's turbulent political scene at the time. When Robin came up with the idea for the song 'Odessa' – about a shipwrecked sailor who's homesick – not only did they have a great song, but a new album title too. They also had an idea of what the album's overall concept could be. Robin's inspiration for 'Odessa' was the 1925 Russian silent film classic *Battleship Potemkin*: about the mutiny of the crew on a Russian battleship and the tragic aftermath. 'I was very affected by it', Robin said. 'Then the idea of the marine influences came in. We wanted to do a story set in Russia, of a man on an iceberg, floating free, thinking back on his life. In a sense, it was music that was pre-*Titanic*'.

However, a Bee Gees concept album, in the truest sense, was not to be. Instead, *Odessa* became a double album of songs bearing no relation to each other. That said, it *is* an album of generally very good songs, including the brilliant title track, 'First Of May', 'Marley Purt Drive' and 'Lamplight'. Drummer Colin Petersen recalled the country influence on

Odessa songs like 'Marley Purt Drive' and 'Give Your Best': 'It was my idea that we do that sort of thing, and Maurice is the one who will take more time out to listen to what I have to say; although, within the group, the okay has to come from Barry'.

For Barry, the album was never finished: 'Everything got out of hand and we didn't know which way we were heading. We never really finished the album. It was our own production and we were very proud of it, but it all turned out different. It marked a period of breaking up, and we weren't talking to each other, so we weren't in the studio together half the time and weren't as friendly toward each other'.

Maurice later described the album as going 'up and down in places, but a lot of people regard it as our *Sgt. Pepper*. To us, I don't think it was the best album we made, but the main title 'Odessa', I loved'. Responding to Maurice's comment, Barry said, 'I guess I have strong personal feelings about it because it was a time when the group was splitting up'.

The decision to release 'First Of May' as the lead single was riddled with controversy and was the catalyst for Robin's eventual exit. Ironically, Robin's final appearance with The Bee Gees beforehand was on *The Tom Jones Show* on 21 February, performing a unique arrangement which segued 'I Started A Joke' – on which Robin sang the lead with Barry on backing vocal – into 'First Of May' which Barry sang entirely on his own. In what can, in hindsight, be looked upon as a cruel twist, the song's final lines left Barry in the spotlight while Robin was in darkness, followed by Maurice on piano and Colin on drums fading to darkness a little later. In 2003, referring to his split from the band, Robin flippantly told *Mojo* magazine, 'We had egos'.

Perhaps the primary example of how one of the greatest vocal harmony groups in the history of popular music enjoyed no harmony amongst themselves at the time, is the fact that *Odessa* has not one but three instrumentals on it. Those tracks didn't even demonstrate the group's individual musical prowess – save for Maurice's piano on 'Seven Seas Symphony' – but served as more of a showcase for arranger Bill Shepherd and the orchestra.

Upon its release, *Odessa* wasn't particularly well-received by the critics, but it still made the UK top ten and the US top twenty album charts. Over the years, however, critical appreciation has grown, and many now regard *Odessa* as the most crucial of the group's 1960s albums. It's also considered to be one of the most imaginative, ambitious and interesting albums of their career – the title track epic being particularly admired for its quality.

Odessa is famed for its lavish red flocked gatefold sleeve embossed in gold. While the cover was quite unique, its production caused some issues at the printworks of Ernest J. Day & Co. Ltd. The Bee Gees' road manager Tom Kennedy recalled, 'The fibres were like itching powder, and they brought the whole plant to a stop. When they were making the album covers and were sticking the flock on, it was getting in the air, causing rashes, and they had to stop production on it'.

Except for the 1974 Japanese reissue, all later *Odessa* pressings came in regular card sleeves without flocking. British and German editions opted to brand the album 'The Original', by prefacing the title with a rubber-stamped graphic.

In keeping with the title track's theme, the inner gatefold depicts a child being thrown from a sinking ship into the safe hands of people in one of the lifeboats.

When it comes to Bee Gees collectors, *Odessa* has a special fascination and comes with bragging rights. In some South American countries, it was split into two single albums, while, in addition to the regular release, the Netherlands and West Germany issued a single LP – *Best of Odessa* – through record clubs. Numerous reissues over the years have added to the plethora of original releases. It's not uncommon for the devoted fan or completist to own upwards of 30 copies of *Odessa* in various formats.

In 1970, with the future of the group uncertain, Polydor in the UK reissued the first *Odessa* disc as part of their budget-priced 99 series, under the title *Marley Purt Drive*, after one of the album's strongest cuts. The sleeve design – by Hamish Grimes and Gustav Karl Moody (more commonly known as Hamish & Gustav) – was a garish affair, with a photograph of the three Gibb brothers posing by a crudely-cropped ship's mast. It omits Colin Petersen from the line-up as if purposely denying him his legacy as part of the group. Petersen's departure had been acrimonious, not so much from the Gibbs' perspective, but from Robert Stigwood's – legal proceedings continuing for a number of years before matters were concluded.

The second *Odessa* disc was released as *Sound of Love* in the same series but was actually released before *Marley Purt Drive*. Polydor's German budget label Karussell issued this album alone without its companion. The sleeve design was again by Hamish & Gustav who, thankfully, adopted a more tasteful approach than on their previous effort. Issued with a pleasant blue/grey background, a decoupaged violet frame presents an earlier-period photo of Barry, Robin, and Maurice posing by a globe; although, interestingly, it's not the same photo shoot used for the promotion of the 1967 single 'World'.

With the Bee Gees' increased popularity in the mid-1970s, RSO compiled a single Odessa album for the US and Canadian markets, released in September 1976 following the group's *Main Course*-led career resurgence.

When the album was initially reissued on CD in Europe, the instrumental track 'With All Nations (International Anthem)' was absent. No reason has ever been given for this puzzling omission. It can't be for lack of CD space, as it was included on US editions with plenty of room to spare.

In 2009, Reprise released a three-CD box set edition containing mono and stereo mixes of the original album. The third disc – enticingly titled *Sketches For Odessa* – contained demos, alternate versions, and two previously unreleased songs. The set saw the return of the flocked cover but in the form of a box housing the three CDs, a sticker, poster and informative booklet written by the sets' compiler Andrew Sandoval. Those who ordered early directly from the record company in the US, were rewarded with an *Odessa* T-shirt.

Odessa was included in Robert Dimery's book *1001 Albums You Must Hear Before You Die*.

'Odessa (City On The Black Sea)' (Barry Gibb, Robin Gibb, Maurice Gibb)

Recorded at IBC Studios, London: 17 October 1968 and other unknown dates

The title track is perhaps the most ambitious song The Bee Gees had created to date. It was inspired by a travel brochure Robin had seen.

It opens with a swirling orchestra simulating a storm at sea, followed by gentler cello and classical guitar in the aftermath, which backs the maudlin scene-setting introduction. The verses are presented in the form of letters to the protagonist's wife, within which he addresses her variously as 'cherub' and 'treasure'. He ponders his fate as the sole survivor of the British ship *Veronica*, which the introductory narrative tells us sank on 14 February 1899 under the command of Captain Richardson.

In verse one, the accompaniment is primarily acoustic guitar with occasional piano accents, while Robin muses about 'filing this berg to the shape of a ship' and asking his wife to tell the vicar to 'pray that I don't melt away'. The first chorus is big and powerful, with all three brothers adding tight harmonies to Robin's overlaid lead vocal.

Verse two is slightly faster than the first, and the guitar is joined by bass and strings. The second chorus is far more intense than the first, augmented with a cello part filtering through into a full-blown solo played by Paul Buckmaster and a wordless chant reminiscent of 'Every Christian Lion Hearted Man Will Show You' from *Bee Gees 1st*. The instrumental builds in intensity before the coda revisits the opening orchestral storm setting and vocal part to finish.

As revealed on the demo that appeared on the *Sketches For Odessa* disc in 2009, Barry originally narrated an introduction in a faux-American accent. The ship's name was originally intended to be *Onstrauss,* and it was Dutch, not British. The year she sank was 1866, but the date remained as 14 February. In his spoken word, Barry also adds that the ship 'was lost at sea and was wiped off the British royal register of shipping. There were no survivors'. The original title 'Odessa (City On The White Sea)' was likely changed because Odessa is actually a port on the Black Sea (marginal to the Atlantic Ocean, lying between Europe and Asia). The White Sea is connected to the northwest coast of Russia, and is indirectly connected to the Arctic Ocean.

Early on, the song was being considered as the album's lead single. Being over seven minutes long, the intention was to split the song over both sides of the 7", but the flow of the song would have been lost. However, the days of the three-minute pop song *were* being challenged by the likes of Richard Harris' 'McArthur Park' and The Beatles' 'Hey Jude', which were both hits in 1968, and neither of which were split over two sides of their respective singles. But deciding it wasn't in their best interests to follow that trend, the song was eventually dropped from consideration as an extract, and remained an album cut.

Robin was not best-pleased by this turn of events, saying, 'I worked and worked on that 'Odessa' track, and I got a ring from Robert Stigwood to say it was the greatest pop classic he had ever experienced. He said it was stupendous, and I used to get calls from him at three and four and five and six in the morning telling me the same thing. I thought it was going to be the new single'.

Who knew at the time that this would be such a critical decision and would determine The Bee Gees' fate?

'You'll Never See My Face Again' (Barry Gibb, Robin Gibb, Maurice Gibb)
Recorded at IBC Studios, London: 17 October 1968
A haunting track with Barry taking the lead vocal. The song has a slight country feel with guitars to the forefront. In light of the dissension and

tension amongst the brothers at the time, one wonders if any of the lyrics might've been more pointed than usual. It's one of the stronger tracks on a generally good but inconsistent album.

'Black Diamond' (Barry Gibb, Robin Gibb, Maurice Gibb)
Recorded at IBC Studios: 3 October 1968
Considered by some as a lost classic, this was the first song recorded when the group returned to England after initial *Odessa* sessions in New York City and was the first song not to feature lead guitarist Vince Melouney, who'd left the group after those New York sessions. It was recorded twice – the first version was released on *Sketches For Odessa* in 2009, and the second was the album take. Showcasing Robin's strong lead vocal, the intro features Maurice playing guitar, and Bill Shepherd's orchestral arrangement. Barry didn't feature on the demo at all. The beginning is similar on both versions, but there are vastly different lyrics in the verses.

Welsh singer Stephen Morgan's superb cover version – which appeared on the *Ordinary People ... Living Ordinary Lives* Bee Gees tribute album in 2002 – breathed new life into the song, and brought it solidly into the 21st century.

'Marley Purt Drive' (Barry Gibb, Robin Gibb, Maurice Gibb)
Recorded at Atlantic Studios, New York: 15 August 1968; IBC Studios, London: November 1968
Over fifty years before he publicly declared himself a 'bluegrass artist' to celebrate the 2021 release of *Greenfields* – an album of bluegrass and country duets of Bee Gees songs – Barry recorded the now-classic 'Marley Purt Drive'. Originally titled 'Marley Purt Drive (Area Code 213)', this fine rocking track is somewhat reminiscent of The Band's 'The Weight', which was released a few weeks before 'Marley Purt Drive' was recorded.

Recorded at Atlantic Studios in New York, Barry was joined by legendary bluegrass musician Bill Keith from the Jim Kweskin Jug Band on banjo and pedal steel, Maurice on bass, Vince Melouney on guitars and Colin Petersen on drums. It was later completed with an orchestra, at IBC in London in November.

The lyric's surreal narrative tells of a financially modest married man with fifteen children, who one Sunday takes a drive out to Pasadena to get some respite from his circumstances, only to return and discover – without explanation – that he now has twenty more children to look after!

An earlier mix with a false start followed by one count, and with the original New York vocal, later appeared on *Sketches For Odessa*.

'Marley Purt Drive' was released as a single in South Africa in July 1969 and was also included on a compilation album – *No One's Gonna Change Our World* – assembled by comedian Spike Milligan, featuring sleeve notes by Prince Philip, the Duke of Edinburgh. The charity album – released in the UK on 12 December 1969 – was for the benefit of the World Wildlife Fund, and is widely known as being the first release of the Beatles song 'Across The Universe'. The Bee Gees' contribution was the album's longest track, clocking in at 4:26.

The song became a regular part of the concert set until 1974, and it was occasionally played as an impromptu warm-up during soundchecks well beyond that time.

When Polydor in the UK later issued the two *Odessa* LPs as single albums as part of their budget-priced 99 series, the first disc was issued as *Marley Purt Drive*, emphasising the song as a strong title track.

Notable cover versions include those by Jose Feliciano – who scored a hit with it in Australia, Canada and the US in 1970 – and Lulu (Maurice's wife at the time), on her highly-regarded *New Routes* album, which was recorded at the legendary Muscle Shoals Sound Studios in Alabama, and co-produced by future Bee Gees producer Arif Mardin.

'Edison' (Barry Gibb, Robin Gibb, Maurice Gibb)
Recorded at Atlantic Recording Studios, New York: 21 August 1968; IBC Studios, London: November 1968

'Edison' started life as 'Barbara Came To Stay', as featured on the 2009 *Sketches For Odessa* disc. The title may have been inspired by the brothers' mother, Barbara Gibb.

The melody remained the same in the revised version, but the lyrics were developed into a tribute to American inventor Thomas Alva Edison. The lyric is very clever, referring to Edison's inventions in the lines, 'He made electric lights to read', 'He gave us cylinders to please' and 'Station to station, many wires'.

'Edison' seemed to have turned out far better than its 'Barbara Came To Stay' prototype; however, it's album filler, and probably wouldn't have made the cut if *Odessa* had been stripped down to a single album at the time.

'Melody Fair' (Barry Gibb, Robin Gibb, Maurice Gibb)
Recorded at IBC Studios, London: 25, 26 and 27 October 1968

Once described by Maurice as 'one of our best productions in simplicity and warmth', 'Melody Fair' is the album's most commercial song. Barry recalled, 'I think 'Melody Fair' was written in the studio; we used to write a lot of stuff on the spot in the studio. We often used to go to recording studios without any songs at all. Because the time was booked, we had to be there. So, we'd turn up at seven at night, and we'd basically start writing and cutting the backing track of a song that wasn't finished. 'Melody Fair' was probably influenced by 'Eleanor Rigby' – I was wanting to make the same kind of statement'.

The first demo was recorded on 26 October 1968, and a second more upbeat version the following day. Both demos appeared on *Sketches For Odessa*. With Barry singing lead, only Maurice appears to be providing support vocals, along with Bill Shepherd's beautiful orchestral arrangement. The drums were removed from the final recording.

Despite its commercial potential, 'Melody Fair' was released as a single in Japan only in 1971: two years after it appeared on *Odessa*. Maurice explained that this was because it was used in the 'motion picture *Melody* or *S.W.A.L.K.*, David Putnam's first film. He used a lot of our earlier singles. A lovely movie based on kids falling in love for the first time'.

The group performed the song in its entirety on their Japanese tour in March 1972, and as part of the medley section on the Japanese leg of the 1989 *One for All* tour. The *Melody* movie was a big hit in South Africa too, so it was appropriate that both 'First Of May' and 'Melody Fair' – which featured in it – were performed at the *One Night Only* concert stop in Pretoria in 1998.

In 1974, The Bee Gees' little brother Andy formed his first band in the Isle of Man, with guitarist John Alderson, bassist Jerry Callaghan and drummer John Stringer. Barbara Gibb named the group Melody Fayre – with altered archaic spelling – after this song.

In 1994, Eggbert Records released a tribute album called *Melody Fair*, which featured many great cover versions of Bee Gees songs, including a revitalised rendition of the title track by California band The Jigsaw Seen.

'Suddenly' (Barry Gibb, Robin Gibb, Maurice Gibb)
Recorded at IBC Studios, London: 17 October 1968

'Suddenly' – originally titled 'How Can You Tell' – was Maurice's only solo vocal on *Odessa* and was indeed his first complete lead vocal on any Bee Gees song since their Australian era. It suits his voice well, and it would seem likely that he wrote the song. However, like every song on *Odessa*, it was credited to all three brothers regardless of who actually wrote it. This policy– amongst a litany of other issues – was also causing frustration among the sibling trio, as they felt that they weren't being appropriately accredited for their respective contributions.

In 1969, British producer Mike Batt covered 'Suddenly' as the B-side of his Beatles cover single 'Your Mother Should Know'. He would go on to record the classic albums *Schizophonia* and *Tarot Suite* but will always be best remembered for writing the theme song to the animated children's TV programme *The Wombles* and its subsequent spin-off pop hits.

'Whisper Whisper' (Barry Gibb, Robin Gibb, Maurice Gibb)

Recorded at Atlantic Recording Studios, New York: 13 and 14 August 1968; IBC Studios, London: November 1968

The orchestra's ascending chromatic string introduction creates an air of suspense, but gives no indication of what's to follow. The first four verses represent a dialogue between a drug dealer and his customer – controversial in any era, but quite shocking that it was The Bee Gees doing it.

The tempo picks up for the final part, which sees Barry doing his best John Lennon impression, accented with horn stabs and subject matter of a sexual nature. The song continues to spiral towards its dramatic and sudden finish. It's an interesting track.

According to Bee Gees historian Joe Brennan, the album recording of 'Whisper Whisper' is a composite of three sections recorded at different sessions. An alternate take of part two with a vocal recorded at the New York sessions, appears on *Sketches For Odessa*.

Only one cover of this song is known to exist – by Washington, D.C. grunge band Action Figures, appearing on the highly-acclaimed 1994 Bee Gees tribute album *Melody Fair*.

'Whisper Whisper' made a surprise appearance on the soundtrack of the 2021 Disney movie *Cruella*, alongside tracks by The Electric Light Orchestra, Supertramp, Blondie, Queen, The Doors and The Clash.

'Lamplight' (Barry Gibb, Robin Gibb, Maurice Gibb)

Recorded at IBC Studios, London: 25 October 1968 and other unknown dates between 24 November and 27 December 1968

In terms of Bee Gees' lore, manager Robert Stigwood's decision to relegate the Robin-led 'Lamplight' to the B-side of the Barry-helmed 'First Of May' single, is one of the most notorious chapters in the lengthy annals of their career. Slighted, Robin took his leave from the group he'd helped to build over the previous decade.

As the brothers would later admit, Stigwood's decision, in retrospect, only brought forward what was inevitable. Eight years of paying their dues in Australia without much success, followed by the sudden impact of success and all its associated pressures, had cast a heavy shadow on the brothers' working and personal relationships. Weary from touring and endless recording sessions, and stoked by immaturity, the cauldron of turmoil began to boil over.

During an April 2021 guest appearance on music producer Rick Rubin's *Broken Record* podcast, Barry referred to the song as 'brilliant', saying he'd played it quite recently for the first time in years and 'it should have been released as a single'.

Ironically, in Germany – where the group were very popular – 'Lamplight' was the first choice for the single A-side, and it was initially issued in a picture sleeve with 'Lamplight' as the main title. This was soon withdrawn and replaced with a different sleeve favouring 'First Of May' as the A-side.

A demo of 'Lamplight' recorded on 25 October 1968 – which appears on the *Sketches For Odessa* CD – omits the familiar introduction sung in French:

Allons viens encore chérie
J'attendais an après an
Sous la lampe dans la vieille avenue

This closely translates to the English-language bridge:

Come home again dear
I have waited year after year
Under the lamp in our old avenue

A source for the translation has never been identified.

'Sound Of Love' (Barry Gibb, Robin Gibb, Maurice Gibb)
Recorded at Atlantic Recording Studios, New York: 20 August 1968; IBC Studios, London: November 1968

'Sound Of Love' is a fine ballad with a powerful Barry lead vocal, built around Maurice's simple but effective piano work.

When Polydor in the UK later issued the two *Odessa* LPs as single albums, the second disc was issued as *Sound of Love*, emphasising the song as a strong title track.

A cover version was on the market before The Bee Gees' take was released. Decca Records released a single by Paul Slade on 21 February 1969: five weeks before *Odessa* hit the stores.

Two other notable covers followed in 1970: the legendary Etta James gave the song a different groove on her album *Etta James Sings Funk*, while The Sandpipers' harmony-laden version appears to pre-empt Barry's exaggerated vibrato from 'How Can You Mend A Broken Heart'.

'Give Your Best' (Barry Gibb, Robin Gibb, Maurice Gibb)
Recorded at Atlantic Recording Studios, New York: 20 August 1968; IBC Studios, London: November 1968

On an album best-known for its lush orchestral support, this fun, upbeat country/rock song is a real standout. Drummer Colin Petersen said it was the best session he ever played on. Bluegrass musicians Bill Keith and Benjamin Franklin 'Tex' Logan Jr. were brought in especially for the New York sessions, playing banjo and fiddle, respectively.

The song appeared in the 1971 movie *Melody*, but it's not known whether the introductory banter 'It's a square dance Mr. Marshall, it's a square dance on the floor, it's a square dance Mr. Perkins, it's a square dance to be sure, to be sure' had any bearing on lead character Melody Perkins' surname.

The original vocal take with different lyrics appears on *Sketches For Odessa*.

The brothers' sister Lesley Gibb made her only known appearance on record duetting with Australian country singer Ian B. MacLeod on his 1973 album *Restless*, where the sleeve notes billed Lesley as 'The sister of the world-famous Bee Gees'. 'Give Your Best' was one of three songs they performed together, although it's the only one penned by her brothers – the others being 'Rings Of Gold' and 'Keep On Smiling'.

'Seven Seas Symphony' (Barry Gibb, Robin Gibb, Maurice Gibb)
Recorded at IBC Studios, London: 19 August 1968

It seems incongruous now – and perhaps it did way back in 1969 – that one of the greatest vocal-harmony groups of all time would put not one, not two, but *three* instrumental tracks on an album. Of the three, 'Seven Seas Symphony' is by far the best. It has a lovely melody, with Maurice's piano at the forefront backed by Bill Shepherd's orchestra – all playing together live. Neither The Bee Gees' band nor the other Gibb brothers participated in the recording of this or the album's other instrumental tracks.

'With All Nations (International Anthem)' (Barry Gibb, Robin Gibb, Maurice Gibb)
Recorded at IBC Studios, London: 17 October 1968

The second of the three instrumental tracks closes side three and is by far the most pretentious, sounding like something that could have come from the famous British film production company Pinewood Studios in the 1940s or 1950s. Gloriously pompous and patriotic, it's similar in places to 'Moon Anthem': an equally grandiose song Robin Gibb recorded later in 1969 to celebrate the first moon landing. However, including 'With All Nations' in particular – although quite bizarre in some ways – only adds to the eccentricity, uniqueness and brilliance of the album overall.

The demo that appeared on the *Sketches For Odessa* CD had a rousing vocal chorus with the three brothers singing stirring, if somewhat twee, lyrics. If one ever doubted the Gibb brothers' British heritage, they should indeed listen to this song.

'I Laugh In Your Face' (Barry Gibb, Robin Gibb, Maurice Gibb)
Recorded at IBC Studios, London: 12 July 1968

This is possibly the earliest song written for *Odessa*, as records show it was penned at the same time as 'I've Gotta Get A Message To You', earlier in 1968. With lead vocals shared by Barry and Robin, this is another sorrow-filled song with some nonsensical lyrics – but, as always, with a great melody and a hook-rich chorus.

'Never Say Never' (Barry Gibb, Robin Gibb, Maurice Gibb)
Recorded at Trident Studios, London: October 1968; IBC Studios, London, on other unknown dates between 24 November and 27 December 1968

'Never Say Never Again' has a very catchy chorus and excellent vocals, but is let down by some inane lyrics. Robin would recall that he wanted to write the song with the line 'You said 'Goodbye', I declared war on Spain', but 'Barry wanted something so normal it was ridiculous. He said my words were so unromantic. But what could be more normal than a man in love wanting to declare war on anything that was to him unlovely?'. The jury's still out on this case, but perhaps the song and its lyric epitomise the pure eccentricity and intrigue of The Bee Gees' songwriting at the time.

With a lead vocal by Barry, a demo of 'Never Say Never' appeared on the *Sketches For Odessa* disc, with intrusive bass and lead guitar too far forward in the mix.

English psychedelic band The Tangerine Peel – who released 'Every Christian Lion Hearted Man Will Show You' as a single on United Artists in 1967 – issued 'Never Say Never' as another A-side, on 14 March 1969, having changed label to MGM Records.

'First Of May' (Barry Gibb, Robin Gibb, Maurice Gibb)

Recorded at Atlantic Recording Studios, New York: 16 August 1968; IBC Studios, London: 24 November 1968

Chart positions: Netherlands: 1, West Germany: 3, Ireland: 4, New Zealand: 4, South Africa: 4, Switzerland: 4, UK: 6, Belgium: 7, Norway: 9, Austria: 10, Canada 14, Australia: 15, France: 18, Spain: 20, Italy: 22, US: 37

'First Of May' is now considered a classic Bee Gees song; one of the prettiest compositions the brothers ever wrote and one of their most popular and enduring.

As mentioned previously, it was the contentious A-side of the only *Odessa* single released in the UK, America, Australia and most of Europe. Originally, the title track was to be the first single, with its lengthy duration spread over both sides. Before the idea was quashed, it was given the catalogue number Polydor 56304, which was then transferred over to 'First Of May'. Whether the 'Odessa' single was actually pressed has never been confirmed; but as none have ever been found over the half-century since its mooted release, it's highly unlikely that it was.

It's a sweet ballad of a long-lost childhood love, sung solely by Barry. He explained that the song title 'was my dog's birthday. When Linda and I first moved into an apartment near St. Paul's Cathedral, we got ourselves a Pyrenean mountain dog and named him Barnaby. The idea came from then. Sad to say, Barnaby's gone, but the song lives on'. Barnaby is seen on the *Cucumber Castle* album cover and TV special, and also in the 'Lonely Days' promotional film clip.

Despite 'First Of May' not being the preferred A-side choice for all concerned, Robert Stigwood's decision to release it was validated when it became another international hit, charting in the top ten across Europe and the UK, and the top twenty in Canada and Australia.

Maurice recalled that when they were writing the song, 'Barry and I were sitting at the piano, and I started playing the chords and Barry started singing 'When I was small and Christmas trees were tall', and I started singing along with it. We put a demo down (at New York's Atlantic Studios on 16 August 1968) with a vocal, and we kept the piano track.

Went back to England, and went into IBC Studios in London, added onto that piano track, and Barry's vocal stayed on as well. We had a choir and an orchestra all on this one piano'.

After its inclusion in the *Melody* film soundtrack in 1971, 'First Of May' had several resurrections. In 1996, the song was used as the theme of the Japanese drama *Wakaba no Koro* and was consequently reissued as a 3' CD-single in Japan, with 'How Deep Is Your Love' as the B-side. It reached number 25 and sold more than 100,000 copies.

Maurice performed the song as a duet with his former wife Lulu on her 2002 TV special *An Audience with Lulu*: subsequently released on her *Greatest Hits* album the following year. In 2005, Robin guested on British boy band G4's cover of the song, which was also released as a Christmas single. The Bee Gees also performed the song during their *One Night Only* concert in South America in 1999.

Cover versions of 'First Of May' number well over 100, with many high-profile artists among them, including Patti Boulaye, Jose Feliciano, Roger Whittaker, Cilla Black, Frank Ifield, The Wolfe Tones, Sarah Brightman and Matt Monro.

'The British Opera' (Barry Gibb, Robin Gibb, Maurice Gibb)
Recorded at IBC Studios, London: October or November 1968

The third and final instrumental on the album is the weakest of the three, although it's not unpleasant in the slightest. It is, however, rather ostentatious, and it's hard to envisage a young group of pop musicians composing this. The Gibbs could certainly have floated musical ideas, but this is far more a showcase of Bill Shepherd's arranging skills than a coherent song. The orchestra works hard to lift the song, but it would possibly have been better suited to a film or television soundtrack rather than being the anticlimactic finale to a rather splendid album.

Odessa – 2009 edition bonus songs

'Nobody's Someone' (Barry Gibb, Robin Gibb, Maurice Gibb)
Recorded at IBC Studios, London: 3 October 1968

Barry sounds more than a little melancholy as he takes the lead vocal on this sad little song. He accompanies himself on 12-string guitar, with Maurice on bass and Colin Petersen on drums.

The song's first release was actually as 'a rather obscure cover version', according to the booklet accompanying the *Odessa* reissue CD. The cover was by an artist known only as Andrew, on his 1997 CD EP *Million Dollar Movie*.

Andrew was actually Andrew Sandoval, a name that should be very familiar to Bee Gees fans, not only as the author of the excellent book *Bee Gees: The Day-By-Day Story, 1945-1972*, but as the compiler of the reissues of *Bee Gees 1st*, *Horizontal*, *Idea* and – rather fittingly – *Odessa*. He also helmed the superb collection *Saved by the Bell: Collected Works Of Robin Gibb 1968-1970*. Modesty obviously prevented him from bragging about how great his 'rather obscure cover version' was.

Andrew's version was quite faithful to The Bee Gees' original but added a nice solo cello in verse one, and some punchy drums from verse two onwards. Strings give this production a polished and classy feel, while a tasteful glockenspiel solo is a tip of the hat to Bee Gees arranger Bill Shepherd, who was fond of such things.

'Pity' (Barry Gibb, Robin Gibb, Maurice Gibb)
Recorded at Atlantic Recording Studios, New York: 19 August 1968
'Pity' was the only song recorded for *Odessa* in New York that wasn't fully completed or remade. It's a solid number that may or may not have fit the disparate song collection that made up the album. It could have potentially replaced one of the album's instrumental tracks. Then again, *Odessa* was a masterpiece as it was, so perhaps we shouldn't speculate as to what it could have been, and instead appreciate it for what it is.

Immediately following Robin's withdrawal, he and the remaining Bee Gees were in separate studios recording new material – Barry, Maurice and Colin at IBC in Marylebone, and Robin at De Lane Lea about a mile away in Soho.

The group minted two new songs that would be issued as a single just two months later: 'Tomorrow Tomorrow' and 'Sun In My Morning'.

On 7 May, The Bee Gees began work on the follow-up to *Odessa*. Eventually, the sessions would produce their next studio set *Cucumber Castle*, named after a fantastical album cut from *Bee Gees 1st*. However, it would be almost a year before the new LP saw the light of day.

Following the relative failure of their previous single earlier in the year, The Marbles followed up in May with 'I Can't See Nobody'/'Little Boy' in a number of territories, oddly excluding the UK. The A-side was a comparatively upbeat and brassy cover of the 1967 Bee Gees song, and the B-side was a new Barry and Maurice composition. Trevor Gordon sings lead on the B-side: a sweet, touching little song. Barry Gibb produced both sides, and Bee Gees arranger Bill Shepherd directed the B-side's accompaniment. The single failed to make the charts.

Before splitting later in the year, The Marbles would release one more single: 'Breaking Up Is Hard To Do'. The B-side in the UK was 'I Can't See Nobody'. Their solitary eponymous album was released in 1970, containing five Gibb brothers compositions. Four had previously been released as either A or B-sides, and the fifth was 'To Love Somebody'.

On 17 May, the BBC aired the 45-minute special *Bee Gees in Concert* as part of their long-running London-based *The Talk of the Town* series – a unique gig where sister Lesley replaced the departed Robin for just the one performance. The set list was 'New York Mining Disaster 1941', 'Kitty Can', 'With The Sun In My Eyes', 'Suddenly', 'To Love Somebody', 'Seven Seas Symphony', 'First Of May', 'In The Morning', 'I've Gotta Get A Message to You', 'Spicks And Specks', 'Sun In Morning' and 'World'.

The Bee Gees appeared on *Top of the Pops* on 29 May, in the form of pre-recorded footage of them performing 'Tomorrow Tomorrow': their new stand-alone single that was released the next day. Being their first new output as a three-piece sans Robin, the single arrived to less than stellar reviews and was followed by an equally mediocre chart-showing: it stalled at number 21 in the UK, and reached only 54 in *Billboard* in the US.

'Tomorrow Tomorrow' (Barry Gibb, Maurice Gibb)

Recorded at IBC Studios, London: 19 and 21 March 1969
Chart positions: Denmark: 1, Netherlands: 3, New Zealand: 3, Norway: 3, Brazil: 4, Switzerland: 6, West Germany: 6, Austria: 7, Belgium: 9, South Africa: 9, Spain: 12, Canada: 19, UK: 23, Italy: 24, Australia: 28, US: 54

On the same day Robin announced he was leaving to pursue a solo career, Barry, Maurice and Colin were in the studio laying down tracks for 'Tomorrow Tomorrow' and 'Sun In My Morning'. Maurice implied that Robin's exit had been foreseen when he said, 'As always, thinking ahead, this was the first track that Barry and I recorded as a duet'.

'Tomorrow Tomorrow' is a departure from the typical Bee Gees style the audiences had become accustomed to. Maurice said, 'I don't think it's us, but I quite like it'. It's not surprising that it wasn't written to the usual formula, as it was originally composed with the intention of being given to Joe Cocker, and it's easy to imagine him singing it. Barry rushed to finish the song quickly, but it never reached Joe, whose management gave him 'Delta Lady' instead.

Robert Stigwood attempted to rescue what he believed to be a good commercial number and released it as a Bee Gees single, despite Barry's protest that it didn't suit their style.

'Sun In My Morning' (Barry Gibb, Maurice Gibb)
Recorded at IBC Studios, London: 19 March 1969

Released as the B-side of 'Tomorrow Tomorrow', 'Sun In My Morning' prepared fans for what was to come. With Robin's departure, Barry and Maurice were able to explore territories previously uncharted by the group, and this is a stylistic step towards the country influence that would surface on their subsequent album *Cucumber Castle*.

It is in part a Barry lead vocal, but on most lines, Maurice joins either in part or in full. The trademark three-part sibling harmonies were no more, but the bold two-part harmony, which would become the norm for the next little while, lifts the song immensely.

Maurice was fond of it, calling it 'a hypnotic song with a lot of feeling'. He continued by saying, 'I love the atmosphere and the string arrangement to the loneliest sound of the organ and the voices'.

Robin found time to co-produce the single 'Love For Living' for British singer Clare Torry, which was released on 20 June. It's a song Robin was apparently very enthusiastic about, insisting strings and brass be added. Clare – best-known now as the legendary voice of Pink Floyd's 'The Great Gig In The Sky' – wrote both the A-side and the B-side – 'Live Tomorrow, Live Today' – but Robin was not involved with the recording of the latter.

Steve Kipner – of Steve & The Board fame – and his new musical partner, fellow Australian Steve Groves, came to England in 1968 and released an eponymous album as Steve & Stevie. Kipner bumped into Barry in early 1969, and one thing led to another. Within no time, Steve & Stevie were signed by Robert Stigwood, and Maurice became their producer.

The duo changed their name to Tin Tin and began writing and recording new material. Maurice was a proactive producer, playing a number of instruments on their recordings. Their first single, 'Only Ladies Play Croquet'/'He Wants To Be A Star', was released on 20 June and features Maurice playing harpsichord, bass, drums and mellotron on the A-side; and bass and piano on the flip. Maurice continued to work with Tin Tin throughout 1969 on what would become their first album, including the 1970 hit single 'Toast And Marmalade For Tea'.

Meanwhile, Robin readied his debut solo single 'Saved By The Bell', which followed his brothers' 'Tomorrow Tomorrow' just under a month later on 27 June. However, his legal commitments to The Bee Gees and their management threatened his impending solo career. As 'Saved By The Bell' climbed the UK singles chart, Stigwood vowed to sue him for breach of contract, and secured an injunction to prohibit him from releasing new music. It would be cancelled in September when a deal was negotiated behind the scenes.

Stigwood's litigiousness did little to impede the single's success, as it became a runaway summer hit in Britain and Germany, peaking at numbers 2 and 5, respectively. It topped the singles charts in Denmark, South Africa, the Netherlands, Ireland and New Zealand, although it was largely ignored in the US, where it stalled at 87.

'Saved By The Bell' (Robin Gibb)
Recorded at De Lane Lea Studio, London: March 1969
Chart positions: Denmark: 1, Ireland: 1, Netherlands: 1, New Zealand: 1, South Africa: 1, UK: 2, Yugoslavia: 2, West Germany: 3, Norway: 4, Australia: 9, Canada: 44

Written by Robin alone, 'Saved By The Bell' would introduce his forthcoming solo album *Robin's Reign*, which would arrive eight months later. Robin and arranger Kenny Clayton co-produced the song. Although Robin was officially alienated from his brothers, his twin brother Maurice played piano, organ, guitar and additional vocals: much to Barry's displeasure. With similar production values, an infectious melody and an irresistible chorus, it's very Bee-Gees-like. Regrettably, the lyrics are banal, but the commercial appeal is undeniable. It was the most successful song of Robin's long and industrious solo career, which lasted until his death in 2012.

To promote the single, Robin performed the song on *Beat-Club* in Germany and *Top of the Pops* in the UK. The song was also a popular part of his solo concerts in the 2000s and appeared on a 2005 live solo album recorded with the Neue Philharmonic Frankfurt Orchestra. It was also occasionally performed in post-reunion Bee Gees concerts. 'Saved By The Bell' and Robin's 1983 hit single 'Juliet' were the only solo Gibb recordings to be performed live by The Bee Gees.

'Saved By TheBell''s mechanical rhythm was courtesy of a Rhythm Ace drum machine: manufactured by the Ace Tone company in Japan. Engineer and inventor Ikutaro Kakehashi founded the company in 1960.

He later established the Roland Corporation – one of the world's premier manufacturers of electronic musical instruments. 'Saved By The Bell' has widely been recognised as the first major international chart hit to employ the technology, which was only a few years old at the time and was a rather remarkable innovation. It could play over 100 rhythm combinations and had sixteen pre-set patterns, with four buttons that added separate sounds mimicking a cymbal, clave, cowbell and bass drum. Robin also used the Rhythm Ace on a number of other tracks on the *Robin's Reign* album.

'Mother And Jack' (Robin Gibb)
Recorded at De Lane Lea Studio, London: March 1969
'Mother And Jack' was the B-side of 'Saved By The Bell'. It was also on the *Robin's Reign* album issued the following year. Whilst Robin's songs could quite often be accused of being somewhat morose, 'Mother And Jack' is quite upbeat, although the typically vague Robin lyrics point to the protagonists being evicted from their house. That being said, it's quite an enticing listen.

'Alexandria Good Time' (Robin Gibb)
Recorded at De Lane Lea Studio, London: March 1969
This was the original B-side chosen for 'Saved By The Bell'. However, due to a technical malfunction, it was withdrawn. The handful of surviving singles show the B-side started in the middle of the song and played to the end, followed by a few seconds of silence before the complete song was played. Why the rectification involved replacing the song with a totally different one – 'Mother and Jack' – is unknown, but its substitute was a far better song. However, the slow-moving organ on the melody line of 'Alexandria Good Time' is actually more characteristic of Robin's output at the time.

The recording received a formal release some 45 years later on the posthumous 2015 set *Saved By The Bell: The Collected Works Of Robin Gibb 1968-1970*.

'Smile For Me' – a Barry Gibb song – was an outtake from the 1968 *Horizontal* sessions and was gifted to the popular Japanese band The Tigers. Sung in English, it became the vocal group's grand crack at international success. As they didn't speak English, they had to be taught to sing the English lyrics phonetically. Barry and Maurice rewrote the song specifically for The Tigers, and it was recorded in London with Barry's uncredited contribution. The song was released as the B-side to 'Rain Falls On The Lonely' in the UK on 11 July, but didn't chart. Two weeks later, on 25 July, it was released in Japan as the A-side, and fared very well, reaching number 3.

While 'I.O.I.O.' was technically the first track recorded for what would become The Bee Gees' next album *Cucumber Castle*, it was pinched from the previous summer's *Idea* sessions. Therefore, 'Don't Forget To Remember' was the first track recorded specifically for the new project. It was released as a single in the UK on 8 August.

'Don't Forget To Remember' (Barry Gibb, Maurice Gibb)

Recorded at IBC Studios, London: 7 May 1969
Chart positions: Denmark: 1, Ireland: 1, Netherlands: 1, New Zealand: 1, South Africa: 1, Norway: 2, Switzerland: 2, UK: 2, Belgium: 3, Austria: 8, West Germany: 9, Australia: 10, Spain: 27, Canada: 39, France: 42, US: 73

A sentimental ballad, 'Don't Forget To Remember' is country-flavoured – a style that Barry and Maurice appreciated and would revisit many times in the coming decades. The record received some flak in the UK for being a rip-off of American country singer Jim Reeves, but Barry denied it was any such thing, saying 'it was a tribute to the late singer'.

English singer Peter Mason – who was being considered as Robin's replacement – sang harmony vocals on the song. Peter also recalled singing on two other songs. Robert Stigwood, however, was not in favour of replacing Robin, and Peter was out within a very short period. His vocals appear to have been wiped from the songs.

The single became a huge global success, topping the charts in a number of territories and achieving top ten placements in many others. Its number 2 peak in the UK was ironic, as it matched Robin's 'Saved By The Bell' chart achievement from some weeks earlier.

Barry later spoke sarcastically of the time: 'I don't remember ... well, some of it maybe. We were all fighting about fame, and Maurice and I became the Everly Brothers, Robert Stigwood became *Jesus Christ Superstar*, Robin became solo, and chaos reigned. Time flies when you're having fun'.

The Bee Gees only very occasionally performed the song in concert, firstly during a few of the early shows on the 1975 North American tour – during the medley portion of their set, combined with 'Odessa' – and also on early dates of the European leg of their 1989 *One For All* tour.

Following Maurice's sudden death in 2003, Barry and Robin sang the song as a tribute at a 2006 Diabetes Research Institute fundraising event in Florida. For this emotional performance, Barry took the first verse and Robin the second.

'The Lord' (Barry Gibb, Maurice Gibb)
Recorded at IBC Studios, London: circa July 1969

'The Lord' was the B-side of 'Don't Forget To Remember' in all territories except Canada. It's a jaunty country number with a touch of gospel thrown in. It has a folky picked guitar introduction that switches to rhythmic strumming and is joined by Maurice's lolloping bass. Barry launches into the lead vocal before being joined by two tracks of Maurice – one high and one low – in bold harmony on the chorus.

Having been brought up as Christians – the brothers even went to a Catholic school for a short period in Australia – the lyric speaks of their beliefs, with the protagonist vowing 'I'm gonna believe in the Lord'.

'The Lord' was one of the last sessions with drummer Colin Petersen before he was fired the following month. It was also one of the songs performed in the 1970 *Cucumber Castle* television special, and the segment shows some great interactions between Barry and Maurice. It's a lot of fun.

'I Lay Down And Die' (Barry Gibb, Maurice Gibb)
Recorded at IBC Studios, London: circa June 1969

Released as the B-side of 'Don't Forget To Remember' in Canada only, 'I Lay Down And Die' is totally compulsive listening, with a big powerful drum sound and a fantastic lead vocal from Barry. The dramatic finish finds him at the very top of his vocal range, and quite simply put – it is awesome.

The song was initially recorded using many backing vocals throughout, and that original version is the one heard on the Canadian single. A different mix with most of the backing vocals left out appeared on the *Cucumber Castle* album in 1970.

In July and August, Robin made a handful of appearances on *Top of the Pops* to promote and perform 'Saved By The Bell', which was still in the UK top five. The Bee Gees also appeared on the program twice in August, supporting the newly-released 'Don't Forget To Remember'. On 21 August, Robin and his brothers appeared on the same episode in separate performances. Australian-born British disc jockey Alan 'Fluff' Freeman was the day's presenter. Almost 40 years later, Robin would pay tribute to him with the song 'Alan Freeman Days', on his final studio album *50 St. Catherine's Drive*, released posthumously in 2014.

The Bee Gees would also make time in August to return to America for a second stint on *The Ed Sullivan Show*, performing 'Don't Forget To Remember'; though the support would be in vain, as the single barely cracked the top 75 on the *Billboard* Hot 100 chart.

In mid-August, Barry, Maurice and Colin began filming a TV special for BBC 2, to accompany and share the title of their forthcoming *Cucumber Castle* album. A few days into production, Robert Stigwood fired Colin from the group. While 'artistic differences' were cited as the reason for his abrupt departure, Colin had allegedly questioned Stigwood's financial management of The Bee Gees – specifically asserting his perception of Stigwood's conflict of interest in serving as both the group's primary manager and their employer. Whilst initially there was some legal to-ing and fro-ing between parties, Petersen was ousted, a financial settlement was reached, and he was uncredited on the eventually-released *Cucumber Castle* album, despite playing on some tracks.

The Bee Gees were now a duo. Accordingly, filming for *Cucumber Castle* was completed with only Barry and Maurice participating, and any scenes featuring Colin were scrubbed. Although production was finished a short time later, the project wouldn't be shown on television until December 1970: nearly eight months after *Cucumber Castle* was released. By that time, Barry, Robin, and Maurice were already reunited and had released new music as a trio.

Young Australian singer Cheryl Lau Sang travelled to the UK in early 1969 and was shortly to return to her homeland when Barry Gibb heard her powerful voice and insisted she stay. He urged Robert Stigwood to sign her so he could write and produce her. Under Stigwood's management, she changed her name to Samantha Sang, and Barry and Maurice set to work writing two songs for her. The resulting single 'The Love Of A Woman'/ 'Don't Let It Happen Again' was released on 15 July and included Barry on backing vocals and guitar, and also production duties. Both songs are powerful ballads, and Sang was well up to the task. Unfortunately, the single failed to hit the charts, though it enjoyed substantial airplay in Australia.

Sang – who'd experienced minor success in Australia in 1967 under the stage name Cheryl Gray – was unknown to The Bee Gees prior to 1969.

She would have to wait a few more years to work with Barry again, when she would re-record 'The Love Of A Woman', and record a song specially penned for her by Barry and Robin called 'Emotion', which would become a global smash hit.

Prior to his sacking from the band, Colin Petersen had entered into artist management, benefitting from the experience of his wife Joanne (née Newfield), who was previously Brian Epstein's personal assistant. Their first signing was Irish singer/songwriter Jonathan Kelly. The single 'Denver'/'Son Jon', which Colin produced, was released on 12 September, followed by Jonathan's eponymous debut album in 1970. Session musicians included Tony Ashton (piano), Kim Gardner (bass) and Roy Dyke (drums) – the group which Vince Melouney produced immediately after departing The Bee Gees in late 1968.

On 4 September, Barry and Maurice logged one more *Top of the Pops* appearance for the year, performing 'Don't Forget To Remember': The Bee Gees final appearance on the program until late-1970.

Four albums into The Bee Gees' international recording careers, Polydor, ATCO, and Spin took the opportunity to issue the compilation *Best Of Bee Gees*. It was first released in the US in June 1969, followed by an October release in the UK.

Best Of Bee Gees (1969)

Release dates: UK: October 1969, US: June 1969
Chart positions: Canada: 5, Australia: 6, UK: 7, US: 9, West Germany: 26
Side 1: 1. 'Holiday' 2. 'I've Gotta Get A Message To You' 3. 'I Can't See Nobody' 4. 'Words' 5. 'I Started A Joke' 6. 'Spicks And Specks'
Side 2: 1. 'First Of May' 2. 'World' 3. 'Massachusetts' 4. 'To Love Somebody' 5. 'Every Christian Lion Hearted Man Will Show You' 6. 'New York Mining Disaster 1941'

Best Of Bee Gees was a useful collection for casual fans, as it contained all the singles released between February 1967 and January 1969, with the exception of 'Jumbo'. If nothing else, it was an impressive reminder of just how much quality material the group had released in less than two years. For most other artists, it would have taken decades to amass a track list this strong.

For those in the UK, the singles 'Holiday' and 'I Started A Joke' would not have registered, nor would the *Bee Gees 1st* album track 'Every Christian Lion Hearted Man Will Show You'. 'Words' makes its first appearance on LP, and in territories other than the US and Canada where it wasn't included among the *Idea* tracks, so does 'I've Gotta Get A Message to You'.

The sound quality across the album varies. Some mastering adjustment seemed to bolster the tracks that first appeared on *Bee Gees 1st*. The stereo mix of 'Words' is unusually bad, with the vocals and piano augmented to the point that the drums were inaudible. Many fans who had only heard 'Words' via this compilation were later surprised to learn it actually had a rhythm section. 'Spicks And Specks' was 'electronically reprocessed' from its original mono master to fit the stereo format; but, rather curiously, on non-ATCO issues outside North America, the *mono* versions of 'Words' and 'I've Gotta Get A Message To You' were used.

Best Of Bee Gees was an unqualified success, reaching the top ten in the UK, US, Canada and Australia. It was the first US Bee Gees album to be certified gold by the RIAA. Given the number of Bee Gees compilation albums that would be issued over the years, *Best Of Bee Gees* has retained a remarkable shelf life, with continual re-releases worldwide.

The first pressing of the German edition somehow ended up with 'Please Read Me' from *Bee Gees' 1st* in place of 'I Can't See Nobody'. The error was remedied for the second pressing.

CD versions issued by Polydor in the 1980s and 1990s had the single 'Tomorrow Tomorrow' instead of 'Spicks And Specks', due to licencing issues with Festival Records in Australia.

On 8 May 2020, Capitol/UMe reissued the album on both black and limited-edition berry-coloured vinyl. The original track list, including 'Spicks And Specks', was reinstated.

The artwork was produced by Haig Adishian, who also created the album covers for Buffalo Springfield's *Retrospective*, Cream's *Goodbye*, and the debut LPs for both Yes and Vanilla Fudge. While the front cover is quite bold with its amber background and cerise titling, it is nonetheless rather uninspiring.

Rather cruelly, guitarist Vince Melouney was not included in either the front or back cover photographs, despite appearing on all but two of the songs. The front cover group photo is from a very early publicity shoot in April 1967 at a time when Melouney had not yet been announced as a group member, and the back cover was from a promotional shoot aboard a ship for the *Odessa* album, after he'd left. These photographs conveniently captured The Bee Gees as a four-piece and very quickly disassociated them from their recently-departed friend and bandmate. It doesn't take much deliberation to conclude that this was Robert

Stigwood's decision. Vince later recalled that when he declared his exit, Stigwood implied that he'd never wanted him or Colin in the group.

That being said, the finalised cover art was not an accurate representation of the group at the time of the album's June release in the US, as Robin had announced his departure several months earlier. By the time the album was released in the UK in October, Colin Petersen was also an ex-Bee Gee.

Former Oasis frontman Noel Gallagher paid an affectionate tribute to *Best Of Bee Gees* by replicating Adishian's instantly-recognisable original colour scheme and typeface on the cover of Noel Gallagher's High Flying Birds' ten-year hits retrospective *Back the Way We Came*: released on 11 June 2021: 'That first Bee Gees *Best of* which I've ripped the cover off, is one of my favourite all-time records', he explained in an interview with Apple Music's Matt Wilkinson. 'We had to come up with an idea for the artwork, and it just happened to be there in my music room at home. And I was like, 'Oh, no *wait* ... actually, that's a fuckin' good idea!''.

Undaunted by Samantha Sang's failure to break into the charts, Barry's next attempt to sponsor a female singer's entry into success was with American soul singer Patricia Ann Cole. Using the professional pseudonym of P. P. Arnold, she was best-known at the time as one of the Ikettes from the Ike & Tina Turner Revue, and also for two minor UK hits: 'The First Cut Is The Deepest' (1967) and 'Angel Of The Morning' (1968). With her signed to the Robert Stigwood Organisation, Barry had plans to produce a whole album of songs for her. Though the album never eventuated, two of the eleven songs Barry produced for Arnold – 'Bury Me Down By The River' and 'Give A Hand, Take A Hand' – were released as a single on 17 October. Both were written by Barry and Maurice. 'Bury Me Down By The River' is a strong country-gospel song, and The Bee Gees' own recording (which Arnold sang on) appeared the following year on the group's next album *Cucumber Castle*. Arnold's backing vocal cameo is a rare instance of a vocalist other than the Gibb brothers appearing on a Bee Gees recording. The B-side 'Give A Hand, Take A Hand' is also very gospel-influenced. The Bee Gees would also release their own recording of this song, but not until the *Mr. Natural* album in 1974.

When Scottish pop/rock quintet Marmalade released The Bee Gees 1966 song 'Butterfly' on 24 October 1969, they were coming off three UK top ten records in the previous eighteen months, including the chart-topper 'Ob-La-Di, Ob-La-Da'. Barry's strong lead vocal on the original 'Butterfly' was replaced in this recording by a more harmony-based take, with some additional orchestral flourishes. Whilst the song was not a hit, it didn't slow Marmalade down fortunately, and they would have a further four top ten hits over the next three years.

Since around August, Maurice had been working with Scottish singer-songwriter Billy Lawrie, who, as Lulu's brother, was Maurice's brother-in-law at the time. The two got on well, writing many songs together over the next few years. 'Roll Over Beethoven'/'Come Back Joanna' was Lawrie's debut single. Maurice produced both single sides and also played bass on the songs. The A-side is a cover of the Chuck Berry classic, and Lawrie penned the B-side. The song is quite different and allowed Maurice room to experiment in the production. The single was released on the Polydor label on 7 November under the artist name Billy M. Lawrie, but it failed to chart.

November also saw the release of a most unusual Gibb brothers composition – the instrumental 'Square Cup', performed by German jazz musician, saxophonist, band leader and conductor Max Greger. Originally demoed in May 1968, the song translated very well to the sax-led big band sound. It was only ever released in Germany, initially as an A-side, but also on a special edition, Polydor compilation album called *Happy New Year*, for the transition from 1969 into 1970. The cassette equivalent was issued as *Best of Polydor* with different artwork.

On 28 November, Robin issued his second solo single of the year: 'One Million Years'. He made a trip to Barcelona in Spain to promote the single. In a rather bizarre multilingual interview, the presenter asked Robin some questions in English, and then translated his answers to French and German while a translator assisted with Spanish. Robin performed 'Saved By The Bell' as he wandered through the construction site of the Basílica de la Sagrada Família, and 'One Million Years' on the stern of a pleasure cruise boat in the harbour surrounded by an audience of tourists.

'One Million Years' (Robin Gibb)
Recorded on 26 September 1969
Chart positions: West Germany: 5, Austria: 8

Due to the legal injunction invoked by former manager Robert Stigwood following Robin's split from The Bee Gees, 'One Million Years' wasn't released until November 1969 (October in Germany), some five months after 'Saved By The Bell'. As such, any momentum that may have been building from that single's success was lost. That may have been Stigwood's intention, as he preferred The Bee Gees as a trio.

With the opening lyric 'I'm dead, my life's been sold', you can quickly appreciate that the song isn't exactly a joyful affair. But with its slow build-up of guitar and drum patterns, and its sad, almost wretched tale of lovelorn despair, it *is* a classic Robin Gibb love song. But not having a commercial hook like 'Saved By The Bell', the single performed dismally on most world charts. Interestingly, it *did* manage to peak at number 5 in Germany and 8 in Austria. Both markets were loyal and consistent for both The Bee Gees and Robin as a solo artist and would remain so for the next 40 years or so. Robin recorded a version of 'One Million Years' in Italian ('Un Million de Ani'), although it was never released officially at the time.

Although the B-side 'Weekend' was included on Robin's debut solo album *Robin's Reign* when it was released the following February, 'One Million Years' was left off the UK and US releases. Due to the single's success in Germany, it *was* on the German release as the final track.

Robin and his then-manager Vic Lewis produced the track. Arranger Kenny Clayton – who would work with Robin throughout his late-1960s solo period – conducted the orchestra. The song once again used the Rhythm Ace drum machine – that debuted on 'Saved By The Bell' – to replicate the snare pattern.

A stereo mix of 'One Million Years' was included on a compilation titled *Gotta Get a Message to You* released on Contour – a Polydor budget label – in 1973. That mix had an altered lead vocal. This version was also included on the *Saved By The Bell: The Collected Works Of Robin Gibb 1968-1970* compilation in 2015.

'Weekend' (Robin Gibb)
Recorded in 1969

The B-side of 'One Million Years' is a more upbeat ballad than the A-side, but only slightly. Robin was never the strongest lyricist, and the intrigue of his slower songs, in particular, was in anticipating which rhyming word would be used. In this case, the words paired with 'weekend' were 'good friend' and 'send'. In Robin's eyes, it was the melody that was most important, and here, it is sweet and quite endearing.

Unlike the A-side, 'Weekend' was included on Robin's debut solo album *Robin's Reign*.

An unusual release on 12 December 1969 was 'Come And Get It'/'No Other Heart' by The Vic Lewis Orchestra and His Singers. While the

A-side was a cover of the Paul McCartney song that Badfinger had just released the week before, Robin wrote the B-side lyrics and Vic Lewis and pianist Ken Thorne wrote the music. At the time, Lewis – a former jazz guitarist and bandleader from Britain – was Robin's manager, and this was recorded at the time Lewis produced some tracks for Robin's first album *Robin's Reign,* which would appear in 1970.

In a year of considerable turmoil, The Bee Gees still collected a few accolades. Germany's *Bravo* magazine awarded them their second Golden Otto award in as many years, as their readers' favourite band, once again beating The Beatles by a significant margin. Barry was recognised for his coveted wardrobe, with the John Stephen Fashion Award, and as Radio Luxembourg's Best Dressed Man. Stephen – dubbed The King of Carnaby Street and The Million Pound Mod – was one of Britain's most influential fashion designers and entrepreneurs, creating a successful empire of men's outfitters throughout central London. Many years later, a cynical Barry would state that he was awarded the accolade only because he spent the most money in Carnaby Street.

However, any celebration of their achievements would be short-lived. In December, Barry and Maurice announced that they also had split in pursuit of individual interests, ending The Bee Gees – for now. Maurice, who was already working with his brother-in-law Billy Lawrie and friends on outside projects, quickly began recording a solo album. Barry would also start working on his solo projects the following year.

Epilogue

1970s

Despite the group's dissolution and all three brothers moving on to pursue separate works by the end of 1969, *Cucumber Castle* was finally released in April 1970 as The Bee Gees' seventh studio album.

The solo projects Barry and Maurice decided to make in lieu of continuing as The Bee Gees, were never released. Each did produce a single – Barry with 'I'll Kiss Your Memory' and Maurice with 'Railroad' – but both failed to ignite interest from all but die-hard fans. During the break, Barry concentrated on songwriting, while Maurice starred in the short-lived West End musical *Sing A Rude Song*, alongside Barbara Windsor.

Recognising their limitations as individual artists and regretting the personal pain they'd inflicted on one another in the process, the three brothers reunited in mid-1970. Robin's first visit to Barry's house since the rift produced immediate results, writing two future classics – 'Lonely Days' and 'How Can You Mend A Broken Heart' – in one afternoon. Though their British fan base had seemingly lost interest in the group due to their public squabbling, the songs would fare well in the United States, peaking on the *Billboard* Hot 100 at numbers 3 and 1 respectively: their biggest statistical successes to date in that country. However, their reunion album *2 Years On* (including 'Lonely Days'), and the follow-up album *Trafalgar* (including 'How Can You Mend A Broken Heart'), were both inconsistent affairs that found the trio struggling to find their way artistically in a shifting pop music landscape. By this time, Australian drummer Geoff Bridgford (ex-Steve & The Board and The Groove) had joined the group along with former Toe Fat member Alan Kendall on guitar, but the ensemble seemed unable to capture the unique sonic cohesion the Gibbs previously had with Vince Melouney and Colin Petersen.

Whilst the hits weren't as forthcoming, The Bee Gees' cachet as a touring band remained intact, performing across the United States, South-East Asia, Australia, and New Zealand to sell-out audiences. The group's next couple of singles, 1972's 'My World' and 'Run To Me', fared reasonably well on the charts. The latter as the group's first UK top ten entry in three years, appearing on their next studio album – the equally uneven *To Whom It May Concern*.

The Bee Gees, after Bridgford's departure, set up shop in Los Angeles to record the country-rock-styled *Life In A Tin Can*, which was released in February 1973. Curiously, it didn't seem to hook into southern California's flourishing musical pulse at the time. Despite an excellent lead single, 'Saw A New Morning', the album sold poorly. The Bee Gees were officially becoming more of a liability for their management and record company than an asset. So, seemingly out of touch with the record-buying public, their next album – *A Kick In The Head Is Worth Eight In The Pants* – was rejected by Atlantic Records.

Never one to lose faith in his protégés, Stigwood arranged for the group to record their next effort with legendary soul/R&B producer Arif Mardin. The ensuing album, *Mr. Natural*, was a welcome change, including more definitively rock-oriented tracks and a strong R&B undercurrent. Though the album garnered positive reviews, it made little impact on most of the world's charts.

The Bee Gees weren't the only ones dismayed by *Mr. Natural*'s lack of success: Atlantic Records was reportedly on the verge of dismissing them from the label. With the group's future hanging in the balance, they returned to work with Mardin on their next studio album, fully aware that it was a make-or-break scenario. Mardin pushed them to stretch and develop their own unique approach to rhythmic pop. To help with the process, an impressive roster of musicians joined the fray. Retaining Alan Kendall on lead guitar, they also hired drummer Dennis Bryon (ex-Amen Corner, Fair Weather), who had already played on the *Mr. Natural* album, and pianist and keyboardist Blue Weaver (ex-Amen Corner, Fair Weather, Strawbs, Mott the Hoople) to become The Bee Gees' band.

In early 1975, The Bee Gees returned to the United States with their band, this time relocating to Miami, Florida, to record at the famed Criteria Recording Studios. They took up residence at the now well-known house located at 461 Ocean Boulevard – the very same digs that had inspired Eric Clapton's comeback album of the same name the previous year. During those sessions, Mardin nudged Barry to experiment with his falsetto voice – a force of nature that would gradually and permanently change The Bee Gees' entire sound.

The resulting *Main Course* was an immediate critical and commercial success, generating their first US number 1 single in four years: 'Jive Talkin''. 'Nights On Broadway' followed as a top ten hit, and 'Fanny (Be Tender With My Love)' reached the top twenty.

Barry began to emerge as the group's creative leader, particularly as *Main Course*'s follow-up *Children Of The World* began to take shape. Engineer Karl Richardson recruited prodigious session player and longtime friend Albhy Galuten to assist him in the booth. The newly forged Gibb-Galuten-Richardson production team remained constant over the next seven years, achieving stratospheric success, including millions in record sales, multiple Grammy Awards, and a steady stream of requests from many other artists, for their services.

On *Children Of The World*, Barry's still-developing falsetto lead dominated the sound. The first single, 'You Should Be Dancing' was another international hit, propelling The Bee Gees to an even greater level of success and renown, particularly in the US.

While the Gibb brothers were in France in early 1977 writing songs for a new studio album, Robert Stigwood asked them to contribute songs to a new film he was producing that was based on a *New York* magazine article – 'Tribal Rights of the New Saturday Night' – which examined the proliferation and culture of urban dance clubs on the US east coast. *Saturday Night Fever* – starring a then-barely-known John Travolta – put the disco phenomenon under a microscope for the world to see.

The Bee Gees' contributions were not incorporated into the film until post-production, and the five new songs included on the soundtrack – 'How Deep Is Your Love', 'Stayin' Alive', 'More Than A Woman', 'Night Fever' and 'If I Can't Have You' (the latter penned by the brothers but recorded by RSO labelmate Yvonne Elliman) – were written in isolation at Château d'Hérouville studio in rural France, a few months before *Saturday Night Fever* had even been mentioned. The near-perfect meshing of The Bee Gees' music and the film's dark, gritty narrative was mostly an accident.

The public reaction to the film and soundtrack was fervent. 'How Deep Is Your Love', 'Stayin' Alive' and 'Night Fever' all reached number one in the US and most other countries around the world, unleashing an unprecedented period of artist domination in popular music history. Yvonne Elliman's 'If I Can't Have You' was the soundtrack's fourth US chart-topper, and Tavares' take on 'More Than A Woman' was also a hit.

Simultaneously, the Gibbs were writing songs for other artists, and the production team was turning them into solid gold and platinum records at a startling pace. Australian singer Samantha Sang's 'Emotion' – written by Barry and Robin – was neck and neck with The Bee Gees' *Fever* singles in the charts. The youngest Gibb brother, Andy – who'd begun writing, recording, and performing on his own in the early-1970s – was also the beneficiary of his elder brothers' winning streak. He'd already scored a US number one hit in the summer of 1977 with his debut single 'I Just Want

To Be Your Everything'. And two more chart-topping singles – '(Love Is) Thicker Than Water' and 'Shadow Dancing' – followed in the first half of 1978.

During the eight-month period beginning in the Christmas season of 1977, the Gibbs wrote six songs that held the number one position in the US for 25 of 32 consecutive weeks. During the week of 8 April 1978, five Gibb-written songs charted simultaneously in *Billboard*'s top ten.

Such chart dominance hadn't been seen since April 1964, when The Beatles had all five of the top five American singles. Barry Gibb became the only songwriter to have four consecutive number one hits in the US, breaking John Lennon and Paul McCartney's 1964 record. The *Saturday Night Fever* soundtrack became the highest-selling album in recording history to that point. By 2015, it had sold more than 40 million copies.

At the close of the year, The Bee Gees' recordings – or those written and produced by different permutations of them – had reportedly accounted for more than 5% of American record sales.

However, amidst all the success, The Bee Gees became victims of overexposure in the name of money and recognition. While Robert Stigwood had been their infallible guiding light for over a decade, his involvement of The Bee Gees and Peter Frampton in the fantastical Beatles tribute film *Sgt. Pepper's Lonely Hearts Club Band* was an embarrassing misstep. The film was savaged by the critics and was a commercial disaster.

Spirits Having Flown – the much-awaited follow-up to *Saturday Night Fever* – was released in February 1979. Selling more than 15 million copies in the US alone, it became the group's most successful studio album ever. It generated three more American number one hits – 'Too Much Heaven', 'Tragedy' and 'Love You Inside Out' – which yielded The Bee Gees a stunning run of six consecutive US chart-topping singles, all between about December 1977 and June 1979.

In June, the group commenced their largest and most successful concert tour to date. With stops in 50 cities, the *Spirits Having Flown* tour took full advantage of the 'Bee Gees fever' that had now permeated popular music.

But by the end of 1979, The Bee Gees' halcyon days were quickly extinguished. The pop-culture wave they'd ridden for the past five years began to crash, and a media-driven backlash against disco and everything it stood for, began choking out anyone and everyone associated with it. While The Bee Gees hardly created any kind of movement, their dominance made them the faces of it – and soon enough, they were the prime targets of the revolt. For the group, the sudden shut-out was frustrating and even frightening.

1980s

Conscious that some respite from The Bee Gees was necessary, the brothers concentrated on songwriting. While all the brothers were active in the process, Barry, Albhy Galuten, and Karl Richardson were the front-facing production team for most of their material for the first half of the decade.

The first major production to surface was Barbra Streisand's *Guilty* album, released in September 1980. It was an unqualified worldwide smash, becoming Streisand's most commercially successful studio work.

The Bee Gees' professional relationship with their mentor and manager Robert Stigwood, had begun to crumble. In October 1980, the brothers sued him and RSO Records, citing unpaid royalties. Stigwood counter-sued for defamation, libel, extortion, and breach of contract. By May 1981, they'd settled the matter out of court.

Certainly, though, their legal battle produced at least a few grey clouds that overshadowed the recording of their next album *Living Eyes*, released in 1981, but creative tension between brothers and their co-producers also didn't help matters. The album fared poorly commercially, missing the top 40 completely in both the US and the UK.

In 1982, Dionne Warwick – an artist the Gibb brothers had long admired – enjoyed great success with her *Heartbreaker* album, again principally written by the brothers and produced by the Gibb-Galuten-Richardson team. The title track soared to number two in the UK, number one in Australia, ten on the *Billboard* Hot 100, and to the top of the US adult contemporary charts. They replicated the approach for Kenny Rogers' 1983 album *Eyes That See In The Dark*. Rogers' duet with Dolly Parton – 'Islands In The Stream' – became the biggest-selling single in the history of the RCA label and one of the top grossing in the country genre to date. Written by all three brothers, it reached number one in the US, Canada, and Australia, peaking at 7 in the UK.

Later in the year, The Bee Gees were commissioned (and contractually obligated to RSO) to contribute five new songs for yet another Robert Stigwood film: the *Saturday Night Fever* sequel, *Staying Alive*. Whilst the Sylvester-Stallone-produced epic was panned, the soundtrack sold over a million copies in the US, and The Bee Gees' single 'The Woman In You' was a top 30 hit.

An unexpected lawsuit from hitherto unknown Chicago songwriter Ronald Selle surfaced that year. Selle claimed the Gibbs had stolen parts of the melody of their 1977 classic 'How Deep Is Your Love' from his 1975 composition 'Let It End'. The landmark case played out for months, with the brothers eventually winning on appeal.

Over a decade after their last solo projects, all three brothers produced individual work in the first half of the 1980s, albeit with each other's assistance. Robin released three albums, *How Old Are You?*, *Secret Agent*, and *Walls Have Eyes*. Maurice released a solo single in 1984, 'Hold Her In Your Hand', included among multiple instrumental tracks he wrote and performed for the soundtrack of the Philippe Mora-directed film *A Breed Apart*. Barry released his first effort *Now Voyager*, complete with an accompanying feature-length video album. While the Gibbs' solo generated a few scattered hits in different parts of the world, they captured only a fraction of the commercial appeal of the songs they were crafting for others in the industry at the time.

In 1985, Barry, Albhy Galuten and Karl Richardson worked as a production team for the final time, producing the *Eaten Alive* album for Diana Ross.

In 1986, The Bee Gees returned to working as a trio. The result was 1987's *E.S.P.*, which returned them to public consciousness and reunited them with their longtime mentor Arif Mardin upon entering a three-album recording deal with Warner Brothers. The first single, 'You Win Again', was a resounding success around the world, reaching number one in the UK, Germany, Ireland, Austria, Norway and Switzerland, and hitting the top ten in many other countries. US radio had yet to release The Bee Gees from their anti-disco grudge, and most programmers passed on it with listeners none the wiser. Still, *E.S.P.* sold more than 2,000,000 copies worldwide and was an important catalyst for the next instalment of The Bee Gees' story.

Ready to capitalise on their return to form, The Bee Gees entered the studio in early 1988 to record their next album. All plans came to a crashing halt when Andy Gibb – aged just 30 – died suddenly on 10 March from myocarditis, an inflammation of the heart muscle due to a recent viral infection. Although Andy's death was unexpected, his brothers did acknowledge that his past drug and alcohol issues had contributed to it.

After a hiatus, the broken-hearted brothers eventually finished *One*, released in the summer of 1989. While the album was less successful in the UK and Europe, the title track became The Bee Gees' first US top ten single in a decade. After the album's release, the Gibbs embarked on their first world tour in ten years.

1990s

The Bee Gees' early 90s works *High Civilization* and *Size Isn't Everything* were self-produced and explored a myriad of different sounds compared to their predecessors. While the albums were successful in the UK and Europe, they were mostly overlooked in North America.

Barry underwent back surgery in 1992, in great pain from arthritis which at one point put his future guitar-playing in great doubt. Maurice, who'd struggled with alcoholism on and off for years, entered rehab and remained sober for the remainder of his life.

The Bee Gees then entered a four-year hiatus, recording one-off projects and slowly preparing tracks for a new album in the process. In early 1997, the long-awaited *Still Waters* arrived and became their most successful album in almost twenty years. It sold more than 5,000,000 copies worldwide, peaking at number two in the UK and Germany. When *Still Waters* reached eleven in the US, it seemed that The Bee Gees had finally escaped the negative weight of their late-1970s image.

The album's release was accompanied by numerous awards and acts of peer recognition across the globe. The Bee Gees were inducted into the Rock and Roll Hall of Fame in May 1997 and were recipients of the Brit Award for Outstanding Contribution to Music from the British Phonographic Industry (BPI), The American Music Awards' International Artist Award of Excellence, and The World Music Legend Award for Outstanding Contribution to the Music Industry the same year.

Beginning what would be a very successful series of one-off concerts branded *One Night Only* in cities around the world, The Bee Gees performed at the MGM Grand Hotel in Las Vegas on 14 November 1997. The concert was filmed for cable television and was released on both DVD/video and CD – the latter selling over six million copies internationally.

2000s

The April 2001 release *This Is Where I Came In* became The Bee Gees' final album of new material as a group. The album's production was purposely unusual, with each brother offering songs they'd written without the others, although there were a few co-written songs. The fragmented approach seemed to reflect the brothers' relationships at the time - it was later disclosed in the press that the group's latter years were steeped in disagreements over their legal, business, and creative affairs.

In the eyes of their audience, however, The Bee Gees appeared to be enjoying their status as elder statesmen of the industry. Barry, Robin, and Maurice were in fine form at the Hammerstein Ballroom of The Manhattan Center in New York City on 27 April 2001, for the taping of *Live by Request*: a television special shown on the US A&E Network.

What would become their final public performance together occurred on 17 June 2001, as energetic headliners of the Wango Tango festival at Dodger Stadium in Los Angeles, where they closed the event's second day with an electric fifteen-song set.

On the 2001-2002 Queen's New Year's Honours List, Barry, Robin and Maurice were made Commanders of the Order of the British Empire (CBE). When Barry and Robin were officially presented with their awards three years later in 2004 at a Buckingham Palace ceremony, sadly, the third member of the trio was not there.

Maurice Gibb died suddenly, aged just 53, on 12 January 2003 at Mount Sinai Medical Centre in Miami Beach, Florida, from complications after surgery for a strangulated intestine. Understandably in shock, Barry and Robin initially announced they intended to carry on the Bee Gees name in his memory but later recanted this, saying they wished to retire it, leaving it to represent the three brothers together.

At the 2003 Grammy Awards in February – just weeks after Maurice's death – The Bee Gees received the Grammy Legend Award. Joining Barry and Robin in accepting Maurice's award in an emotional presentation was Maurice's son Adam.

The remaining Gibb brothers would never produce any new material together. Maurice's stabilising influence on Barry and Robin was greatly missed, and their disparate approaches to making music caused a rift between them that played out publicly in the press. Though Barry and Robin occasionally came together to perform, they continued to work mostly independently and both released recordings with other artists.

On 31 October 2009, Barry and Robin appeared together on an episode of the BBC series *Strictly Come Dancing*, with Robin teasing that more work as a duo was forthcoming. Sadly, it never materialised.

On the eve of the 2012 world premiere of Robin's new album *The Titanic Requiem* in London -written with his son Robin-John to commemorate the 100th anniversary of the sinking of the Titanic – Robin was forced to withdraw due to illness. In November 2011, he had been diagnosed with colorectal cancer, which had metastasised to his liver several months earlier. In April, he contracted pneumonia and fell into a coma. He died in London on 20 May 2012 at the age of 62 from liver and kidney failure. His funeral was held on 8 June 2012 near his home in Thame, Oxfordshire in the UK.

Understandably, Barry took the death of his third brother hard and was not sighted for some time until late 2012, suddenly announcing his first-ever solo tour. Barry designed *The Mythology Tour* concerts to be a celebration of the three brothers' work over the previous 50 years. The show featured his eldest son Stephen and Maurice's daughter Samantha in key roles on stage with Barry, performing songs from 1966 onwards.

Robin's final studio album *50 St. Catherine's Drive*, consisting of recordings made in 2007 and 2008, was released posthumously in September 2014.

In October 2016, Barry released *In the Now*, his third solo album. It received positive reviews around the world and charted in the top three in several countries, including the UK and Australia. In the US, it peaked at number 63.

A year later, Charles, Prince of Wales knighted Barry in a ceremony at Buckingham Palace.

In December 2020, a documentary chronicling the life and music of the Brothers Gibb – *The Bee Gees: How Can You Mend A Broken Heart* – was released to nearly universal critical and public accolades. Renowned American filmmaker and producer Frank Marshall served as director for the documentary, which featured new interviews from Barry, along with former bandmates Vince Melouney, Alan Kendall, Blue Weaver and Dennis Bryon; co-producers Albhy Galuten and Karl Richardson, and musicians Eric Clapton, Lulu, Noel Gallagher, Justin Timberlake, Chris Martin, Nick Jonas, Mark Ronson, and Mykael S. Riley.

In January 2021, on the heels of the documentary and amidst the COVID-19 pandemic, Barry released *Greenfields: The Gibb Brothers Songbook, Vol. 1* - his fourth solo album. It features duets with various American country music and roots artists on eleven Bee Gees songs and one unreleased Barry Gibb song, 'Words Of A Fool', from 1986. The album received very favourable reviews and topped the UK and Australian album charts. In the US, it scored a very respectable number 15 on the *Billboard* 200, while on the US country charts, it peaked at number three. At 74 years of age, Barry Gibb became the oldest artist to reach number one on the Australian ARIA albums chart. That achievement also stretched the brothers' total chart run in their adopted homeland to 57 years, nine months and six days since their first single – 'The Battle Of The Blue And The Grey' – debuted on the 2SM National Top 100 in the week of 12 April 1963.

In July 2021, bronze statues of Barry, Robin, and Maurice – capturing their likenesses as seen in the promotional video for 'Stayin' Alive' filmed in autumn 1977 – were unveiled at the seafront promenade in Douglas, Isle of Man, their place of birth. The statues were cast by artist Andy Edwards, who also created the well-known Beatles statues that stand at Liverpool's Pier Head.

Bibliography

Barnes, Jim & Stephen Scanes - *The Book Top 40 Research* (Australia) 4th Edition 1956-1997

Bilyeu, M., Cook, H., Hughes, A.M., Brennan, J., Crohan, M.,- *Tales of the Brothers Gibb: The Ultimate Biography of The Bee Gees* (Omnibus Press, 2000, 2001, 2003 & 2012)

Casey, Bill - *Nat Kipner and The Bee Gees* Hurstville Library

Casey, Bill - *Ossie Byrne and The Bee Gees* Hurstville Library

Casey, Bill - *Spin Dried* (Moonlight Publishing, 2007)

Crotty, George. *The Australian Festival Record Company: The label listing of singles released in Australia between 1961-1969.* [Australia, n.d.].

Cox, Peter - *Spinning Around: the Festival Records Story* (Powerhouse Publishing, 2001)

Culnane, Paul - Assorted biographies in www.milesago.com

Evans, Raymond – 'To try to ruin: rock'n'roll, youth culture and law and order in Brisbane, 1956-1957', in *The Forgotten Fifties*, edited by John Murphy and Judith Smart, Australian Historical Studies, No. 109, Oct. 1997.

Facer, Hank B - *Spin label discography -MIRLDiscography No. 24*, February 1982 (Museum of Indigenous Recording Labels, 1982

Hayton, John and Isackson, Leon, *Behind The Rock*, Select Books, Australia, 1980

Beck, Christopher, *On Air : 25 Years Of TV In Queensland*, One Tree Hill Publishing, Australia, 1984

Leaf, D., Bee Gees – *The Authorized Biography*

McLean, David - *Collected Stories of Australian Rock'n'Roll*, Canetoad Publications

McRobbie, Alexander – *The Fabulous Gold Coast*

Miller, Harry M -*My Story,* (Macmillan, 1983)

Sandoval, A., *Bee Gees – The Day-By-Day Story, 1945-1972*

Spencer, Chris, *Who's Who Of Australian Rock*, Five Mile Press, Australia, 1997

McFarlane, Ian, *The Encyclopaedia Of Australian Rock & Pop*, Allen and Irwin, Australia, 1999

Newspapers & Magazines
Australia
Australian Cash Box
Australian Women's Weekly incl. Teenager's Weekly
Everybody's

Go-Set
TV Times
TV Week

UK
Beat Instrumental
Disc & Music Echo
Fab 208
Melody Maker
New Musical Express
Rave
Record Mirror

US
Billboard
Goldmine
Record World

Websites
Joseph Brennan's Gibb Songs: www.columbia.edu/~brennan/beegees/
45cat.com
BMI.com
Discogs.com
Newspapers.com
National Film & Sound Archive
National Archives Australia – www.naa.gov.au
OfficialCharts.com
Tvpopdiaries.co.uk

Sleeve Notes
Baker, Glenn A. and Byfield, Mark, *Brilliant From Birth* CD (The Bee Gees), Festival,
Australia, 1998
Byfield, Mark and Crohan, Mark, *Assault The Vaults* CD (Various Artists), Festival,
Australia, 1998
Sandoval, A. – *The Studio Albums 1967-68* (Reprise)
Sandoval, A. - *Odessa* (Reprise)
Tales From The Brothers Gibb box set liner notes

On Track series

Tori Amos – Lisa Torem 978-1-78952-142-9
Asia – Peter Braidis 978-1-78952-099-6
Barclay James Harvest – Keith and Monica Domone 978-1-78952-067-5
The Beatles – Andrew Wild 978-1-78952-009-5
The Beatles Solo 1969-1980 – Andrew Wild 978-1-78952-030-9
Blue Oyster Cult – Jacob Holm-Lupo 978-1-78952-007-1
Marc Bolan and T.Rex – Peter Gallagher 978-1-78952-124-5
Kate Bush – Bill Thomas 978-1-78952-097-2
Camel – Hamish Kuzminski 978-1-78952-040-8
Caravan – Andy Boot 978-1-78952-127-6
Cardiacs – Eric Benac 978-1-78952-131-3
Eric Clapton Solo – Andrew Wild 978-1-78952-141-2
The Clash – Nick Assirati 978-1-78952-077-4
Crosby, Stills and Nash – Andrew Wild 978-1-78952-039-2
The Damned – Morgan Brown 978-1-78952-136-8
Deep Purple and Rainbow 1968-79 – Steve Pilkington 978-1-78952-002-6
Dire Straits – Andrew Wild 978-1-78952-044-6
The Doors – Tony Thompson 978-1-78952-137-5
Dream Theater – Jordan Blum 978-1-78952-050-7
Elvis Costello and The Attractions – Georg Purvis 978-1-78952-129-0
Emerson Lake and Palmer – Mike Goode 978-1-78952-000-2
Fairport Convention – Kevan Furbank 978-1-78952-051-4
Peter Gabriel – Graeme Scarfe 978-1-78952-138-2
Genesis – Stuart MacFarlane 978-1-78952-005-7
Gentle Giant – Gary Steel 978-1-78952-058-3
Gong – Kevan Furbank 978-1-78952-082-8
Hawkwind – Duncan Harris 978-1-78952-052-1
Roy Harper – Opher Goodwin 978-1-78952-130-6
Iron Maiden – Steve Pilkington 978-1-78952-061-3
Jefferson Airplane – Richard Butterworth 978-1-78952-143-6
Jethro Tull – Jordan Blum 978-1-78952-016-3
Elton John in the 1970s – Peter Kearns 978-1-78952-034-7
The Incredible String Band – Tim Moon 978-1-78952-107-8
Iron Maiden – Steve Pilkington 978-1-78952-061-3
Judas Priest – John Tucker 978-1-78952-018-7
Kansas – Kevin Cummings 978-1-78952-057-6
Led Zeppelin – Steve Pilkington 978-1-78952-151-1
Level 42 – Matt Philips 978-1-78952-102-3
Aimee Mann – Jez Rowden 978-1-78952-036-1
Joni Mitchell – Peter Kearns 978-1-78952-081-1
The Moody Blues – Geoffrey Feakes 978-1-78952-042-2
Mike Oldfield – Ryan Yard 978-1-78952-060-6
Tom Petty – Richard James 978-1-78952-128-3
Porcupine Tree – Nick Holmes 978-1-78952-144-3
Queen – Andrew Wild 978-1-78952-003-3
Radiohead – William Allen 978-1-78952-149-8
Renaissance – David Detmer 978-1-78952-062-0
The Rolling Stones 1963-80 – Steve Pilkington 978-1-78952-017-0

The Smiths and Morrissey – Tommy Gunnarsson 978-1-78952-140-5
Steely Dan – Jez Rowden 978-1-78952-043-9
Steve Hackett – Geoffrey Feakes 978-1-78952-098-9
Thin Lizzy – Graeme Stroud 978-1-78952-064-4
Toto – Jacob Holm-Lupo 978-1-78952-019-4
U2 – Eoghan Lyng 978-1-78952-078-1
UFO – Richard James 978-1-78952-073-6
The Who – Geoffrey Feakes 978-1-78952-076-7
Roy Wood and the Move – James R Turner 978-1-78952-008-8
Van Der Graaf Generator – Dan Coffey 978-1-78952-031-6
Yes – Stephen Lambe 978-1-78952-001-9
Frank Zappa 1966 to 1979 – Eric Benac 978-1-78952-033-0
10CC – Peter Kearns 978-1-78952-054-5

Decades Series
The Bee Gees in the 1960s – Andrew Mon Hughes et al 978-1-78952-148-1
Alice Cooper in the 1970s – Chris Sutton 978-1-78952-104-7
Curved Air in the 1970s – Laura Shenton 978-1-78952-069-9
Fleetwood Mac in the 1970s – Andrew Wild 978-1-78952-105-4
Focus in the 1970s – Stephen Lambe 978-1-78952-079-8
Genesis in the 1970s – Bill Thomas 978178952-146-7
Marillion in the 1980s – Nathaniel Webb 978-1-78952-065-1
Pink Floyd In The 1970s – Georg Purvis 978-1-78952-072-9
The Sweet in the 1970s – Darren Johnson 978-1-78952-139-9
Uriah Heep in the 1970s – Steve Pilkington 978-1-78952-103-0
Yes in the 1980s – Stephen Lambe with David Watkinson 978-1-78952-125-2

On Screen series
Carry On… – Stephen Lambe 978-1-78952-004-0
David Cronenberg – Patrick Chapman 978-1-78952-071-2
Doctor Who: The David Tennant Years – Jamie Hailstone 978-1-78952-066-8
Monty Python – Steve Pilkington 978-1-78952-047-7
Seinfeld Seasons 1 to 5 – Stephen Lambe 978-1-78952-012-5

Other Books
Babysitting A Band On The Rocks – G.D. Praetorius 978-1-78952-106-1
Derek Taylor: For Your Radioactive Children – Andrew Darlington 978-1-78952-038-5
Iggy and The Stooges On Stage 1967-1974 – Per Nilsen 978-1-78952-101-6
Jon Anderson and the Warriors – the road to Yes – David Watkinson 978-1-78952-059-0
Nu Metal: A Definitive Guide – Matt Karpe 978-1-78952-063-7
Tommy Bolin: In and Out of Deep Purple – Laura Shenton 978-1-78952-070-5
Maximum Darkness – Deke Leonard 978-1-78952-048-4
Maybe I Should've Stayed In Bed – Deke Leonard 978-1-78952-053-8
Psychedelic Rock in 1967 – Kevan Furbank 978-1-78952-155-9
The Twang Dynasty – Deke Leonard 978-1-78952-049-1

and many more to come!

Would you like to write for Sonicbond Publishing?

At Sonicbond Publishing we are always on the look-out for authors, particularly for our two main series:

On Track. Mixing fact with in depth analysis, the On Track series examines the work of a particular musical artist or group. All genres are considered from easy listening and jazz to 60s soul to 90s pop, via rock and metal.

On Screen. This series looks at the world of film and television. Subjects considered include directors, actors and writers, as well as entire television and film series. As with the On Track series, we balance fact with analysis.

While professional writing experience would, of course, be an advantage the most important qualification is to have real enthusiasm and knowledge of your subject. First-time authors are welcomed, but the ability to write well in English is essential.

Sonicbond Publishing has distribution throughout Europe and North America, and all books are also published in E-book form. Authors will be paid a royalty based on sales of their book.

Further details are available from www.sonicbondpublishing. co.uk. To contact us, complete the contact form there or email info@sonicbondpublishing.co.uk